Student Study Guide

for use with

SEXUALITY TODAY
THE HUMAN PERSPECTIVE

Eighth Edition

Gary F. Kelly
Clarkson University

Prepared by
Richelle Frabotta
Social Health Education

Mc
Graw
Hill

Boston   Burr Ridge, IL   Dubuque, IA   Madison, WI   New York   San Francisco   St. Louis
Bangkok   Bogotá   Caracas   Kuala Lumpur   Lisbon   London   Madrid   Mexico City
Milan   Montreal   New Delhi   Santiago   Seoul   Singapore   Sydney   Taipei   Toronto

The McGraw·Hill Companies

McGraw-Hill Higher Education

Student Study Guide for use with
Sexuality Today: The Human Perspective
Gary F. Kelly

1 2 3 4 5 6 7 8 9 0 BKM/BKM 0 9 8 7 6 5

ISBN 0-07-302268-3

www.mhhe.com

CONTENTS

How to Use the Study Guide

The Study Guide for Gary Kelly's *Sexuality Today Eighth Edition* uses a model that reinforces the content of each chapter through a variety of specific tools. These tools include an **annotated outline, learning objectives, key terms and definitions, guided review and study, self-tests, essay questions**, and an innovative feature of **chapter resource reflections**.

Annotated Outline
The annotated outline highlights the key divisions and content of the respective chapter. It utilizes the general outline provided in the text, thereby retaining a consistency between the primary document and the study aide. In addition the learning objectives for each chapter are provided next to the relevant outline topic. This will help when you have questions about the review of the material through the use of the learning objectives. If you need to locate the chapter material that corresponds with a learning objective, locate the learning objective on the annotated outline and return to the appropriate topics in the chapter.

Learning Objectives
Unlike many study guides that contain only a few learning objectives for each chapter this study guide incorporates a substantial number of learning objectives. The motivation was to provide comprehensive resources that would facilitate the mastering of the chapter content. Professors may teach this course in a number of ways and focus on different aspects of the material. Yet, if students can master the content of the chapter they will be prepared for the range of pedagogical and assessment styles used by professors. You may notice a repetition in the presentation of the learning objectives. This was intentional. To reinforce the chapter content a "level" system for the learning objectives was developed.
- When the word "describe" is used for an objective the material generally covers a few paragraphs of material or an entire section of a chapter.
- "Briefly describe" generally covers material that is presented in one long or two short paragraphs. This material is less substantive than that covered under a "describe" objective
- The "list" objectives means that an exercise is listing, or identifying, chapter content.
- There are some "state" objectives, which involve presenting a position with regards to the objective.
- There are also some "compare" and "contrast" objectives that challenge you to look at the content of the material with a focus on similarities and differences.

This "level" approach may be repetitive, but the goal is to help you understand, retain and use the material in the text to the best of your ability.

Key Words and Definitions
This section of the study guide presents the key terms and definitions as used in the text. At a minimum you should be able to recall the terms and definitions. In actuality you should be able to utilize these terms and definitions in short answer and essay questions if challenged to do so.

Self-Tests
The Self-Tests are traditional multiple choice "exams." Remaining consistent with the term and concept focus of the study guide, the multiple-choice questions focus on these items. There is a very "concrete" or "foundational" aspect to these questions. The principle behind this approach is again having you focus on the content of the material and not just the specific application of it. This again is based on the premise that professors will assess the course content in a number of

ways. If you know the terms and concepts contained in each chapter, then you have the potential to recall or utilize that material in an application question, short answer, or essay. The answers for each self-test are provided at the end of the study guide.

Guided Review and Study
The Guided Review and Study utilizes the traditional of a "fill-in-the-blank" approach. When designing this section of the study guide the goal was to ask you to recall key words or concepts presented within the chapter. This section focuses on material that is generally different from the material covered in the Self-Test section. The hope is that this process will allow you to retain more of the conceptual content of the chapter.
- You should attempt to complete this section of the study guide without turning to the back of the guide to learn the answers.
- Take the opportunity to see what you can recall from the chapter.
- Before looking up the answer, consider returning to the chapter and seeing if you can locate the guided review phrase. This effort will reinforce your knowledge of the material in the text chapter.

Essay Questions and Answers
This section of the study guide provides essay questions that connect at least two chapter objectives. The objective was to stimulate thought across learning objectives so that you may begin to see connections between concepts presented in each chapter. You should use these essay questions, unless directed to do otherwise by your course professor, as another reinforcement tool in preparation for your exams. Do not presume that your professor will merely select these questions from the study guide and do not presume that the "answers" provided at the back of the study guide are the specifics that the professor wants incorporated into their essays. Rather, use these essay questions as a tool through which you can develop an articulate response that incorporates relevant facts and concepts presented in the chapter.

In light of this intent, the "answers" provided at the end of the study guide are given in a "bulleted" manner and not an essay format. These "essay points" are just that, points that should be included in an essay that related to the content of the essay question and drawn from the chapter material. Your professor may use some of these questions, or the content of them, as "short answer" questions or they may do the same for actual essay questions. The hope is that after writing responses to the questions you can assess you readiness to present your thoughts, based on the chapter content, in an essay. **As a cautionary note** please remember that if an essay is required by your professor you will need to provide an "introduction" to your essay, complete the "body" of your essay, and finish your essay with a "conclusion." In this traditional format, you need to remember that the "body" of your essay needs to be the substantial portion of your written response. If a "short answer" is requested then the focus is on the "body" of the essay and not the "introduction" and "conclusion."

Chapter Resource Reflections
Each of the chapter resource reflections challenges you to reflect on the supplemental materials that are sometimes overlooked by students. Sometimes you can tend to focus on the narrative content of chapters, but these other materials provide opportunities for critical reflection about the impact of the content issues of each chapter. These reflections examine the various "case study" examples, the "cross-cultural perspectives," some of the highlighted "readings," and each of the "self-evaluation" exercises. You may be tempted to skip these reflections, but try not to. Use them as another tool to deepen your understanding of the nature and reality of the human sexual experience, and in particular your own human sexual experience.

McGraw-Hill Resources: Reflecting on Sexuality
These experiences were designed to take you beyond the materials presented in the text through the use of the Internet. They were not designed as "trendy" experiences to get you outside the parameters of the text. They were designed to reinforce the materials covered in the text and to link you to quality resources that can be assessed via the Internet. Some of the activities take you to content specific sites that are designed by organizations with specific areas of expertise. Other activities engage you in a review of questions and responses designed to answer questions about sexual topics. Each experience, if undertaken, should provide an additional learning opportunity that hopefully benefits your personal and sexual life.

Being an Excellent Student

Most students who are in college want to be good students, and most students have some particular goal in mind, which is probably why they chose the particular college or university they are attending. As you chose your college or university, and perhaps even an area of major interest or concentration, you had certain goals in mind, which likely included doing well in school, earning good grades, and graduating.

Unfortunately, many students do not do as well in college as they had hoped and expected. Let's examine some of the reasons for this disappointing outcome to see how to avoid them and to learn, instead, how to be a good student and guide your behavior to improve your chances of achieving your goals.

A common definition of education is that it is "how people learn stuff." For most of our history, educators have focused on the "stuff." Teachers were required to be masters of their respective academic fields. Even today, some states have requirements that speak only to the need to be qualified in the subject matter one teaches, not in the teaching methods themselves.

In the 1960s, we became more interested in the "people" part of the definition, which was evidenced by moving to strategies like open classrooms and free universities. The idea was that, given the opportunity to do so, people will naturally learn. Although these experiments were dismal failures, they taught us something.

The key to the definition of education is the word *how*. Today, thanks to a wealth of research on the principles that guide the phenomenon of learning, and on the nature of learning and memory, we know much more about how learning occurs and how we can make it better. By using these principles, we can become better students.

Formulating the Plan

Anything worth having is worth planning for. Whether you hope to learn to teach, to fly, to write for profit, or to change diapers correctly, you have in mind a goal. An everyday question from the first days in elementary school is, "What do you want to be when you grow up?" The answer to this question is one way of formulating a goal. Now that you are a college student, many people will expect you to know what you want to do for a profession or career. Yet you may not have the foggiest notion, or you might have an idea that is still slightly foggy. That is OK. What is clear, however, is that you want to succeed in your college courses. This is a relatively long-range goal, and as such can serve a purpose in keeping you on track.

But our day-to-day behavior is often hard to connect to our long-range goals. We need short-term goals to keep us organized and to be sure that the flow of our activities is in the direction we want to be going. To accomplish our long-range goals, we need to focus on three types of short-term goals. First, we need goals for the day; second, we need goals for the week; and third, we need goals for the semester or term. Let's look at each of these separately.

Goals for Today

It is helpful to keep a daily checklist, diary, or schedule as a reminder of what must be done each day. Check off the things as you accomplish them. A pocket calendar is particularly helpful for this task.

Goals for the Week

Students who are successful in college also schedule their time weekly. Sometime during the course of registration, you made up a schedule showing your classes for the whole week. If you have a job, you must allow time for that, too. Also, many college or university students have family obligations that need to be considered as well. Finally, everyone needs some time for relaxing, eating, sleeping, and playing (even in graduate school we were advised that we needed to find some time to have fun in order to keep our balance). With all these things in mind, it is no wonder many students find little time to study.

But good students do all these things, too, yet they study. Do they have more time? No, we all have the same amount of time. But successful students schedule their time carefully. So, make up a weekly schedule and block off time for all these necessary events: classes, work, relaxation, eating, sleeping, playing, family, and studying. Students who actually schedule their time and keep to their schedules are amazed at how much time they find they have!

As you make up your weekly schedule, you may find your study time in a large block. If this is true, please remember to take a short break every twenty to thirty minutes. This is called distributed practice and is far more efficient than studying for hours on end. After the first twenty or thirty minutes, most of us become much less efficient anyway. When you take that break, reward yourself somehow; then get back to your studying. Something I always tell my students is never to try to read a whole chapter in one sitting--in fact, when I am preparing for a new class, or have changed texts in a class I have been teaching, I take that advice myself!

Goals for the Semester

At the beginning of each semester, we find ourselves immersed in many new courses. Often, you will be confronted by several new professors with whom you have never worked before. It is difficult to sort out the expectations and demands of these several courses. However, it is important to organize the information that will be needed for completing all of the course requirements in order to be successful in the courses.

If you can, obtain a large wall calendar, and mark on it all the dates of tests, exams, and term paper due dates, being sure to write on the calendar the course for which each date applies. Now, estimate how long it will take you to make final preparations for those exams, and mark those dates as warning or alert dates. Look over the dates on which papers are due, and see if they are bunched together. If your college is typical, they will probably be close. You can help yourself to avoid the last-minute all-nighters if you simply determine a spread of due dates for yourself, and mark those on the calendar too. As you do this step, please be sure to avoid any days that have personal significance for you, such as birthdays, anniversaries, and so on. This calendar gives you an overview of major dates in your semester.

If you have followed this carefully, you now have a large semester calendar plastered on your wall, a weekly schedule of major life events, classes, and study times taped over your desk, and a daily checklist of must-do items in your pocket or purse. **So, your scheduling is on its way. Let's look now at other important strategies.**

Attending Classes

Many students believe that, since they are in college, they can decide whether to go to class at all. This is true. Some students also believe that attendance in class is not important to their grade. This is not true! Some colleges or universities have attendance requirements, so that if students miss a given number of

classes it will either lower their grade a full letter grade, or the instructor may drop the student from the course; some instructors have in-class activities that count toward students' grades, so if students are not in class, they do not get credit for participating. Even without such strategies, students who do not attend class sessions almost always do more poorly on the tests and exams. Perhaps they were absent when a crucial item was discussed, or when the instructor lectured over the material this examination requires. Remember, that more often than not, instructors will include information in their lectures that is not in your textbook, and that information (whether from class lecture, videos shown in class, guest lectures, and so on) is fair game for tests. Moreover, if you are not there, the instructor cannot get to know you, and therefore cannot give you the benefit of the doubt on your answers. It should come as no surprise that in study after research study, the data clearly show that those students who attend class regularly receive the highest grades and actually learn more, too! So, the first rule of being an effective student is to attend classes. Besides, how else can you get your money's worth?

But okay, now that you've determined you will go to every class, what will you do?

Benefiting from Lectures

Sometimes students think that if they come to class and "pay attention," they will remember what the instructor talked about; they think that if they take notes, they will miss much of what the instructor says. But sitting and paying attention is difficult. For one thing, most people can think much faster than they can speak. While the instructor lectures at 80 words per minute, the student thinks at about 350 words per minute! If the student is using this extra "thinking capacity" to focus on what the instructor is saying, it is fine. This rarely lasts more than five minutes at a time, however. Most of the time, this extra "thinking capacity" is used in daydreaming!

Daydreaming can be helpful in resolving our emotional problems, planning the course of our lives, and avoiding work. Often, it is motivated by the desire to avoid work. For whatever motive, however, daydreaming is not compatible with attending a lecture. Human beings simply cannot attend to more than one stimulus at one time. And you have to admit, your daydreams can be ever so much more interesting than your professor's lectures.

Attending lectures is best done while taking notes. Use plenty of paper, and leave blank lines at regular intervals, or leave wide side margins. You will use these spaces later (they are not wasted!). If the instructor permits it, be brave and interrupt with questions if you do not understand what is being said. One thing I try to stress to my students is that I may know what I am talking about, but it may be unclear to them--and if it's unclear to one student, it may well be unclear to other students. So, for the sake of the other students who didn't understand what I was talking about, each student should take on the responsibility of asking me to clarify what I said, or to expand in a way that will help them understand. Remember that lectures have a way of progressing and building on earlier information. It is important to understand each point, or later points will be lost. (But please, DO NOT ask the person sitting next to you what the professor said--it disrupts the class, disturbs your neighbor, and you are likely NOT to get an accurate response!)

When you take notes, write out the major points, and try to just make simple notes on the supporting minor points. If you miss something, and you cannot ask a question about it, approach the instructor immediately afterward, when it is likely to still be fresh in both your minds. DO NOT try to write down every word, and DO try to use abbreviations or symbols, or, you could do what I did--learn shorthand! (Or, make up your own.)

Often my students will ask if they may tape record my lectures. Personally, I have no objection to having students do this. In fact, I did this my first term back in college but found it was terribly tedious trying to transcribe the lecture. The students for whom this may be particularly helpful are those who have visual, auditory, or motor impairments. However, do not ever tape record a lecture without first asking for and obtaining the professor's permission.

Within one or two hours after the lecture, on the same day, go back over your notes, and do two things. First, fill in the rest of the minor points. This often amounts to completing the sentence or other element. Second, write brief summaries and any questions that you now have in the blank spaces (lines or margins) you left earlier (clever of you to leave those spaces!). These few minutes spent reviewing and organizing your notes will pay off in greatly improved memory. The questions you have you can ask in class, or during the instructor's office hours, and reap two benefits. First, you will get the answers. Second, you will demonstrate that you are a serious student, and that will impress your instructor.

One other thing about going to class. While this is not always true, I have found that typically my best students sit in front. And most students seem to have a need to have "their seat," while a few students have a need to move around, sitting in one seat one day and a different seat the next. It wasn't until my graduate school days that I realized why I needed "my seat"--as a student, we are being overwhelmed with new information, a stressful experience; we need some structure we can count on to reduce that stress. So, if you are one of those who likes to wander, be considerate of your classmates' needs for stress reduction.

By the way, to get the most out of the lectures, do complete the assigned reading BEFORE the class begins so you are familiar with the material. This will help you keep up with what the instructor is talking about, will reduce the amount of information you do not understand, but may also bring up important questions for you to ask in class if the instructor does not talk about them.

Reading for Learning

We all know how to read. You are proving it by reading these words. Hopefully, you are also realizing some ideas as a result of reading. If you are only reading words, please WAKE UP! STOP DAYDREAMING!

We can read a variety of things: newspapers, movie reviews, novels, magazines, and textbooks. Textbooks are unlike all the others, and must be read with a strategy all their own.

There are many reading and studying strategies, and all of them work to an extent. Perhaps you learned one or more in the course of going to high school. Perhaps you even took a how-to-study course when you entered college. If so, you probably learned one or two of these systems. If you have one you like, that works for you, keep it. If you are interested in learning a new one, read on.

The PQ4R Method

One of the most successful and most widely used methods of studying written material was the SQ3R method, first developed at The Ohio State University. Researchers had noted that students who were more successful were more active readers. More recently, this method has been updated to the PQ4R Method, which adds an additional step. This method teaches you the same skills that have made many thousands of students successful. If you use this method when you read and study, you will be more successful, too. I have outlined the steps below and the text describes this method in Chapter 13.

The P stands for PREVIEW. After you have read the overview or chapter outline, and the list of learning objectives, you should survey the chapter in the text. This is also called skimming. Look at the headings and subheadings, and get the gist of the major points in this chapter. Check off each point in the outline of this Study Guide as you pass it in the pages of the text.

The Q stands for QUESTION. Reading is greatly enhanced if you are searching for the answers to questions. For this text, the Student Study Guide provides learning objectives that can serve as questions. For other texts, make up questions for yourself, based on the chapter overview or on your own survey of the chapter. Be sure that you have at least one question for each major unit in the chapter; you will be less efficient at studying those units for which you do not have questions.

The first of the four Rs is for READ. As you read, look for the answers to the questions you posed, or to the study or learning objectives furnished for you. When you find material that answers these questions, put a mark (X) or a "post-it" note in the margin next to that material. This will help now, since you are actively involved, and later, when you review. It is a good idea to wait to underline or highlight lines of text until after you have read the entire chapter at least once, so you will know what is and what is not most important. (In fact, while some "authorities" suggest you underline or highlight no more than 10% of what you are reading, I find that when most of us begin to underline or highlight, we wind up doing it to most of the chapter--I suggest not doing it at all because it becomes too passive, which counteracts your attempts to read "actively.")

The second R stands for REFLECT. As you are reading, stop every so often and reflect on the material to increase its meaningfulness. This includes analyzing the material, thinking about how to apply it to your own life, interpreting the information, and connecting it with information you already have in your long-term memory.

The third R is for RECITE. One of the oldest classroom techniques in the world (Aristotle used it) is recitation. In the classroom version, the teacher asks the questions and the students answer them. Unless you can get your teacher to study with you regularly, you'll have to play both roles. Periodically stop in your reading and say aloud (if possible) what the author is telling you. Try to put it in your own words, but be sure to use technical terms as you learn them. If you are not in a situation where you can recite out loud, do it in writing. Just thinking it is not enough. When should you pause to recite? A good rule of thumb is that each time you come to the end of a major subheading, you should recite. One professor encourages his students to recite at least one sentence at the end of each paragraph, and two or three or more sentences at the end of each subunit (when you come to a new heading).

People who do not use recitation usually forget half of what they read in one hour, and another half of the half they remembered by the end of the day. People who use recitation often remember from 75 to 90 percent of what they studied. This technique pays off. By the way, if anyone questions why you are talking to yourself, tell them that a psychologist recommended it.

The fourth R is for REVIEW. You should review a chapter soon after you have studied it (using the PQ and first 3Rs). You should review it again the day or evening before a test. It is not usually helpful to cram the night before a test, and particularly not the day of the test! That type of studying does not produce good memory, and is likely to make you more anxious during the test itself.

Taking Tests

One of the things students fear most is failure. Failure signifies that things are not going well, and alerts us to the possibility that we may not achieve our goals. Unfortunately, many students see tests and exams as opportunities to fail. They prepare by becoming anxious and fearful, and trying to cram as much as possible right before the exam. These students rarely do well on the exam. They often fail, thus accomplishing just what they feared.

Taking tests requires strategy and planning. First, it is helpful to know what type of tests you will have. Your instructor probably told you during the first class meeting, or it may be in the class syllabus or course outline. If you do not know, ask.

If you are going to be taking essay exams, the best way to prepare is by writing essays. Before you do this, it is a good idea to find out what types of questions the instructor asks, and what is expected in a response. Again, it is helpful to ask the instructor for this material. Perhaps you can even see some examples of essay questions from previous years--some instructors at some colleges have copies of their exams on file in the department office or in the library. By finding out what is expected, you can formulate a model against which you can evaluate your answers.

Now, using the learning objectives, or some essay questions you wrote, actually sit down and write out the answers. I have prepared at least two essay questions for each chapter in this text. HINT: If you usually feel more anxious during a test, it may help you to practice writing your essays in the room in which the test will be given. Simply find a time when the room is vacant, and make yourself at home.

If your instructor gives multiple-choice tests, then you should practice taking multiple-choice tests. For each chapter, either use questions provided in the Student Study Guide, or make up your own. You may find it helpful to work out an arrangement to pool questions with other students, thereby reducing the amount of work you have to do, and developing a network of friends. Or, you may ask your professor if he or she would entertain the idea of having students write some of the exam questions--some of my professors did that in my undergraduate classes, and it is something I sometimes have my students do.

Whichever way you do it, the important thing is to prepare for tests and exams. Preparation is about 95 percent of the secret to getting a good grade. (Yes, there is some actual luck or chance involved in test scores, as even your instructor will admit!) Preparation is not only a good study and review technique, but also helps to reduce anxiety.

Dealing with Test Anxiety

Anxiety can be a helpful response when it occurs at low levels. In 1908, Yerkes and Dodson showed that the amount of anxiety that could benefit performance was a function of the difficulty and complexity of the task. As the difficulty of the task rose, anxiety became less helpful and more likely to interfere with performance.

If you have ever been so anxious in a test situation that you were unable to do well, even though you knew the information, you have test anxiety. If you get your exams back, and are surprised that you marked wrong answers when you knew the correct answers, or if you can only remember the correct answers after you leave the examination room, you too may have test anxiety.

Strategy Number One: Effective Study

Use study habits that promote learning and make the best use of time. Strategies, such as scheduling your time and using the PQ4R system, reduce anxiety by increasing confidence. As you come to realize that you know the material, your confidence rises and anxiety retreats.

Strategy Number Two: Relaxation

Each of us develops a unique pattern of relaxation. Some people relax by going to a specific place, either in person or mentally. Others relax by playing music, by being with friends, by using autogenic relaxation phrases, or by meditating. Whatever you do, be aware of it, and try to practice relaxation techniques. If you are good at relaxing, try thinking about those situations that make you anxious, and relax while you think of them. To do this, allow yourself to think only briefly (fifteen to thirty seconds at a time) of the situation that makes you anxious, and then relax again. After a number of such pairings, you will find that thinking about that situation no longer makes you anxious. At this point, you may be surprised to find that the situation itself also no longer produces anxiety. You may find that it is helpful to think about these anxiety-provoking situations in a sequence from those that produce very little anxiety to those that are more anxiety-evoking. Such a list, from low to high anxiety, might look something like this:

1. Your instructor announces that there will be a test in four weeks.
2. Your instructor reminds you of the test next week.
3. As you study, you see on the course outline the word *test*, and remember next week's test.
4. One of your friends asks you if you want to study together for the test, which is the day after tomorrow.

5. You choose not to go out with your friends because of the test tomorrow.

6. As you get up in the morning, you remember that today is the day of the test.
7. You are walking down the hall toward the classroom, thinking about what questions might be on the test.
8. The instructor enters the classroom, carrying a sheaf of papers in hand.
9. The instructor distributes the papers, and you see the word *test* or *exam* at the top.
10. After reading the first five questions, you have not been able to think of the answer to any of them.

If you work at it gradually and consistently, pairing these types of thoughts (briefly) with relaxation and remembering to let go and relax after each one, this will dispel test anxiety and make test taking a more productive and successful experience.

Strategy Number Three: Thinking Clearly

Most students who have test anxiety think in unclear and unproductive ways. They say to themselves things like: "I can't get these answers correct . . . I don't know this stuff . . . I don't know anything at all . . . I'm going to fail this test . . . I'm probably going to flunk out of school . . . I'm just a dumb nerd." These thoughts share two unfortunate characteristics: they are negative and they are absolute. They should be replaced.

When we tell ourselves negative and absolute thoughts, we find it impossible to focus on the test material. The result is that we miss questions even when we know the answers. Our thinking prevents us from doing well.

A good strategy for replacing these negative and absolute thoughts is to practice thinking positive and honest thoughts, such as: "I may not know all the answers, but I know some of them . . . I don't know the answer to that right now, so I will go on to the next one and come back to that . . . I don't have to get them all right . . . I studied hard and carefully, and I can get some of them correct . . . I am a serious student, and have some abilities . . . I am prepared for this test, and know many of the answers . . . This test is important, but it is not going to determine the course of my entire life and if I don't do well, it doesn't mean I'm a horrible person or a dummy."

By thinking clearly, honestly, and positively, we quiet the flood of anxiety and focus on the task at hand. Students who use this technique invariably do better on the tests. It takes practice to think clearly, but it is worth the effort. After a while, you will find that it becomes natural and does not take any noticeable effort. And as anxiety is reduced, more energy is available for studying and for doing well on examinations. The eventual outcome is more enjoyment with learning, better learning, more success in college, and the achievement of your goals.

Strategy Number Four: Guided Imagery

Something I often do with my students before a test is to have them relax (see strategy Two), close their eyes, and visualize themselves walking into a tall building. They go into the elevator in the building and take it to the top floor, which is fifty-six stories up. They walk out of the elevator, and go to the stairwell, then climb to the top of the building. There is no railing on the top of the building. I direct them to walk over to the very edge of the building and put their toes at the very edge, then look down. I ask them to think about how they are feeling as they are looking down onto the street from the top of this building. I then tell them to back up, have the realization that they can fly--just spread out their arms and they can fly. Then they are directed back to the edge of the building, knowing that they can fly. They put their toes on the edge, look down, then

spread their arms and fly, eventually flying down to land safely on the ground below. Next I have them visualize themselves in the classroom; on the desk before them is their test. They look at the test and see themselves reading the questions, saying "I know that answer. Yes, I remember learning that." They visualize themselves being successful, answering all the questions correctly, feeling good about themselves. Then I have them visualize getting their tests back, with a big "A" on the test.

Some students are much better able to visualize than others. You can try combining strategy two with this strategy to help you improve your visualization, since it can be an effective success strategy.

Strategy Number Five: Do the Easy Ones First

One technique I learned while studying for the GRE (Graduate Record Exam) was to read each question and answer the ones I knew, then go back to the harder ones. Two things to watch out for on this: first, be sure you get the answers in the right place--sometimes when we skip a question or two, we wind up marking the wrong space, so check that your answer to question 10 is in space 10; second, you may find you're stumped by the first several questions--don't let that throw you, just keep going because there is bound to be one you jump on and say, "Yes! I know that one." Answer the easy ones first, then go back to the others after you've built up your confidence seeing you DO know "stuff." Then, always go back over the whole test to be sure you answered every question (the exception here is if you have a professor who takes more than one point off for wrong answers--in that case, it's better not to answer than to answer wrong, but I don't know anyone who does that).

Strategy Number Six: State Dependent Learning

Research has found that we remember information best when we are in the same "state" we were in when we first learned the information. So, for example, you might remember a certain song when prompted by a specific stimulus (seeing someone who reminds you of your "first true love"); or, we will remember things we learned when we were particularly happy if we are again in that mood. This goes for physical contexts as well--so that we have an advantage if we take an exam in the same room where we learned the information in the first place. But it also goes to physical context in terms of our bodies--if you drink coffee or caffeine-laden sodas when you study, try to do the same before your exam. On the other hand, if you don't consume caffeine when you study, by all means, DO NOT suddenly have a cup of coffee before your exam. Because of the power of this phenomenon, you may want to create a particular mental context for yourself when you study so that you can put yourself into the same mental context when you take your exams.

Strategy Number Seven: Take a Break

If you find yourself getting stressed out during the test, take a break. Put your pencil down, breath deeply, you may even want to put your head down on the desk (please, do not fall asleep!). Use the relaxation techniques or the guided imagery strategy; visualize yourself looking at the test and suddenly realizing that you DO know the answers to at least most of the questions. Then go back to taking the test.

Remember, that with all of these test taking strategies, if you don't do the first one, none of the others will help! Passing the course requires that you actively study the material.

Memory Techniques

No matter how much you read, it won't help you if you don't remember *what* you read. The most critical factor in remembering is being able to apply what you have learned. Of course, some things such as people's names, or certain dates, or statistical information are not easily applied to your life, so you'll have to use other techniques. But first, let's talk about the "easy way."

Apply It to Your Life

If you can take the material you are learning and use it in your everyday life, you will remember it without any problem. Connect it with what you already know, either from life experience or other courses you have taken. Sometimes what you are learning fits nicely with what you already knew; sometimes it will contradict what you learned before. This is an opportunity to look at how the new information fits in with the old--were there new research findings? Or, is it merely a difference of opinion? Make these associations--don't keep the information for any class neatly compartmentalized--if you do, you'll have a hard time trying to find it when you need it.

Teach It to Someone Else!

When we start teaching something to someone else, we find we HAVE TO learn it, and by trying to explain the material to another person, we examine it and think about it differently. So, take the material you are learning in this class (or any class) and teach it to someone else. When they ask you questions, you can look them up and find the answers, or think them out together, or ask someone else. As you explain these concepts to someone else (your children, your friends, or even your dog), you will suddenly see them in a totally different light.

Mnemonic Techniques

Some things are just really difficult to apply to your own life. Dates, names, places, statistics, and such may not have a great deal of meaning for you. In that event, use the tricks that memory specialists use--mnemonics. There are many different types. For example, one famous mnemonic is an acronym for remembering the Great Lakes: HOMES=Huron, Ontario, Michigan, Erie, and Superior; or the colors of the rainbow is a man's name: ROY G. BIV=Red, Orange, Yellow, Green, Blue, Indigo, and Violet (if not for this "man," I'd never remember indigo!) You can make up your own acronyms by taking the first initial of any term, person, etc. It's easiest, though, if it's something that makes sense to you.

Another mnemonic technique is called the "method of loci," and I've been told it's one that medical students use to remember body parts. You list the things you need to remember, then visualize yourself walking around a familiar place (like your living room), putting one item on a particular piece of furniture. Then, when you need to remember that item, you go through your "living room" to see where it is.

One other mnemonic technique is the story method. Take the information you need to remember and put it into a story.

Be an "Information Dropper"

This is similar to the suggestion to teach, but less formal. Ask your friends to "indulge" you by listening to what you learned in your Life Span Development class (or any other class). Then *tell*

them what you are learning. You may, in fact, find that you have managed to help one of your friends by sharing this information!

Rote Memory

If you can remember back to grade school, when you learned to multiply, somehow the only way that seems to happen is by repeating the multiplication tables over and over and over again. Personally, I think this is about the worst way to learn most anything, but for some things (like multiplication tables) it works. The Flashcards that are included in each chapter of this Study Guide are a way to help you learn through repeating the material you don't know until you are able to answer the questions posed without looking at the reverse side of the cards. Hopefully you will then go further, and apply the information to other areas of your life.

Most Important

Remember this: professors don't actually "teach" their students, rather, they facilitate learning so students end up teaching themselves. While we try really hard to motivate our students, keep them interested, and present information in a way that helps students to understand, the ultimate responsibility for learning rests with the student. Some students have learned *despite* their professors, others don't learn even with the very best of professors. So, keep your goals in mind, study hard, ask questions, and aim for success!

Time Management Tips

- You might want to take the "tried and true" approach of planning out your known commitments for the entire semester once you receive the course syllabi.

- You can then add special projects or meetings to this schedule. What professors often find is that students forget when an assignment is due. Assignments can quickly backup in the "queue," that wonderful waiting-line. Then students panic or spend those late evenings and early mornings generating those papers and producing those projects. This is a great method if you like the feelings generated by stress and a lack of sleep, but one can hardly imagine that the feelings are worth it. Additionally the quality of the work may get you by but is it really the type of work you want to submit? Remember that you are acquiring knowledge and skills that will be useful in your career, even in those general education courses that provide a foundation for conversations and human interaction within future work settings.

- In addition to planning the due dates for your assignments at the beginning of the semester, begin working on these assignments early and in segments. Don't wait to produce the entire research paper or project. Undertake the process in stages. For example, in completing a research paper begin with your literature search. Use academically based search tools to locate relevant articles and books. Obtain copies of these documents earlier in the semester, or as early as possible. Read an article ever few days or at least one a week for each assignment. Make notes in the margins, in the source document, or on note cards. Then when you are ready to produce the paper or project refer to these notes. Not that this will "solve" all of your scheduling concerns, but in should make your papers and projects manageable.

- Additionally, you can incorporate the use of this study guide into your time management plans. Use the learning objectives as a means of guiding your reading of the chapter. You might even consider using this outline for taking notes while reading, or for that matter as a note taken guide if your class in predominantly a lecture class. After reading and attending lectures use the guide as a review tool to prepare you for your quizzes or exams. Based on the assessment methods used by your professor use the appropriate reinforcement tools. The self-tests and guided review for multiple choice tests. The guided review and essay questions for essay and short answer exams. Finally, you can use the chapter resource reflections to provide a more personal reflection that may, depending on your professor's expectations, be incorporated into essay responses.

How to Use the Internet

Although the Internet is opening up the world to many individuals in a vast array of mediums (i.e. computers, television, cellular phones) you need to be cautious regarding its use in academia. Determining the **credibility** of the sources of information is a major task. Unfortunately, if you simply use the Internet search engines they will find a wide variety in terms of the quality and type of "hits" you get. For example, if you simply type "sex" in a search engine they will generate many commercial sites that are selling sexual products and not sites that are appropriate for academic research or presentations. It only takes a few dollars a month and an opinion or product to produce a web site. For this reason it is suggested that you use sites that are associated with a long standing credible organization or that they use "gateway" sites that screen other sites and only refer individuals to quality sites. McGraw-Hill has developed a Human Sexuality drop-in center at http://www.mhhe.com/socscience/sex/ which provides hyperlinks to other researched sites, and of course the Online Learning Center for the eighth edition of *Sexuality Today* located at www.mhhe.com/kelly8 is also a tremendous resource for students and instructors alike.

Further Resources

SexSource CD-ROM
Packaged free with each new copy of the textbook, the SexSource CD-ROM gives students access to the best of multimedia materials for sexuality. It includes short video clips that illustrate key concepts in the textbook and issues important to today's students, as well as practice quizzes for each chapter. (0073135003)

Online Learning Center- The official website for the text contains Chapter Outlines, Practice Quizzes that can be e-mailed to the professor, and links to relevant Internet sites. www.mhhe.com/kelly8.

For those of you with "Print Disabilities" including blindness, visual impairment, learning disabilities or other physical disabilities, please check out the **Recording for the Blind and Dyslexic website** at **www.rfbd.org** or call customer service at **(800) 221-4792**. This educational library has 77,000 taped titles including textbooks, and reference and professional materials for people who cannot read standard print because of a disability.

ACKNOWLEDGEMENTS

I so valued the opportunity to contribute to this Study Guide! It's quite a group effort, and one that would not have happened without the leadership and exceptional communication skills of Kirsten Stoller at McGraw Hill. Certainly Dr. Kelly's experienced words of wisdom are the cornerstone of this project. Mary Lee Harms was delightful to work with and is a knowledgeable copy editor. I found it rewarding to work with these professionals who understand and value the subject of sexuality and worked diligently to make this knowledge available to you. Thanks!

I must acknowledge the support I received from family and friends while working on this project. It seems that life will continue to happen despite deadlines! Betsy Frabotta, Tom Spencer and Angel Hansford were instrumental in their cheerleading efforts and with running guard so I could focus on the tasks at hand. My friend and colleague, Colleen Mercuri-Johnson, is always an open port in the midst of my storms. And I would be remiss if I did not acknowledge my students at Miami University Middletown and Sinclair Community College who are my inspiration to do this job that I love.

I am passionate about the teaching of the subjects in this textbook and study guide. I can think of nothing more important than endeavoring to learn more about sexuality both personally and through academic study. Our sexuality is what draws us together. It is the only common bond among humans… what a powerful gift. Respect it and respect yourself. Enjoy!

Richelle Frabotta, MSEd

CHAPTER 1
HISTORICAL, RESEARCH, AND CROSS-CULTURAL PERSPECTIVES ON SEXUALITY

CHAPTER OUTLINE

Learning Objectives

THE METHODS OF SEXOLOGICAL RESEARCH

SELF-EVALUATION

CHAPTER LEARNING OBJECTIVES

1. Consider the term "sexual ambivalence" and its cultural relevance.

2. Describe the European cultural influence on North American sexuality.

3. Describe the influence of homogeneous and heterogeneous cultures on sexuality.

4. List four categories of Western nation's sexual permissiveness.

5. Contrast the cultural acceptance of voyeurism and exhibitionism.

6. Describe the differences between Mangaia and Japanese and Chinese and African cultures regarding sexual behaviors and attitudes.

7. Describe cross-cultural influences regarding perceptions of same-gender behavior.

8. Describe the role of same-gender behaviors in preindustrial societies.

9. Describe Victorian perceptions of human sexuality.

10. List the six broad approaches and influences regarding patterns of change.

11. Briefly describe the influence of each broad approach and influence regarding patterns of change.

12. List two perspectives of biological essentialism.

13. Briefly describe the position of the social constructionists.

14. Briefly describe why a "reasonable approach" of variability is preferred.

15. Describe how politics and traditional values are involved with the social dimensions of sexuality.

16. List the three categories of attitudes.

17. List two 18th century negative attitudes regarding masturbation.

18. Briefly describe the perception of Krafft-Ebing toward masturbation.

19. State the opinions regarding masturbation by prevailing professionals.

20. Contrast the perceptions of young individuals from the 1950s with the 1980s and mid-1990s regarding sex.

21. Consider the differences between the terms "non-marital sex" and "hooking up".

22. Describe the research findings regarding attitudes toward "hooking up" and casual sexual encounters.

23. Compare and contrast the "double standard" as seen in America, Japan, Finland and two areas in the former Soviet Union.

24. Describe attitudes regarding same-gender sexual expressions.

25. Identify three positive and affirming concepts about human sexuality that have emerged within the last thirty years.

26. Describe the historical perceptions regarding sex and romance.

27. Describe and contrast the views regarding comprehensive sexuality education.

28. Consider when sex research became a credible scientific course of study

29. List three sex researchers from the 19th century that significantly impacted and shaped public concepts about human sexuality.

30. Identify the sex research focus of the early and mid twentieth century.

31. Describe the influence of Krafft-Ebing, Freud, and Ellis regarding early sex research.

32. Describe the significance of Kinsey's research and the questions it has raised.

33. Describe the flaws in early sex surveys.

34. Describe the two major research efforts of Masters and Johnson.

35. List the survey studies of the 1970s, 1980s, and 1990s.

36. List the topics of the "other sex" surveys of the 1990s.

37. Describe the findings of the of the early 1990s sex research.

38. Describe the significance of the National Health and Social Life Survey (NHSLS).

39. Describe the process of selecting samples.

40. List two types of bias in sex research.

41. List four types of talking surveys.

42. Describe a reason for gender discrepancies in sex surveys.

43. Describe both case studies and clinical research.

44. List both the topic and who conducted the major observation research study.

45. Distinguish between the concepts of ethnography and ethnosexuality.

46. Describe a challenge to anthropologists conducting field studies.

47. List the keystone of scientific research.

48. Describe the principles of informed consent.

49. List and describe three additional ethical challenges for researchers.

50. Describe a challenge to anthropologists conducting field studies.

51. List the keystone of scientific research.

52. Describe the principle of informed consent.

53. List and describe three additional challenges for researchers.

KEY WORDS

Biological essentialism: a theory that human traits and behaviors are primarily formed by inborn biological determinants such as genes and hormonal secretions, rather than by environmental influences.

Case study: an in-depth look at a particular individual and how he or she might be helped to solve a sexual or other problem. Case studies may offer new and useful ideas for counselors to use with other patients.

Clinical research: the study of the cause, treatment, or prevention of a disease or condition by testing large numbers of people.

Controlled experiment: research in which the investigator examines what is happening to one variable while all other variables are kept constant.

Ethnography (eth-NAH-gruffy): the anthropological study of other cultures.

Ethnosexual: referring to data concerning the sexual beliefs and customs of other cultures.

Eurocentric (ur-oh-SEN-trick): a cultural attitudinal framework typical of people with western European heritages.

Hooking up: engaging in sexual behavior in which there is no particular future commitment.

Informed consent: the consent given by research subjects indicating their willingness to participate in a study, after they are informed about the purpose of the study and how they will be asked to participate.

Latency period: a stage in human development characterized, in Freud's theory, by little interest in or awareness of sexual feelings.

Metrosexual: popular term to describe straight men who care about their appearance and good taste.

Penile strain gauge: a device placed on the penis to measure even subtle changes in its size due to sexual arousal.

Plethysmograph (pleh-THIZ-ma-graff): a laboratory measuring device that charts physiological changes over time. Attached to a penile strain gauge, it can chart changes in penis size. This is called penile plethysmography.

Retrosexual: popular term to describe men who, as a declaration of their masculinity, reject spending time on grooming and taste.

Random sample: a representative group of the larger population that is the focus of a scientific poll or study in which care is taken to select participants without a pattern that might sway research results.

Sample: a representative group of a population that is the focus of a scientific poll or study.

Sexology: the scientific study of human sexuality.

Sexosophy: the philosophies and ideologies relating to human sexuality.

Sexual ambivalence: the struggle to balance inner sexual insecurities with prevailing social conflict; the apparent inconsistencies with a consistent sexual message and what we specifically consider proper and appropriate.

Sexual health: the concept that recognizes the existence of particular personal and public health issues relating to sexuality

Sexual pleasure: the concept that people have a right to positive enjoyment of their sexuality.

Sexual rights: a political concept that calls for the clarification of human rights and freedoms regarding sexual orientation and behavior.

Sexual revolution: the changes in thinking about sexuality and sexual behavior in society that occurred in the 1960s and 1970s.

Social constructionism: a theory that holds that human traits and behaviors are shaped more by environmental social forces than by innate biological factors.

Variable: an aspect of a scientific study that is subject to change.

Voyeurism (VOYE-yu-rizm): sexual gratification from viewing others who are nude or are engaging in sexual activities.

SELF-TEST

When responding to the following multiple-choice questions, choose the "best" answer. The "best" answer is the one that corresponds to the information contained in your text.

1) Human sexuality
   a) provides a consistent set of guidelines and values to follow.
   b) is a realm of contrasts and contradictions, social trends and cultural imperatives.
   c) allows people to aspire to a set of standards that support a unified culture.
   d) is ever-changing depending upon which researcher is most prominent.

2) The residents of the Finnish village of Kutemajarvi were trying to hold a sex fair that would feature
   a) a booth offering free condoms.
   b) scenes from a dungeon where people were engaging in sadistic and masochistic sex play.
   c) a kissing booth where people could donate $10 to charity in exchange for a kiss.
   d) pleasant outdoor locations for couples to share sexual activity.

3) Someone who engages in voyeurism gains sexual satisfaction by
   a) taking off their clothes where others can see them.
   b) seeing others nude.
   c) seeing others involved in sexual acts.
   d) both b and c

4) In Japanese culture female sexuality is often
   a) widely accepted.
   b) ignored or subjugated.
   c) silently avoided.
   d) externally hidden, while privately celebrated.

5) Many societies find themselves caught between emerging attitudes of greater sexual freedom and
   a) conflict with adolescent puberty rituals.
   b) traditional values that discourage sexual expression.
   c) religious rites.
   d) dating rituals.

6) The period during the 1960s was often referred to as
   a) the sociosexual revolution.
   b) the psychosexual revolution.
   c) the hippie sex happening.
   d) the sexual revolution.

7) The pattern of change that included a counterculture movement that questioned rules, regulations, and decisions is
   a) Media and Internet Attention.
   b) Changing Roles of Women.
   c) New Approaches to Morality and Personal Autonomy.
   d) HIV and AIDS.

8) Which is the category of attitude that believes the primary purpose of sexual activity is reproduction?
   a) procreational
   b) traditional
   c) relational
   d) recreational

9) Which of the following 18th century observations compounded the negative view of masturbation?
   a) criminally deviant people observed masturbating
   b) church officials wanting to control sexual behaviors
   c) people in mental institutions observed masturbating
   d) children frequently seen masturbating

10) The prevailing professional opinion regarding masturbation is
   a) that it is a normal part of human sexual expression.
   b) that, if done excessively. it is a minor sexual deviance.
   c) a moral issue that is sinful.
   d) psychopathological.

11) College students who are currently dating need to be aware of which of the following "double standards?"
   a) traditional
   b) transitional
   c) relational
   d) conditional

12) Hooking up is relatively acceptable and commonplace; however,
   a) women are the predominant gender initiating casual sex.
   b) the older generation is not participating.
   c) it is predominant among only one age group.
   d) there still exists a difference in acceptability based on gender.

13) The concept of "sexual health"
   a) recognizes that humans will experience negative sexual experiences.
   b) grew out of a World Health Organization conference in 1975.
   c) is so new that a large portion of industrialized nations have not yet added the concept to their national discussions.
   d) suggests that sexual dysfunctions and disorders are declining.

14) Comprehensive sexuality education
   a) recognizes cultural differences exist, and education should be presented in a manner sensitive to those differences.
   b) emphasizes the need to teach young people skills to communicate effectively.
   c) suggests that the educational process is a lifelong one.
   d) all of the above.

15) Medical and Mental health professionals have, at times, classified certain differing forms of orientations, behaviors, and expressions of gender as all but one of the following:
   a) sick.
   b) criminal.
   c) acts of God.
   d) sinful.

16) The politics of sexuality education have been referred to as a
   a) Sexual War.
   b) Family Values War.
   c) Religious War.
   d) Culture War.

17) Which of the early sexual researchers took a stand on rights for people who were gay or lesbian?
   a) Magnus Hirschfeld
   b) Richard von Krafft-Ebing
   c) Sigmund Freud
   d) Henry Havelock Ellis

18) Which of the early sexual researchers viewed masturbation as the cause of sexual deviations?
   a) Henry Havelock Ellis
   b) Richard von Krafft-Ebing
   c) Sigmund Freud
   d) Magnus Hirschfeld

19) Which of the following individuals was not one of the early marriage researchers?
   a) Robert Latou Dickinson
   b) Helena Wright
   c) Theodoor van de Velde
   d) Robert Davidson

20) All of the following were early sex surveys *except*
   a) The Hunt Report.
   b) The Redbook Survey.
   c) The Glamour Survey.
   d) The Hite Report.

21) When conducting survey research, the early surveys should have been more concerned about
   a) increasing the number of surveys distributed.
   b) decreasing the number of surveys distributed.
   c) how to get the participants.
   d) inviting minority groups to participate.

22) Which of the following is believed to be the "best" designed research study to investigate human sexual behavior?
   a) National Health and Family Life Survey
   b) National Health and Social Life Survey
   c) National Health and Sexuality Living Survey
   d) National Health and Social Living Survey

23) The National Longitudinal Study of Adolescent Health took how many years to complete?
   a) 3 years, 1994-1996
   b) 3 years, 1992-1994
   c) 5 years, 1994-1998
   d) 5 years, 1992-1996

24) Which of the following pairs represent forms of research bias?
   a) volunteer and response
   b) volunteer and answer
   c) contributor and response
   d) age and gender

25) All of the following are means of talking surveys *except*
   a) face-to-face interviews.
   b) telephone interviews.
   c) completion of questionnaires.
   d) observing behaviors.

26) In surveys of sexual behavior, there has been a consistent pattern in the data that is based on
   a) gender discrepancy.
   b) age differences.
   c) attitudinal divergences.
   d) communication differences.

27) When an anthropologist conducts research that collects information that describes the sexual practices of a particular culture, they are engaging in what type research?
   a) ethnography
   b) ethnosexual field studies
   c) ethnosociological field studies
   d) ethnosexiography

28) Human subjects have the right to informed consent, which means that
   a) they must be given limited information about the purpose of the study.
   b) they are not informed about physical or psychological harm.
   c) they must be given complete prior information about the study.
   d) they must be given completed information about the study once it is completed.

29) The device, that when combined with the penile strain gauge, measures male erectile responses is a
   a) plethysmometer.
   b) plethysmagraph.
   c) erectograph.
   d) plethysmograph.

GUIDED REVIEW AND STUDY
[Answers are provided at the end of the study guide.]

The guided review and study is designed to develop recall of key concepts from the chapter. The review is in the form of a set of "fill-in-the-blank" questions. The answers for each of the questions can be found at the end of the study guide.

1) The evidence shows that it is not education, but _____, that leads to the most risky sexual decision making.
2) Regarding the range of sexual behaviors, societies and cultures are often classified according to degrees of _____ and _____.
3) Sexuality in America is frequently seen as a _____ or _____ goal orientation.
4) Same-gender behavior in some preindustrial societies is viewed as a stage in _____ _____.
5) Ideals and values about_____ and _____ in Western cultures have seen dramatic shifts in the past two centuries.
6) Traditional gender roles see the man as a _____ _____ for the woman and the woman as a _____ _____ _____ _____ to the man.
7) _____ is a term that is recently coined in response to heterosexual men who are now able to publicly take pride in a well-groomed and stylish appearance.
8) Human personality traits and behaviors, according to _____ _____, are mostly shaped by social influences.
9) Research has found that _____ does not merely refer to actions involving sex organs.
10) College students with _____ sexual partners and who get _____ frequently are less likely to use condoms on a consistent basis.
11) The "reasonable approach" to variability promotes examining the influence of _____ and/or the _____.
12) Regarding sexual attitudes, there appear to be several different _____ attitudinal patterns that exist alongside one another.
13) Early perceptions about masturbation viewed it as the _____ of Onan, or that if sexual fluids were expended, individuals would become _____.
14) In Western culture, there remains a _____ __ _____ regarding gender differences and sexual expression.
15) _____ attraction or orientation has been traditionally used as the norm against which sexual behaviors have been judged.
16) In the mid _____, homosexuality was removed from the American Psychiatric Association list of mental disorders.
17) Appearing in a United Nations document in 1994, _____ _____ recognizes that people must understand that they do not have to submit to unwanted sexual contact and indeed should be able to access birth control and sexually transmitted infection prevention methods.
18) Kinsey applied _____ to sexual behavior instead of drawing conclusions solely from personal observations.
19) _____ sexuality education sees the educational process as a lifelong endeavor regarding sexuality.
20) Although the methodologies are questioned, the _____ research of the 1970s solidified some of the myths and misconceptions about sexual behaviors.
21) The greatest strength of the National Health and Social Life Survey (NHSLS) was that the sample population was _____ selected, unlike most other studies of sexual behavior.

22) The difference between sexology and sexosophy is that the former is rooted in _____, while the latter is rooted in _____ or _____.
23) Sex researchers have the difficult responsibility of ensuring that their own methods and _____ do not distort the outcome of their work.
24) People who volunteer to participate in sexuality studies tend to be more _____ experienced than nonvolunteers.
25) Observational studies may take place in _____ settings or in the field; the former setting was used by Masters and Johnson.
26) In a controlled experiment, a particular _____ is studied or manipulated by the researcher.
27) When conducting ethical research, researchers must protect subjects from both _____ and _____ harm.
28) There is an increasing use of the _____ to gather _____ data.
29) Mandated reporting can create a(n) _____ _____ for a researcher who receives information about a sex crime.

ESSAY QUESTIONS
[Answers are provided at the end of the study guide.]

1) What do you think about this statement by Goldenberg, "…sexuality is something about which human beings are startlingly ambivalent"? Identify other examples of how Americans express this ambivalence. Now consider your own sexual values and behaviors. Do you practice sexual ambivalence?

2) Describe European as well as homogeneous and heterogeneous cultural influences on sexuality.

3) Describe the influence of five broad approaches and influences regarding patterns of change regarding sexuality.

4) Describe the perception of Krafft-Ebing toward masturbation along with the opinions of other professionals regarding this behavior.

5) Describe the processes for selecting research samples as well as two types of biases in sex research.

6) Describe the principle of informed consent as well as three additional ethical challenges faced by researchers.

CHAPTER RESOURCE REFLECTIONS

Cross-Cultural Perspective

As you read "The Influence of Carnival in Brazil," how would you envision yourself celebrating Carnival is Brazil? What cultural influences regarding such a celebration would you bring from your culture? Would you be able to let yourself enjoy the celebration from their cultural perspective? What cultural influences would promote your joining in the celebration? What cultural influences would restrain your participation?

As you read "He's going metro – or is it bi-metro?" can you relate to more intricate grooming habits for men? Do you or do you have male friends who classify themselves as metrosexual? How do you think this cultural phenomenon of better male grooming has impacted our traditional beliefs about being a "real man"?

Case Study

Many, if not all of us, have preconceived notions regarding sexuality, relationships, and often marriage. After reading Anil's story, what are your thoughts about the efforts he made to become a loving and sexually adequate husband? If you were Anil, what would you have done?

Chastity Belts

After reading the story about present day chastity belts, what was your initial response? Would you wear one if asked by your partner? Why or why not? Would you ask your partner to wear one? Why or why not?

Self-Evaluation: You and Your Sexuality

Initially, students may find it difficult or challenging to explore their sexuality from a personal perspective. In this chapter, two opportunities are provided. One opportunity examines your attitudes, whereas the other examines a variety of potential sexual behaviors. The attitude questionnaire even asks that you have a conversation with your parents or people who raised you. This can be scary, as some students have never had a conversation, at least in any detail, with their parents or guardians. The attitude activity may be more frightening for older adult students because they will be talking with their aging parents, who may be perceived as nonsexual people, about sexual topics. Take both of these activities as your initial steps to exploring not only the vast field of human sexuality, but also your personal journey into understanding your own sexual life and sexuality.

MCGRAW-HILL RESOURCES
REFLECTING ON SEXUALTY

Remember that this section of the study guide takes you beyond the text to explore other resources in the field of human sexuality. The experience attempts to expand on at least one concept covered in the chapter.

Access the McGraw-Hill web pages associated with sexuality at
      http://www.mhhe.com/socscience/sex

Scroll down and "click" on the hyperlink for "Resource Room."

Scroll down and "click" on the hyperlink for "Web Resources."

Scroll down and "click" on the hyperlink for "Electronic Journal of Human Sexuality."

Scroll down the Web site until you reach the listing for "Research Papers," for the current journal edition, or continue scrolling down until you see the "Table of Contents" for previous journal editions. "Click" on the hyperlink of your choice.

Once at this site, select and read one of the research articles. In particular, pay attention to the type of research study conducted. Can you ascertain any biases in the research?

CHAPTER 2
FEMALE SEXUAL ANATOMY AND PHYSIOLOGY

CHAPTER OUTLINE

SELF-EVALUATION

You and Your Body

CHAPTER LEARNING OBJECTIVES

1. List and describe the functions of the external female sex organs.

2. List and describe the function of the clitoris, including the parts of the organ.

3. Describe a problem of and treatment for the clitoral prepuce.

4. Describe the procedure for conducting female genital cutting.

5. Describe the purposes of female genital mutilation.

6. Describe different cultural perceptions regarding female genital cutting.

7. Describe the structures, functions, and potential concerns regarding the vagina and surrounding muscles.

8. Describe concerns with the procedure of douching.

9. List the five types of hymens.

10. Describe the social and medical concerns regarding the hymen.

11. Describe the procedure for women examining their genitals.

12. List six disorders of the female sex organs.

13. Describe the causes of and treatments for disorders of the female sex organs.

14. List and describe the parts and functions of the uterus.

15. Describe why cervical cancer is a concern for women.

16. Identify five sex-related factors associated with higher risk for cervical cancer.

17. Consider the new Pap test screening guidelines from the American Cancer Society.

18. Describe how a pelvic exam is conducted.

19. List and describe two procedures for examining suspicious cells of the cervix.

20. List and describe the parts and functions of the ovaries.

21. List and describe the parts and functions of the fallopian tubes.

22. List and describe two stages of cervical cancer.

23. List and describe three additional disorders associated with the uterus.

24. Describe two anatomical abnormalities associated with the uterus.

25. Describe the parts of the breast.

26. Describe the process of lactation.

27. Describe three facts about breast cancer.

28. Describe genetic concerns associated with the female breasts.

29. Describe the process for undertaking breast self-examination.

30. Describe the recommendations for mammograms.

31. List and describe two procedures for addressing malignant breast tumors.

32. Briefly describe perceptions of menarche and menopause.

33. List the glands and hormones associated with the menstrual cycle.

34. Describe the four-phase process of menstruation.

35. Describe the difference between PMS and PMDD.

36. Identify the newest treatment approach for women dealing with menstrual cycle discomforts.

37. Describe the hormonal and physiological body changes associated with menopause.

38. Describe the benefits and risks of hormone replacement therapy.

39. Describe the sexual implications of menarche and menopause, as well as the relationship to a positive self-perception.

KEY WORDS

Acute urethral syndrome: infection or irritation of the urethra.

Areola (a-REE-a-la): darkened, circular area of skin surrounding the nipple of the breast.

Bartholin's glands (BAR-tha-lenz): small glands located in the opening through the minor lips that produce some secretion during sexual arousal.

Cervical intraepithelial neoplasia (CIN) (ep-a-THEE-lee-al nee-a-PLAY-zhee-a): abnormal, precancerous cells sometimes identified in a Pap smear.

Cervix (SERV-ix): lower "neck" of the uterus that extends into the back part of the vagina.

Cilia: microscopic, hairlike projections that help move the ovum through the fallopian tube.

Circumcision (SIR-cum-sizh-uhn): of clitoris—surgical procedure that cuts the prepuce, exposing the clitoral shaft.

Clitoridectomy (clih-torr-ih-DECK-tah-mee): surgical removal of the clitoris; practiced routinely in some cultures.

Clitoris (KLIT-a-rus): sexually sensitive organ found in the female vulva; it becomes engorged with blood during arousal.

Corpus luteum: cell cluster of the follicle that remains after the ovum is released, secreting hormones that help regulate the menstrual cycle.

Cystitis (sis-TITE-us): a nonsexually transmitted infection of the urinary bladder.

Diethylstilbestrol (DES) (dye-eth-al-stil-BES-trole): synthetic estrogen compound once given to mothers whose pregnancies were at high risk of miscarrying.

Dysmenorrhea (dis-men-a-REE-a): painful menstruation.

Endometrial hyperplasia (hy-per-PLAY-zhee-a): excessive growth of the inner lining of the uterus (endometrium).

Endometriosis (en-doe-mee-tree-O-sus): growth of the endometrium out of the uterus into surrounding organs.

Endometrium: interior lining of the uterus, innermost of three layers.

Estrogen (ES-tro-jen): hormone produced abundantly by the ovaries; it plays an important role in the menstrual cycle.

Fallopian tubes: structures that are connected to the uterus and lead the ovum from an ovary to the inner cavity of the uterus.

Fibroid tumors: nonmalignant growths that commonly grow in uterine tissues, often interfering with uterine function.

Fibrous hymen: condition in which hymen is composed of unnaturally thick, tough tissue.

Follicles: capsules of cells in which an ovum matures.

Follicle-stimulating hormone (FSH): pituitary hormone that stimulates the ovaries or testes.

Fundus: the broad top portion of the uterus.

Glans: sensitive head of the female clitoris, visible between the upper folds of the minor lips.

Gonadotropin-releasing hormone (GnRH): (go-nad-a-TRO-pen): hormone from the hypothalamus that stimulates the release of FSH and LH by the pituitary.

Hormone replacement therapy (HRT): treatment of the physical changes of menopause by administering dosages of the hormones estrogen and progesterone.

Hot flash: a flushed, sweaty feeling in the skin caused by dilated blood vessels; often associated with menopause.

Hymen: membranous tissue that can cover part of the vaginal opening.

Hysterectomy: surgical removal of all or part of the uterus.

Imperforate hymen: lack of any openings in the hymen.

Infibulation (in-fib-you-LAY-shun): surgical procedure, performed in some cultures, which seals the opening of the vagina.

Interstitial cystitis (IC): a chronic bladder inflammation that can cause debilitating discomfort and interfere with sexual enjoyment.

Introitus (in-TROID-us): the outer opening of the vagina.

Invasive cancer of the cervix (ICC): advanced and dangerous malignancy requiring prompt treatment.

Isthmus: narrowed portion of the uterus just above the cervix.

Labia majora (LAY-bee-uh mah-JOR-uh): two outer folds of skin covering the minor lips, clitoris, urinary meatus, and vaginal opening.

Labia minora (LAY-bee-uh mih-NOR-uh): two inner folds of skin that join above the clitoris and extend along the sides of the vaginal and urethral openings.

Lactation: production of milk by the milk glands of the breasts.

Lumpectomy: surgical removal of a breast lump, along with a small amount of surrounding tissue.

Luteinizing hormone (LH) (LEW-tee-in-ize-ing): pituitary hormone that triggers ovulation in the ovaries and stimulates sperm production in the testes.

Mammography: sensitive X-ray technique used to discover small breast tumors.

Mastectomy: surgical removal of all or part of a breast.

Menarche (MEN-are-kee): onset of menstruation at puberty.

Menopause (MEN-a-pawz): time in midlife when menstruation ceases.

Menstrual cycle: the hormonal interactions that prepare a woman's body for possible pregnancy at roughly monthly intervals.

Mons: cushion of fatty tissue located over the female's pubic bone.

Myometrium: middle, muscular layer of the uterine wall.

Oocytes (OH-a-sites): cells that mature to become ova.

Os: opening in the cervix that leads into the hollow interior of the uterus.

Osteoporosis (ah-stee-o-po-ROW-sus): disease caused by loss of calcium from the bones in postmenopausal women, leading to brittle bones and stooped posture

Ova: egg cells produced in the ovary. A single cell is called an ovum; in reproduction, it is fertilized by a sperm cell.

Ovaries: pair of female gonads, located in the abdominal cavity, that mature ova and produce female hormones.

Ovulation: release of a mature ovum through the wall of an ovary.

Oxytocin: pituitary hormone that plays a role in lactation and in uterine contractions.

Pap smear: medical test that examines a smear of cervical cells to detect any cellular abnormalities.

Perimenopause: the time of a woman's life surrounding menopause, characterized by symptoms resulting from reduced estrogen levels.

Perimetrium: outer covering of the uterus.

Polycystic ovary syndrome (PCOS) (PAH-lee-SIS-tick): a disorder of the ovaries that can produce a variety of unpleasant physical symptoms, often because of elevated testosterone levels.

Premenstrual dysphoric disorder (PMDD): severe emotional symptoms such as anxiety or depression around the time of menstruation.

Premenstrual syndrome (PMS): symptoms of physical discomfort, moodiness, and emotional tensions that occur in some women for a few days prior to menstruation.

Prepuce (PREE-peus): in the female, tissue of the upper vulva that covers the clitoral shaft.

Prolactin: pituitary hormone that stimulates the process of lactation.

Prolapse of the uterus: weakening of the supportive ligaments of the uterus, causing it to protrude into the vagina.

Prostaglandin: hormonelike chemical whose concentrations increase in a woman's body just prior to menstruation.

Pubococcygeus (PC) muscle (pyub-o-kox-a-JEE-us): part of the supporting musculature of the vagina that is involved in orgasmic response and over which a woman can exert some control.

Shaft: in the female, the longer body of the clitoris, containing erectile tissue.

Smegma: thick, oily substance that may accumulate under the prepuce of the clitoris or penis.

Urinary meatus (mee-AY-tuss): opening through which urine passes from the urethra to the outside of the body.

Uterus (YUTE-a-rus): muscular organ of the female reproductive system; a fertilized egg implants itself within the uterus.

Vagina (vu-JI-na): muscular canal in the female that is responsive to sexual arousal; it receives semen during heterosexual intercourse for reproduction.

Vaginal atresia (a-TREE-zha): birth defect in which the vagina is absent or closed.

Vaginal atrophy: shrinking and deterioration of vaginal lining, usually the result of low estrogen levels during aging.

Vaginal fistulae (FISH-cha-lee *or* -lie): abnormal channels that can develop between the vagina and other internal organs.

Vaginismus (vaj-uh-NIZ-mus): involuntary spasm of the outer vaginal musculature, making penetration of the vagina difficult or impossible.

Varicose veins: overexpanded blood vessels; can occur in veins surrounding the vagina.

Vulva: external sex organs of the female, including the mons, major and minor lips, clitoris, and opening of the vagina.

Vulvar vestibulitis: one form of vulvodynia that often interferes with sexual penetration of the vagina.

Vulvodynia: a medical condition characterized by pain and burning in the vulva and outer vagina.

SELF-TEST

When responding to the following multiple-choice questions, choose the "best" answer. The "best" answer is the one that corresponds to the information contained in your text.

1) The external female sex organs consist of all of the following *except*
   a) mons.
   b) labia majora.
   c) labia vagina.
   d) clitoris.

2) The function of the external labia is to
   a) cover the outer, least sensitive sex organs of the women.
   b) protect the outer sex organs of the women.
   c) cover and protect the clitoris.
   d) cover and protect the inner sex organs of the women.

3) The clitoral hood is also called the
   a) prepuce.
   b) clitoral sheath.
   c) labia minora.
   d) clitoral meatus

4) Bartholin's glands are sometimes referred to as
   a) the g-spot.
   b) vulvovaginal glands.
   c) Skene's glands.
   d) functional tissue.

5) The most sensitive portion of the vulva is the
   a) labia majora.
   b) clitoral shaft.
   c) clitoral glans.
   d) clitoral prepuce.

6) Clitoridectomies were thought to "cure" which of the following:
   a) masturbation and prevent insanity.
   b) masturbation and pregnancy.
   c) prevent insanity and pregnancy.
   d) adultery and masturbation.

7) Some cultures also practice _____ where the labia minora and sometimes the labia majora are removed and the sides of the external portion of the vagina are sewn together.
   a) afibulation
   b) anfibulation
   c) infibulation
   d) defibulation

8) Which country has policies regarding health care providers assisting with female genital mutilation (FGM)?
   a) Iran
   b) Sudan
   c) Egypt
   d) England.

9) The two sets of muscles surrounding the vaginal opening are the
   a) sphincter vulvi and levator ani muscles.
   b) sphincter vaginae and levator labial muscles.
   c) sphincter ani and levator vaginae muscles.
   d) sphincter vaginae and levator ani muscles.

10) Studies continue to demonstrate that, contrary to popular notions, douching is
    a) necessary before a pap smear.
    b) only for women under 35 years old.
    c) a healthy practice.
    d) actually dangerous.

11) A surgical procedure in which the physician places stitches in the labia to help women who did not want their husbands to know they were not virgins is a
   a) lover's gift.
   b) passion knot.
   c) virginal knot.
   d) lover's knot.

12) It's a good idea for women to examine their genitals
   a) daily.
   b) bi-annually.
   c) weekly.
   d) monthly.

13) Cystitis is also referred to as
   a) primary urethral infection.
   b) acute urethral syndrome.
   c) acute urethral infection.
   d) primary urethral syndrome.

14) In one study, _____ of several hundred surveyed indicated that they were currently experiencing vulvar pain.
   a) 90%
   b) 80%
   c) 65%
   d) 45%

15) The inner most layer of the uterus that is rich in blood vessels and glands is the
   a) endometrium.
   b) perimetrium.
   c) myometrium.
   d) isthmetrium.

16) All but one of the following are sex-related factors associated with a higher risk for cervical cancer.
   a) late adolescence initiation of sexual intercourse
   b) ten or more sexual partners
   c) history of pelvic inflammatory disease (PID) or (sexually transmitted disease (STI)
   d) having a partner with multiple sex partners

17) Which of the following is not one of the five sex-related factors associated with a higher risk for cervical cancer?
   a) 15 or more sex partners
   b) very early initiation of sexual intercourse
   c) history of PID or an STI
   d) having a partner who has been with multiple sex partners

18) An aggressive diagnostic procedure used to investigate suspicious cells detected during a Pap smear:
   a) dissection and curettage.
   b) dilation and cervicalcision.
   c) dilation and curettage.
   d) D, C and C

19) All of the following are associated with the ovaries and fallopian tubes *except*
    a) the ova.
    b) the follicles.
    c) the oocytes.
    d) the follicular ligaments.

20) Recent research has indicated that mammalian ovaries may indeed continue to
    a) produce hormones in a woman in her 90's.
    b) produce new oocytes and follicles even into young adulthood.
    c) ovulate occasionally even after completing menopause.
    d) maintain a ration of healthy viable oocytes after completing menopause.

21) The condition in which the ligaments that support the uterus become weakened and the uterus extends into the vagina is
    a) polycystic ovary syndrome.
    b) prolapse of the cervix.
    c) prolapse of the uterus.
    d) partial uterine collapse.

22) During lactation, which hormone stimulates milk production?
    a) prolactin
    b) oxytocin
    c) androgen
    d) estrogen

23) Several nongenetic factors have been identified that may influence a woman's risk for breast cancer. Which of the following is not in that list?
    a) weight
    b) age
    c) monogamous sexual relationship
    d) onset of puberty

24) The best time to undertake breast self-examination is
    a) at the beginning of the menstrual cycle.
    b) at the end of the menstrual cycle.
    c) midway through the menstrual cycle.
    d) once you have begun menstruating.

25) Two procedures used to treat malignant tumors of the breast are
    a) mastectomy and breastectomy.
    b) mastectomy and lumpectomy.
    c) lumpectomy and breastectomy.
    d) malignantectomy and breastectomy.

26) The onset of menarche is generally between _____, whereas the onset of menopause is generally between _____.
    a) 9 and 16; 35 and 40.
    b) 9 and 12; 45 and 60.
    c) 9 and 16; 45 and 55.
    d) 8 and 14; 55 and 60.

27) All of the following are parts of the menstrual cycle *except*
   a) postovulatory preparation.
   b) luteal secretion.
   c) menstruation.
   d) preovulatory preparation.

28) PMS refers to
   a) preliminary menstrual syndrome.
   b) post menstrual syndrome.
   c) premenarch syndrome.
   d) premenstrual syndrome.

29) The years surrounding menopause are usually termed
   a) premenopause.
   b) perimenopause.
   c) primary menopause.
   d) programmed menopause.

30) HRT refers to
   a) hormone research and testing.
   b) hormone replacement testing.
   c) hormone replacement therapy.
   d) hormone research therapy.

GUIDED REVIEW AND STUDY
[Answers are provided at the end of the study guide.]

1) The entire area of the vulva is considered to be a major _____ zone for females, because it is generally very sensitive to sexual stimulation.
2) The _____ contains two columns and two bulbs of spongy tissue which become _____ with blood during sexual excitement causing the entire structure to become erect.
3) The vaginal opening, or _____, leads into the vagina.
4) Appropriate stimulation of the _____ is usually necessary for women to reach orgasm.
5) If _____ collects around the shaft of the clitoris, mild infections may result.
6) _____ is often deeply embedded in a particular culture's way of life reflective of historical patriarchal traditions.
7) The inner part of the vagina is not particularly _____.
8) _____ refers to tension and pain associated with involuntary contractions of the outer vaginal muscles.
9) The vagina has its own _____ and a rather delicate balance of naturally-occurring microorganisms that are important to its health.
10) When the hymen completely covers the opening of the vagina, it is referred to as a/an _____ hymen.
11) One of the most common bacteria to cause cystitis is _____.
12) Vaginal _____ occurs when the inner surfaces of the vagina shrink and narrow.
13) The neck of the uterus is called the _____, and the top is called the _____.
14) The most recent American Cancer Society recommends that women begin pap smears by the age of _____ or _____ years after becoming sexually active.

15) For a pelvic exam, a _____ is first carefully inserted into the vagina to hold open its walls.

16) Another term for miscarriage is _____.

17) _____ are cells in the ovarian follicles that potentially develop into ovum.

18) The fingerlike projections of the fallopian tubes are referred to as _____.

19) Cancer of the _____ is a common type of malignancy in women, second only to cancer of the breast.

20) Studies have shown that there is a _____ incidence of cervical cancer among women who have been sexually active with several men.

21) _____ is a disorder in which the uterine lining grows outward into the organs surrounding the uterus.

22) The darkened circular area of skin surrounding the nipple is called the _____.

23) Breast self-examinations should include both a _____ examination and a _____ examination.

24) _____ is a special X-ray picture taken of the breast that can detect even small lumps.

25) First menstruation is referred to as _____, and cessation of menstruation is referred to as _____.

26) The menstrual cycle is divided into four stages: the follicular phase, _____, luteal secreation and _____.

27) During ovulation the hypothalamus triggers the release of the _____ hormone from the pituitary.

28) Pain associated with menstruation is called _____.

29) Women who are more comfortable with their own sexuality tend to be more comfortable with _____ and _____.

30) The more severe psychological symptoms associated with PMS are sometimes classified as premenstrual _____ disorder.

31) _____ are now being prescribed to help women dealing with menstrual cycle discomforts.

32) The sexual implications of aging stem from both _____ and biological changes.

33) _____ is a hormonelike chemical believed to be involved in producing PMS.

34) Decreased estrogen production in women may lead to a weakening of the bones which is referred to as _____.

35) Menopausal women may experience a sweaty feeling that is associated with dilation of blood vessels in the skin. This is sometimes called a _____ _____.

36) A number of studies of HRT have demonstrated a statistical relationship between treatment with estrogen and _____ and _____ cancer.

ESSAY QUESTIONS
[Answers are provided at the end of the study guide.]

1) Identify the external and internal female sexual organs, as well as two cultural or social issues that involve these organs.

2) Identify six disorders of the female sex organs as well as the symptoms, causes, or treatments for these disorders.

3) Briefly discuss the importance of a routine pelvic exam as well as describing medical conditions that can result from pelvic abnormalities.

4) Briefly discuss the importance of and procedures for conducting a self-breast exam.

5) Describe the hormonal and physiological changes associated with menopause as well as the risks and benefits of hormone replacement therapy.

CHAPTER RESOURCE REFLECTIONS

Case Study-New Material

Should Karina feel "guilty" about how others perceive her? Why or why not? Should college students be concerned about alcohol consumption and engaging in sexual behaviors? Why or why not?

Cross-Cultural Perspective

As you read the cross-cultural "celebrations" about menarche, what are your reactions to the various celebrations? If you were a parent living in one of these cultures, do you believe you would "celebrate" the cultural norm? Why or why not?

Risks of Estrogen

After reading the story on the Hormone Quandary, and presuming there are no new research findings by the time you are menopausal; (a) if female, would you utilize HRT? Why or why not? (b) if female or male, would you want you female partner to utilize HRT? Why or why not? Do you think that the government should put more money toward researching the effects of HRT?

Self-Evaluation: You and Your Body

Although this activity is included in the main text chapter on female anatomy and physiology, it is important for both sexes to be comfortable not only with their bodies but also the bodies of their partners, whether of the opposite or same sex. This is not an easy undertaking in a society that focuses on the value and beauty of a "perfect" body as generally presented by models and encouraged by the media. Yet, it is important to take the time to reflect on these questions, as our body image and level of acceptance can impact our expressions of sexuality. So please take time to carefully reflect on these questions. If there are things you can change and want to change, or things you need to accept and want to accept, then take a few moments to investigate how you can make that happen. Develop a set of goals and a plan and do the best you can to have the body you want and accept.

MCGRAW-HILL RESORUCES
REFLECTING ON SEXUALTY

Remember that this section of the study guide takes you beyond the text to explore other resources in the field of human sexuality. The experience attempts to expand on at least one concept covered in the chapter.

Access the McGraw-Hill Web pages associated with sexuality at:
    http://www.mhhe.com/socscience/sex

Scroll down and "click" on the hyperlink for "Resource Room."

Scroll down and "click" on the hyperlink for "Web Resources."

Scroll down and "click" on the hyperlink for "a status report on breast implant safety."

Read the article by Marian Segal. After reading this article, would you, if female, choose to get breast implants? Why or why not? If you are male, would you support your female partner, your female friends, or your sister getting breast implants? Why or why not? Base your response on the information contained in the article.

CHAPTER 3
MALE SEXUAL ANATOMY AND PHYSIOLOGY

CHAPTER OUTLINE

SELF-EVALUATION

    Your Sexuality Education: Past, Present, and Future

CHAPTER LEARNING OBJECTIVES

1. Describe the structures and functions of the lobes of the testes.

2. Describe the structures and purpose of the scrotum.

3. Describe the controversy regarding testicular support.

4. Describe the reasons for and the process of conducting a testicular exam.

5. Describe the consequences of testicular cancer treatments.

6. List and describe six disorders of the testes.

7. Describe the structures and functions of the penis.

8. Describe the general process of erection in men.

9. Describe the muscular and chemical process of erection.

10. Describe the characteristics of an average penis.

11. Describe how penis size can affect the physiological process in penis-vagina intercourse.

12. Describe two procedures and concerns regarding penis enlargement.

13. Describe the pros and cons of male circumcision.

14. List and describe erectile disorders of the penis.

15. Describe how vigorous stimulation can damage the penis.

16. List and describe three congenital penile conditions.

17. Describe the structures and functions of the internal male organs.

18. List and describe two types of prostatitis.

19. Describe the treatments for prostate enlargement.

20. Describe the procedure for examining the prostate.

21. List the hormones and cells associated with sperm production.

22. Describe how sperm are expelled from the body.

23. List and describe two ejaculatory problems.

24. Describe the concerns regarding sperm count.

25. Describe aging changes in the male body.

26. Describe the phenomena of "andropause."

27. Describe the benefits and risks of testosterone replacement therapy.

28. Describe ways in which men can survive the male climacteric.

Agenesis (absence) of the penis (ae-JEN-a-ses): a congenital condition in which the penis is undersized and nonfunctional.

Anejaculation: lack of ejaculation at the time of orgasm.

Anorchism (a-NOR-kiz-um): rare birth defect in which both testes are lacking.

Benign prostatic hyperplasia (BPH): enlargement of the prostate gland that is not caused by malignancy.

Bulbourethral glands: another term for Cowper's glands.

Circumcision (SIR-cum-sizh-uhn): in the male, surgical removal of the foreskin from the penis.

Corona: the ridge around the penile glans.

Cowper's glands: two small glands in the male that secrete an alkaline fluid into the urethra during sexual arousal.

Cryptorchidism (krip-TOR-ka-diz-um): condition in which the testes have not descended into the scrotum prior to birth.

Cyclic GMP: a secretion within the spongy erectile tissues of the penis that facilitates erection.

Ejaculation: muscular expulsion of semen from the penis.

Epididymis (ep-a-DID-a-mus): tubular structure on each testis in which sperm cells mature.

Epididymitis (ep-a-did-a-MITE-us): inflammation of the epididymis of the testis.

Epispadias (ep-a-SPADE-ee-as): birth defect in which the urinary bladder empties through an abdominal opening and the urethra is malformed.

Erection: enlargement and stiffening of the penis as internal muscles relax and blood engorges the columns of spongy tissue.

Foreskin: fold of skin covering the penile glans; also called the prepuce.

Frenulum (FREN-yu-lum): thin, tightly drawn fold of skin on the underside of the penile glans; it is highly sensitive.

Glans: in the male, the sensitive head of the penis.

Hypospadias (hye-pa-SPADE-ee-as): birth defect caused by incomplete closure of the urethra during fetal development.

Interstitial cells (in-ter-STIH-shul): cells between the seminiferous tubules that secrete testosterone and other male hormones.

Interstitial-cell-stimulating hormone (ICSH): pituitary hormone that stimulates the testes to secrete testosterone; known as luteinizing hormone (LH) in females.

Monorchidism (ma-NOR-ka-dizm): presence of only one testis in the scrotum.

Orgasm: pleasurable sensations and series of contractions that release sexual tension, usually accompanied by ejaculation in men.

Penis: male sexual organ that can become erect when stimulated; it leads urine and sperm to the outside of the body.

Peyronie's disease (pay-ra-NEEZ): development of fibrous tissue in spongy erectile columns within the penis.

Phimosis (fye-MOE-sus): a condition in which the penile foreskin is too long and tight to retract easily.

Priapism (pry-AE-pizm): continual, undesired, and painful erection of the penis.

Prostate: gland located beneath the urinary bladder in the male; it produces some of the secretions in semen.

Prostatitis (pras-tuh-TITE-us): inflammation of the prostate gland.

Retrograde ejaculation: abnormal passage of semen into the urinary bladder at the time of ejaculation.

Scrotum (SKROTE-um): pouch of skin in which the testes are contained.

Semen (SEE-men): mixture of fluids and sperm cells that is ejaculated through the penis.

Seminal vesicle (SEM-un-al): gland at the end of each vas deferens that secretes a chemical that helps sperm to become motile.

Seminiferous tubules (sem-a-NIF-a-rus): tightly coiled tubules in the testes in which sperm cells are formed.

Shaft: in the male, cylindrical base of penis that contains three columns of spongy tissue: two corpora cavernosa and a corpus spongiosum.

Sperm: reproductive cells produced in the testes; in fertilization, one sperm unites with an ovum.

Spermatocytes (sper-MAT-o-sites): cells lining the seminiferous tubules from which sperm cells are produced.

Testes (TEST-ees): pair of male gonads that produce sperm and male hormones.

Testicular failure: lack of sperm and/or hormone production by the testes.

Testosterone (tes-TAHS-ter-one): major male hormone produced by the testes; it helps to produce male secondary sex characteristics.

Testosterone replacement therapy: administering testosterone injections to increase sexual interest or potency in older men; not considered safe for routine use.

Urethra (yu-REE-thrah): tube that passes from the urinary bladder to the outside of the body.

Vasa efferentia: larger tubes within the testes into which sperm move after being produced in the seminiferous tubules.

Vas deferens: tube that leads sperm upward from each testis to the seminal vesicles.

SELF-TEST

When responding to the following multiple-choice questions, choose the "best" answer. The "best" answer is the one that corresponds to the information contained in your text.

1) All of the following are parts of the male testes *except*
   a) interstitial cells.
   b) perididymis.
   c) vasa efferentia.
   d) seminiferous tubules.

2) The cremasteric muscle
   a) suspends the testes in the scrotum.
   b) suspends the scrotum from the body.
   c) regulates scrotal temperature.
   d) expels semen from the testes.

3) Severe testicular injury, causing pain and swelling for a day or more, may be associated with
   a) erectile disorders.
   b) premature ejaculation.
   c) infertility.
   d) birth defects.

4) Testicular cancer is relatively rare and primarily affects men who are between the ages of
   a) 45 and 65.
   b) 35 and 50.
   c) 15 and 30.
   d) 20 and 35.

5) All of the following, if found, should be reasons for concern after conducting a testicular self-examination *except*
   a) any "light" feeling in a testicle.
   b) swelling of lymph nodes in the groin.
   c) swelling or tenderness of the breasts.
   d) a painless lump on the testicle.

6) When both testes are completely lacking at birth, the disorder is know as
   a) cryptorchidism.
   b) monorchidism.
   c) testicular failure.
   d) anarchism.

7) Epididymitis, inflammation of the epididymis, is relatively common and caused by
   a) a severe blow to the testicles where bruising results.
   b) many different types of bacteria.
   c) prolonged sexual arousal.
   d) a genetic trait passed from the father.

8) The ridge that is around the edge of the penile glans is referred to as the
   a) frenulum.
   b) corona.
   c) forona.
   d) coronal meatus.

9) The "spongy" penile tissue that encases the urethra is referred to as the
   a) corpus spongiosum.
   b) corpora cavernosa.
   c) corpora spongiosum.
   d) urethral spongiosum.

10) The complex phenomenon of erection involves a carefully balanced interaction among all but one of the following:
   a) muscle tissue.
   b) the nervous system.
   c) cyclic GMP.
   d) the epididymis.

11) The vagina, during sexual arousal, balloons or opens in the inner
   a) one fifth.
   b) three fourths.
   c) two thirds.
   d) one half.

12) Studies on penis size have sometimes been conducted to gather information about how likely it is
   a) for the penis to increase by 75% during sexual activity.
   b) for a condom to slip off or break during sexual activity.
   c) for a woman, during sexual activity, to refuse penetration due to girth, width, and length.
   d) for the testicles to change color taking on a bluish tone during sexual activity.

13) Circumcision has been part of the religious ceremony of which faith?
   a) Roman Catholic
   b) Christian
   c) Jewish
   d) Native American

14) The medical condition that has been cited as a good reason for circumcision is referred to as
   a) phimosis.
   b) painful foreskin.
   c) penilmosis.
   d) penile adhesions.

15) A condition that involves continual, painful, and undesired erection of the penis is called
   a) penilpism.
   b) priapism.
   c) dysmenoriasm.
   d) pyronie's disease.

16) This sac-like structure is approximately 2 inches long and produces secretions which constitute about 70% of seminal fluid.
   a) prostate
   b) testes
   c) seminal vesicles
   d) urethral glands

17) These glands are responsible for secreting a clear, sticky alkaline substance, or pre-ejaculatory fluid, that coats the inner lining of the urethra.
   a) prostate glands
   b) urethral glands
   c) cowper's glands
   d) kelly's glands

18) Men who suffer from prostatitis have an
   a) inflammation of the bladder.
   b) inflammation of the penile tissues.
   c) inflammation of the prostate.
   d) inflammation of the posterior penile tissues.

19) The recommended age at which men should begin to have regular prostate exams is
   a) 25.
   b) 35.
   c) 45.
   d) 55.

20) The PSA test refers to the
   a) penile-specific antigen test.
   b) prostate cancer specific antigen test.
   c) prostate specific antigen test.
   d) penile cancer specific antigen test.

21) The two pituitary hormones associated with producing sperm in males are
   a) ICSH and FSH.
   b) ICSH and LH.
   c) LH and FSH.
   d) FSH and SSH.

22) The condition in which there is an organic problem that causes an absence of semen and a dry orgasm is referred to as
   a) retrograde ejaculation.
   b) retarded ejaculation.
   c) retrosexual ejaculation.
   d) anejaculation.

23) Healthy sperm can swim against mucous currents and gravitational pull at approximately
    a) 55 inches a day.
    b) 65 inches a day.
    c) 5 to 9 inches an hour.
    d) 3 to 7 inches an hour.

24) All but which of the following have been identified as factors possibly contributing to low sperm count?
    a) pollutants in the environment
    b) fetal exposure to estrogen in the uterus
    c) drinking excessive amounts of Mountain Dew
    d) changes in diet

25) The form of hormonal therapy that seems to improve sexual interest and potency in men is referred to as
    a) estrogen replacement therapy.
    b) androgen replacement therapy.
    c) testosterone replacement therapy.
    d) hormonal replacement therapy.

26) The normal treatment for testicular cancer is
    a) chemotherapy.
    b) radiation therapy.
    c) removal of both testicles.
    d) removal of the cancerous testicle.

27) Regarding penis size, most researchers believe that the effect that applies to male erect penises is
    a) a continual unequalizing effect.
    b) a situational equalizing effect.
    c) an equalizing effect.
    d) a situational unequalizing effect.

GUIDED REVIEW AND STUDY
[Answers are provided at the end of the study guide.]

1) Men are not often are not well informed about their _____ or about significant _____ that can affect their sexual and reproductive health.
2) Just before birth, the testes move through the _____ canal and into the scrotum.
3) The testicular cells that produce testosterone are referred to as Leydig or _____ cells.
4) The cremasteric muscles help to regulate testicle _____.
5) The survival rate for testicular cancer is about _____ percent if not treated within the first three months.
6) _____ is the condition in which the testes have not descended into the scrotum before birth.
7) Prolonged sexual arousal without an orgasm is not dangerous or permanently damaging but only rather _____.
8) The two most sensitive areas of the penile glans are the _____ and _____.
9) Erection of the penis is controlled by a _____ and is mostly a (an) _____ reaction.

10) Two perineal muscles, the _____ and _____, show bursts of sexual activity just prior to erection.
11) _____ is a chemical that causes the muscle cells to relax, allowing the arteries to open so that blood flows into the open spaces in the erectile tissues.
12) Most penis enlargement techniques use some form of _____ device that has been known to cause injury to the penis.
13) Surgical interventions should not be considered for penile enlargement unless the erect penis is less than _____ inches, and the man is experiencing significant _____ problems with sex.
14) The buildup of material under the foreskin of the penis is called _____.
15) Two congenital conditions resulting from difficulties in fetal development of the penis are _____ and _____.
16) _____ groups feel that the pain associated with circumcision is an unnecessary trauma for a newborn.
17) _____ disease occurs primarily in older males and involves the development of gouch, fibrous tissue around the corpora cavernosa.
18) Another name for Cowper's glands are _____ _____.
19) Semen or _____ fluid is a milky, sticky, alkaline substance that helps to transport sperm through the penis.
20) _____, inflammation of the prostate gland, may be either acute or chronic.
21) Benign prostatic _____ refers to nonmalignant prostatic enlargement.
22) During sexual excitement and activity, the sperm are moved from the _____ in the testes up to the _____ through each vas deferens.
23) _____ and _____ can occur separately as part of male sexual response.
24) _____ is an option for men who have lower-than-normal levels of testosterone for their age as shown by appropriate medical tests.
25) Although ejaculation is a _____ phenomenon, it is possible for men to learn how to control the length of time it takes to reach orgasm and ejaculation.
26) _____ changes in the aging male body cause more testosterone to be bound to blood proteins or plasma.

ESSAY QUESTIONS
[Answers are provided at the end of the study guide.]

1) Identify the external and internal male sex organs as well as briefly discussing their functional purpose.

2) Briefly discuss the importance of, procedure for, and potential consequence of not conducting regular testicular exams.

3) Describe the "relative" importance of penis size, as well as two procedures and relevant concerns regarding penis enlargement procedures.

4) Describe conditions that affect the prostate as well as treatments to correct these conditions.

5) Describe the changes, concerns, and treatments of the aging sexual male's body.

CHAPTER RESOURCE REFLECTIONS

The Circumcision Decision

After reading the article, "The Circumcision Decision," would you have a male child circumcised? Why or why not? Discuss this topic with your partner or a family member who is male. Do you share the same views about male circumcision? Finally, since the medical recommendations do not support circumcision, do you believe a male child, upon reaching adulthood, should be able to sue his parents for genital mutilation? What argument would you offer to support an adult males' law suit?

Case Study

Pretend you are Roland. Would you respond to his suitemates' reaction the same way Roland did? Why or why not? What other alternatives would you consider if you were Roland? How do these alternatives respect the rights of all parties?

Jake has body image issues regarding his prosthetic testicle and penis size. In your experience, do you think men are greatly concerned with the appearance of their genitals? If you were raising a boy, would you encourage him to be concerned with the appearance of his genitals? What might you unintentionally say that would cause him concern about his genital appearance? What messages are prevalent in our culture that influences boys and men regarding genital image? If you had concerns about the appearance of your genitals, what communication techniques would you utilize to work with a partner regarding your concerns?

Manopause

We are all aging, even those of you in your late teens or early twenties. Your body and bodily functions will not remain the same but will continue to decline. In light of the discussion of the physical and psychological changes presented in the article, along with the recommendations for maintaining one's vitality, who can you do now, at your present age, to create a body and life that attempts to maximize your vitality?

Self-Evaluation: Your Sexuality Education

Sexuality education, for us, our partners, and our children, is not an easy task. Many of us believe we know a lot about human sexuality...but are you well educated? This subject area is very complex, and even sexuality educators find that they are personally, as well as professionally, continuing to learn throughout their lives. Everyone should see sexuality education as a lifelong learning opportunity. This self-evaluation exercise provides you the opportunity to examine your past, present, and future. Looking at our past can sometimes be difficult. Yet, we need to know from where we have come to know what we need to do to get to where we want to be in our lives, especially in our sexual lives. Our present is generally impacted by our past. Often difficulties in our present can be traced to our past; including difficulties we were having in the broad area of human sexuality. Again, take time to do this exercise with the goal of taking stock of the influences in your life, where you presently stand, and where you want to be regarding knowledge about human sexuality. This is especially true regarding knowledge that can be obtained through educational endeavors.

Remember that this section of the study guide takes you beyond the text to explore other resources in the field of human sexuality. The experience attempts to expand on at least one concept covered in the chapter.

Access the McGraw-Hill Web pages associated with sexuality at:
> http://www.mhhe.com/socscience/sex

Scroll down and "click" on the hyperlink for "Resource Room."

Scroll down and "click" on the hyperlink for "Web Resources."

Scroll down and "click" on the hyperlink for "go ask Alice or www.goaskalice.columbia.edu."

Scroll down and "click" on Sexual Health.

Scroll down and "click" on the hyperlink for one of the issues under "Men's Sexual Health" that deals with anatomy of the penis.

Read the question and response. You should be able to briefly describe the condition that was presented in the question, the potential "cause" of the condition, and the recommended course of action. On a more practical note, what was something you learned about this concern with the male anatomy?

CHAPTER 4
HUMAN SEXUAL RESPONSE

CHAPTER OUTLINE

CHAPTER LEARNING OBJECTIVES

1. Briefly describe cultural influences regarding sexual response.

2. List and describe the Masters and Johnson four-phase model of human sexual response.

3. Describe concerns with the Masters and Johnson four-phase model.

4. List and describe Helen Kaplan's three-phase model of human sexual response.

5. Briefly describe the nature and perceptions about sexual desire.

6. Describe the general physiological similarities of the sexual responses of males and females.

7. Describe general differences in sexual responses, especially in women.

8. Describe a concern regarding the concept of sex stimulation.

9. List and describe the two "systems" involved in sexual arousal.

10. Describe the concept and variability of sexual arousability.

11. Briefly describe the involvement of psychological arousal in sexual arousal.

12. List and describe the stages of sexual response activation.

13. Compare and contrast gender differences regarding sexual arousal.

14. Describe how individuals learn to be sexual.

15. Describe gender stereotypes regarding sexual arousal.

16. Describe the physiological responses of females during the excitement phase.

17. Describe the physiological response in females in the plateau phase.

18. Describe the physiological response in females in the orgasmic phase.

19. Describe the physiological response in females in the resolution phase.

20. Describe what is known about multiple orgasmic females.

21. Describe the controversy regarding types of female orgasms.

22. Describe what is known and the controversy about the "G Spot."

23. Describe what is known about female ejaculation.

24. Describe the process and benefits of Kegel exercise.

25. Describe the physiological response of males in the excitement phase.

26. Describe the physiological response of males in the plateau phase.

27. Describe the physiological response of males in the orgasm phase.

28. Describe the physiological response of males in the resolution phase.

29. Describe the refractory period and its physiological consequences.

30. Describe the controversy regarding multiple orgasms in males.

31. Describe the influence of and controversy about the influence of hormones regarding sexual arousal response.

32. List and describe the "effects" of hormonal secretions.

33. Describe the effect of testosterone in males and females.

34. Describe the physiological effect of aging regarding female sexual response.

35. Describe the physiological effect of aging regarding male sexual response.

KEY WORDS

Activating effect: the direct influence some hormones can have on activating or deactivating sexual behavior.

Androgen (ANN-dra-gin): a male hormone, such as testosterone, that affects physical development, sexual desire, and behavior. Testosterone is produced by both male and female sex glands and influences each sex in varying degrees.

Central arousal system: internal components of sexual arousal that come from the cognitive and emotional centers of the brain, forming the foundations for sexual response.

Climax: another term for orgasm.

Desire phase: Kaplan's term for the psychological interest in sex that precedes physiological sexual arousal.

Ejaculatory inevitability: the sensation in the male that ejaculation is imminent.

Excitement: the arousal phase of Masters and Johnson's four-phase model of the sexual response cycle.

G spot: a vaginal area that some researchers feel is particularly sensitive to sexual stimulation when its underlying spongy tissues are engorged with blood.

Organizing effect: manner in which hormones control patterns of early development in the body.

Orgasm (OR-gaz-em): a rush of pleasurable physical sensations associated with the release of sexual tension.

Orgasmic release: reversal of the vasocongestion and muscular tension of sexual arousal triggered by orgasm.

Peripheral arousal system: external components of sexual arousal that reach the brain and spinal cord from the skin, genitals, and sense organs.

Plateau phase: the stable, leveled-off phase of Masters and Johnson's four-phase model of the sexual response cycle.

Refractory period: time following orgasm during which a man cannot be restimulated to orgasm.

Resolution phase: the term for the return of a body to its unexcited state following orgasm.

Sexual dysfunctions: difficulties people have in achieving sexual arousal and in other stages of sexual response.

Skene's glands: secretory cells located inside the female urethra.

SELF-TEST

When responding to the following multiple-choice questions, choose the "best" answer. The "best" answer is the one that corresponds to the information contained in your text.

1) The researcher/s who provided the most thoroughly researched information on how the human body responds to sexual stimulation is/are
   a) Margaret Mead.
   b) Gary Kelly.
   c) William Masters and Virginia Johnson.
   d) Helen Kaplan.

2) All of the following are phases of the four-phase model of sexual response *except*
   a) excitement.
   b) desire.
   c) plateau.
   d) orgasm.

3) Which phase of Kaplan's model is associated with sexual dysfunctions?
   a) desire
   b) orgasm
   c) vasocongestion
   d) resolution

4) All but one of the following are factors of human sexual desire:
   a) biological
   b) psychological
   c) cultural
   d) spiritual

5) In human sexual response, which of the following has been found to be very similar in both sexes?
   a) desire
   b) resolution
   c) excitement
   d) orgasm

6) Some women, when not reaching orgasm during sexual intercourse, experience feelings of
   a) excitement.
   b) guilt.
   c) relief.
   d) sadness.

7) All models of sexual arousal seem to include stimuli that are both
   a) external and subjective.
   b) internal and objective.
   c) internal and external.
   d) organic and tactile.

8) Research studies have found that women are less likely than men to pick up on what type of sexual cues regarding their own sexual arousal?
   a) psychological
   b) neurological
   c) organic
   d) physiological

9) All of the following factors are associated with sexual response *except*
   a) stabilizing emotions.
   b) activating emotions.
   c) deactivating emotions.
   d) automatic mechanisms.

10) There is evidence that when a person's nervous system has been excited by some non-sexual stimulus, that individual will react in a way that suggests that may make them
   a) spontaneously move into a fantasy state.
   b) more susceptible to sexual arousal as well.
   c) less interested in acting sexually.
   d) need to take a moment to gather their thoughts.

11) The level of sexual interest and desire people have influences that ways in which they
   a) perceive sexual cues.
   b) behave toward an individual or group of people.
   c) process and interpret sexual words and information.
   d) perform daily tasks and functions.

12) Women's self-reported feelings about sexual arousal and their evaluations of their own sexual responses tend to be consistently more_____ than men.
   a) positive
   b) confusing
   c) negative
   d) none of the above

13) The subjective experience of orgasm, or the degree of pleasure described, seems to be affected by the
   a) sexual situation in which it occurs.
   b) intensity of physical stimulation.
   c) perceived emotional intentions of the partner.
   d) length of time the couple is able to spend engaged sexually.

14) Unlike males, females appear to have the potential to experience _____ during their sexual response.
   a) delayed orgasms
   b) multiple orgasms
   c) a nonrestimulating resolution phase
   d) a longer refractory period

15) All of the following are categories of female orgasm *except*
   a) uterine.
   b) clitoral.
   c) vaginal.
   d) cervical.

16) The G spot in women is generally found
   a) in the posterior vagina.
   b) in the anterior vagina.
   c) on the anterior clitoris.
   d) on the posterior clitoral shaft.

17) Grafenberg hypothesized that the Skene's glands might be similar to which of the male glands?
   a) Cowper's
   b) testes
   c) prostate
   d) pituitary

18) What plays an important role in how female orgasm, the G spot, and female ejaculation are perceived?
   a) parental approval of sex behaviors
   b) religion
   c) social factors
   d) none of the above

19) The first sign of the excitement phase in males is
   a) thickening of the scrotal tissue.
   b) erection of the nipples.
   c) erection of the penis.
   d) vasocongestion of the penis.

20) During the plateau phase of male sexual response, the testes increase in size by about
   a) 25 percent.
   b) 50 percent.
   c) 10 percent.
   d) 100 percent.

21) When the male senses that an orgasm is imminent, is it referred to as
   a) orgasmic inevitability.
   b) ejaculatory reality.
   c) orgasmic preclusion.
   d) ejaculatory inevitability.

22) All but one of the following usually lead to a more rapid return of the penis to its fully flaccid state.
   a) thinking sexual activity
   b) walking
   c) urinating
   d) feeling hungry

23) The period of time during which a man cannot be restimulated to ejaculation is referred to as
   a) the nonorgasmic period.
   b) the delayed orgasmic period.
   c) the refractory period.
   d) the sedated period.

24) Positive correlations have been seen in all of the following groups regarding the influence of hormones and sexual arousal or sexual activity *except*
   a) aged males.
   b) certain males.
   c) adolescent males.
   d) adolescent females.

25) Two effects associated with hormones and sexual response are
   a) organizing and effecting.
   b) activating and categorizing.
   c) organizing and classifying.
   d) activating and organizing.

26) Testosterone is classified as a "male hormone" or
   a) estrogen.
   b) progesterone.
   c) androgen.
   d) karagen.

27).There is evidence that, in aging individuals, a decrease in both sexual desire and frequency of sexual activity is
   a) rapid.
   b) gradual.
   c) systematic.
   d) critical.

28) All of the following are effects of aging on female sexual response *except*
   a) changed resolution phase.
   b) orgasm taking longer.
   c) fewer orgasmic contractions.
   d) less enlargement of clitoris.

29) Older men have greater difficulty
   a) being socially aroused to sexual stimuli.
   b) controlling their psychological urges.
   c) controlling their physiological urges.
   d) achieving full penile erection.

30) All of the following are changes in the male sexual response *except*
   a) reduced orgasmic contractions.
   b) less forceful semen ejaculation.
   c) shortening of refractory period.
   d) lengthening of refractory period.

31) The average length of time for men in their late fifties to achieve another erection after ejaculation is
   a) 2 to 3 hours.
   b) 12 to 24 hours.
   c) 24 to 36 hours.
   d) 12 hours.

GUIDED REVIEW AND STUDY
[Answers are provided at the end of the study guide.]

1) Human sexual response is not confined to reactions of the sex organs but involves marked changes throughout the body, especially in the _____ and _____.
2) The _____ phase is characterized by the body showing signs of arousal.
3) The desire phase of sexual response represents a _____ component that can lead to physical response.
4) Some researchers maintain that they have been unable to distinguish a measurable _____ in either men or women.
5) There seem to be _____ differences in the orgasms of males and females.
6) In the field of sexology, it is now widely accepted that there is no such thing as sex drive in the sense that some identifiable _____ need is generated during times of sexual abstinence.
7) _____ suggest that sexual motivation may affect an innate drive for reproduction to assure survival of the species, but evidence for the theory remains only suggestive.
8) All models of sexual arousal seem to recognize that _____ processes are an essential component of the process.
9) The tendency to become sexually aroused is meditated by both _____ and _____ factors.
10) Beyond automatic response, the brain's responses are more _____ in regulating whether sexual response will continue to be facilitated or inhibited.
11) There is general agreement among the majority of sexologists that people _____ to be sexual.
12) There does not seem to be a measurable difference in the ways men and women cognitively process sexual information, but there are distinct differences in the _____ of such information.
13) The process of _____ causes a slippery, alkaline fluid to seep through the lining of the vagina.

14) Many women show a darkening of the skin through the neck, breasts, and upper abdomen and it is termed the _____ _____.

15) Just preceding the orgasmic phase of sexual response in women, there is a sensation of _____ during which time the pulse rate reaches its peak.

16) Masters and Johnson proposed that most, if not all, women have the _____ for more than one orgasm.

17) The two different nerve pathways to the sex organs are the _____ nerves and the _____ nerves.

18) _____ is the German physician associated with the "G spot" in women.

19) The _____ muscle surrounds the vagina and is the focus of Kegel exercises.

20) Kegel exercises have been recommended for _____ women and seem to help the vagina and uterus return to normal shape and tone.

21) _____ in the pelvic area during early sexual arousal contributes to erection of the penis.

22) The _____ does not change markedly during the plateau phase of sexual response.

23) Males often have strong _____ muscle contractions throughout the body during orgasm and usually exhibit _____ pelvic thrusting.

24) About _____ percent of the penile erection is lost immediately after orgasm and ejaculation.

25) The refractory period in aging men _____ increases with age.

26) Recent studies demonstrate that the central arousal system is probably more dependent on the presence of _____ for _____ than is the peripheral arousal system.

27) In certain males, but not all, low _____ levels have been associated with difficulty achieving erections.

28) _____ effect refers to ways in which hormones control patterns of early development in the body.

29) The research on women has yielded a clearer relationship between levels of _____ and levels of sexual desire.

30) _____ toward one's own sexual functioning can play an important role in maintaining sexual functioning in older age.

31) Regarding sexuality and the aging, in the simplest language, there is a need to _____ it or _____ it.

32) Men may fear sexual _____ which usually means erection problems of various sorts.

ESSAY QUESTIONS
[Answers are provided at the end of the study guide.]

1) Compare and contrast the Masters and Johnson four-phase model of human sexual response with Kaplan's three-phase model.

2) Compare and contrast gender differences regarding sexual arousal as well as gender stereotypes associated with sexual arousal.

3) Briefly discuss both what is known about multiple orgasms for females and males and controversies surrounding the types of female orgasms.

4) Describe hormonal effects on sexual arousal, including the effects of testosterone in both males and females.

5) Briefly describe the physiological effects of aging on both male and female sexual response.

CHAPTER RESOURE REFLECTIONS

Cross-Cultural Perspective

As you read this cross-cultural perspective, the first challenge is to suspend any ethnocentrism, essentially the use of your cultural perspective as the means of evaluating other cultural experiences. Our Western culture has, and continues to be, influenced by Judeo-Christian religions, and many of you may come from one of those traditions. Without challenging your religious or spiritual beliefs, there may be a need to examine those beliefs along with the beliefs and practices presented in this writing. You may first have to examine what your religious or spiritual beliefs really say about sex and sexuality. From the Judeo-Christian tradition, the "Song of Songs" is a wonderful scriptural resource for examining the nature of sexuality within those traditions. Once you have explored your foundations, consider the Eastern concepts presented in the reading. There is the clear possibility that the traditions are not oppositional but rather can complement one another, while remaining true to your religious or spiritual beliefs. Continue your educational journey and see what you can learn from the holistic traditions of the East.

Treatment Options

If female, after reviewing the various "treatment options," which do you think you would consider using? What criteria would you use while considering these options? Many of these options are in their experimental stages. Do you support more funding for researching treatment options to encourage and potentially enhance female sexual desire, function, and arousal? Who should pay for research? Should insurance companies cover the costs of sexual function treatment? What if other countries had more options with better research supporting those options...should the U.S. FDA allow them into the country?

HBO – Sopranos

Eastern spiritual sexual practices are not new, just new to our Western consciousness. Since Eastern practices are ancient, does that make them more credible? What do you think about Westerners attempting to practice parts or certain techniques of a tradition? Is it important to understand the history of a spiritual practice?

Self-Evaluation: Sexual Arousal and Response in Your Life

Here is another activity that provides an opportunity for self-knowledge and potential growth. After completing the evaluation, you may find that you are quite content with the knowledge you obtain about yourself. Yet, if carefully examined, there is always the possibility that some area of the evaluation gave you pause to think about yourself and your sexuality. Once you identify areas with which you are not as happy or content as you would like to be, the goal is to attempt to address those issues. You don't have to face those issues alone. Utilize the services of your college or university often offered through the counseling center or seek referrals to local professionals who can help you to work with any issues so that you can have a healthy sexuality and sexual life.

Remember that this section of the study guide takes you beyond the text to explore other resources in the field of human sexuality. The experience attempts to expand on at least one concept covered in the chapter.

Access the McGraw-Hill Web pages associated with sexuality at:
> http://www.mhhe.com/socscience/sex

Scroll down and "click" on the hyperlink for "Resource Room."

Scroll down and "click" on the hyperlink for "Web Resources."

Scroll down and "click" on the hyperlink for "Go ask Alice" or "www.goaskalice.columbia.edu."
 * Click on hyperlink for "sexuality."

Scroll down and "click" on hyperlink for "prolonging arousal/lasting longer." (under "about sexual difficulties")

Based on what Alice maintains is a reason for male animals orgasming quickly, do you believe the recommended "stop-smart" method as a "practical" solution? Why or why not? Regarding the second question, do you agree with Alice's advice? Why or why not?

CHAPTER 5
DEVELOPMENTAL AND SOCIAL PERSPECTIVES ON GENDER

CHAPTER OUTLINE

SELF-EVALUATION

Masculinity and Femininity in Your Life

CHAPTER LEARNING OBJECTIVES

1. Briefly describe controversies regarding the perception of the sexes.

2. List and describe the types of intersexuality.

3. Describe three cross-cultural views of intersexuality.

4. Describe the controversy regarding intersexuality in western culture.

5. Describe the concepts of gender identify and gender role.

6. List and describe the general components of the factors of sexual differentiation.

7. List and describe the four levels of biological sex.

8. Describe the process of creating a personal perspective of one's gender.

9. Consider how gender roles may become self-fulfilling prophecies.

10. Describe the chromosomal prenatal factors of sexual differentiation.

11. Describe the fetal gonadal factors regarding sexual differentiation.

12. Describe the fetal hormonal factors involving sexual differentiation.

13. Describe possible genetic factors in regard to fetal development that challenge it as the "default" gender.

14. Describe rare problems seen in early stages of sexual differentiation.

15. Describe the influence of DHT in genital development.

16. Describe the perceived influences of hormones of brain development and sex differentiation.

17. Describe the sexual influences of hormones that result in sexual differentiation variations.

18. Describe the perceived effects of fetally androgenized females.

19. List and describe the effects of two synthetic hormones on sexual differentiation.

20. Describe the effect of androgenital syndrome on male and female sexual differentiation.

21. Describe the physiological effects of androgen insensitivity syndrome.

22. Describe the gender effects of androgen insensitivity syndrome.

23. Describe the multiplier effect of hormones at the social environmental level.

24. List and describe three findings of sexual differentiation at puberty.

25. Describe two general factors regarding adult gender identity.

26. List and briefly describe three models regarding the concept of masculinity and femininity.

27. List and describe "exaggerated" extremes of the bipolar model.

28. Briefly describe, compare, and contrast androgyny with traditional feminine manners.

29. Describe how transgendered individuals are perceived both socially and professionally.

30. Briefly describe what is known about transsexualism.

31. Describe the continuum for transgenderism

32. Briefly describe evolutionary psychology and sociobiology.

33. Briefly describe a controversy regarding the evolutionary approach.

34. Describe general qualitative differences between males and females.

35. Describe the difference in males and females in cognitive and motor function.

36. Describe the facts of brain differentiation in males and females.

37. Briefly describe the learning process in gender role development.

38. List and describe the three phases of the psychodynamic gender differentiation model.

39. Describe social learning theory when applied to gender development.

40. Describe cognitive development theory as it applies to gender development.

41. Briefly describe gender schema theory.

42. Briefly describe behavioral genetics as it applies to gender development as well as controversy regarding this position.

43. Describe the multifactorial "web" approach to gender as presented by Maccoby.

44. Describe cultural influences regarding the acceptance of gender difference in males and females.

45. Describe gender influences of educational institutions on gender discrepancies.

46. Briefly describe changing perceptions and discrepancies of gender in the workplace.

47. Describe how the field of academia and the field of science continue to perpetuate gender disparity.

48. Describe the general nature of feminists in American

49. Describe two waves of feminists' activities in American history.

50. Describe how contemporary feminists have influenced perceptions of sexuality.

51. List three traditional male roles that may make men uncomfortable.

52. Describe objectives and outcomes of asserting masculinity as a cultural movement in North America.

53. Describe the general consequences of the level of male interaction within a culture.

54. Describe how gender roles are influenced by cultural values.

55. Describe the influence of gender roles on mate selection.

56. Describe gender differences in males and females regarding psychological and behavioral problems.

KEY WORDS

Androgen insensitivity syndrome: a developmental condition in which cells do not respond to fetal androgen, so that chromosomally male (XY) fetuses develop external female genitals. There also is a feminization of later behavioral patterns.

Androgyny (an-DROJ-a-nee): the presence of high frequencies of both masculine and feminine behaviors and traits in the same individual.

Anti-Müllerian hormone: secretion of the fetal testes that prevents further development of female structures from the Müllerian ducts.

Conception: the process by which a sperm unites with an egg, normally joining 23 pairs of chromosomes to establish the genetic "blueprint" for a new individual. The sex chromosomes establish its sex: XX for female and XY for male.

Congenital adrenal hyperplasia: a genetic disorder that masculinizes chromosomal females and seems to lead to a masculinization of behavior as well.

Core gender identity: a child's early inner sense of its maleness, femaleness, or ambivalence, established prior to puberty.

DAX-1: the region on the X chromosome that seems to play a role in sexual differentiation.

DHT-deficiency syndrome: a condition in which chromosomally male fetuses have underdeveloped male genitals and may be identified as girls at birth. However, at puberty, they begin to develop masculine secondary sex characteristics and seem to maintain masculine patterns of behavior.

Differential socialization: the process of treating boys and girls differently as they are growing up.

Dihydrotestosterone (DHT): a chemical produced by the fetal testes that promotes further development of the testes, scrotum, and penis in the fetus.

Fetally androgenized females: a condition in which hormones administered during pregnancy caused chromosomally female (XX) fetuses to have masculinization of genitals and perhaps of later behavioral patterns, even though they were raised as girls.

Gender dysphoria (dis-FOR-ee-a): another term sometimes used to describe a gender identity disorder.

Gender identity: a person's inner experience of gender: feelings of maleness, femaleness, or some ambivalent position between the two.

Gender identity disorder: the expression of gender identity in a way that is socially inconsistent with one's anatomical sex.

Gender role: the outward expression and demonstration of gender identity, through behaviors, attire, and culturally determined characteristics of femininity and masculinity.

Gender schema: a complex cognitive network of associations and ideas through which the individual perceives and interprets information about gender.

Gonads: sex and reproductive glands, either testes or ovaries, that produce hormones and, eventually, reproductive cells (sperm or eggs).

H-Y antigen: a biochemical produced in an embryo when the Y chromosome is present; it plays a role in the development of fetal gonads into testes.

Hyperfemininity: a tendency to exaggerate characteristics typically associated with femininity.

Hypermasculinity: a tendency to exaggerate manly behaviors, sometimes called machismo.

Intersexuality: a combination of female and male anatomical structures, so that the individual cannot be clearly defined as male or female.

Müllerian ducts (myul-EAR-ee-an): embryonic structures that develop into female sexual and reproductive organs unless inhibited by male hormones.

Multiplier effect: the combining of biological and socioenvironmental factors more and more with one another in the process of human development.

Pseudohermaphrodite: a person who possesses either testes or ovaries in combination with some external genitals of the other sex.

Secondary sex characteristics: the physical characteristics of mature women and men that begin to develop at puberty.

Sexual differentiation: the developmental processes—biological, social, and psychological—that lead to different sexes or genders.

SRY: the sex-determining region of the Y chromosome.

Transgenderism: a crossing of traditional gender lines because of discomfort and nonconformity with gender roles generally accepted by the society.

Transsexualism: a strong degree of discomfort with one's identity as male or female characterized by feelings of being in the wrongly sexed body.

True hermaphrodite: a person who has one testis and one ovary. External appearance may vary.

Wolffian ducts (WOOL-fee-an): embryonic structures that develop into male sexual and reproductive organs if male hormones are present.

SELF-TEST

When responding to the following multiple-choice questions, choose the "best" answer. The "best" answer is the one that corresponds to the information contained in your text.

1) The Connecticut individual who was examined in 1843 by a physician and determined to be a "man" and was allowed to cast a deciding vote was
   a) James Suydam.
   b) Levi Suydam.
   c) John Money.
   d) Levi Schwartz.

2) All of the following refer to categories in which there is some mixture of male and female anatomical characteristics *except*
   a) intersexuality.
   b) true hermaphrodites.
   c) pseudohermaphrodites.
   d) pseudointersexuals

3) The "third gender" of India was referred to as
   a) *kwolu-aatmwol.*
   b) *berdache.*
   c) *hijra.*
   d) *berjra.*

4) The inner experience of one's gender is referred to as
   a) gender role.
   b) gender interiorialis.
   c) gender identity.
   d) gender differentiation.

5) Prenatal factors of sexual differentiation occur at
   a) implantation.
   b) conception.
   c) blastocyst development.
   d) human gamete development.

6) All of the following are expressions of biological sex *except*
   a) relational sex.
   b) genetic sex.
   c) gonadal sex.
   d) body sex.

7) Biological levels of sex interact with all listed below except one:
   a) environmental influences
   b) digestion of food products
   c) hormonal concentrations in the bloodstream
   d) cultural imperatives

8) The gene on the Y chromosome that seems to play a major role in the development of the male organs is labeled
   a) MSG.
   b) SMG.
   c) MYC.
   d) SRY.

9) A fertilized egg cannot survive with which of the following chromosomal types?
   a) X
   b) XYY
   c) Y
   d) XXX

10) Of the duct systems present in the embryo, which of the following represent potential male reproductive structures?
    a) Müllerian ducts
    b) Wolffian ducts
    c) Pregenital ducts
    d) Reprogenital ducts

11) All of the following appear more frequently in men than women *except*
    a) mental retardation.
    b) learning disabilities.
    c) most speech pathologies.
    d) variant sexual behaviors.

12) This substance has been identified as the chemical agent that helps transform the fetal gonads into testes.
    a) H-R antibody
    b) H-Y antibody
    c) H-R antigen
    d) H-Y antigen

13) Congenital adrenal hyperplasia is also referred to as
   a)   estrogenital syndrome.
   b)   androgenital syndrome.
   c)   pseudoandrogenital syndrome.
   d)   "masculinization" syndrome.

14) In androgen insensitivity syndrome, the developing fetus is
   a)   unable to limit the effects of estrogens.
   b)   unable to respond normally to the testosterone secreted by the pituitary.
   c)   unable to enhance the effects of estrogens.
   d)   unable to respond normally to the testosterone secreted by the fetal testes.

15) The process by which biological and social-enviornmental factors build upon one another has
been referred to as the
   a)   multiplier effect.
   b)   biosocioenvironmental effect.
   c)   sociocultural effect.
   d)   biocultural effect.

16) It can be seen that prenatal factors set the stage for the development of later
   a)   gender identity and sexual orientation.
   b)   gender roles and sexual identity.
   c)   gender roles and gender identity.
   d)   sexual identity and sexual orientation.

17) The belief that boys and girls are treated differently as they are raised is known as
   a)   gender specific socialization.
   b)   sexual differentiation.
   c)   differentiation of gender.
   d)   differential socialization.

18) Evidence shows that even young children have all of the following feelings *except*
   a)   sensual.
   b)   procreative.
   c)   romantic.
   d)   sexual.

19) Physical changes during puberty are referred to as the development of
   a)   pubertal sex characteristics.
   b)   tertiary sex characteristics.
   c)   secondary sex characteristics.
   d)   procreative sex characteristics.

20) The amount of experience with sex and romance gained during adolescence is affected by all
of the following factors *except*
   a)   exposure to sex education.
   b)   exposure to media.
   c)   peer group influence.
   d)   social class.

21) The presence of high levels of masculine and feminine behaviors in a single individual is called
   a) bisexuality.
   b) bidrogeny.
   c) androsexuality.
   d) androgyny.

22) Hypermasculinity, which is a tendency to exaggerate those behaviors that are perceived as male, is sometimes called
   a) machiculinity.
   b) machismo.
   c) antihyperfemininity.
   d) hypofemininity.

23) The psychologist associated with the development of an inventory measure that assesses androgyny is
   a) Alfred Kinsey.
   b) Gary Kelly.
   c) Sandra Bem.
   d) David Benjamin.

24) Individuals who cross the usual boundaries that delineate "expected" gender roles can be categorized, for discussion purposes, in all the following *except*
   a) transdysphoria.
   b) transgenderism.
   c) gender identity disorder.
   d) gender dysphoria.

25) Some recent evidence suggests that transgendered identities may well be shaped by the same
   a) biological and environmental factors as bisexuals.
   b) biological and environmental factors as homosexuals.
   c) biological and environmental factors as people who are intersexed.
   d) biological and environmental factors as all gender identities.

26) One's gender identity and gender role are not necessarily related to
   a) core gender identity.
   b) affectional orientation.
   c) sexual orientation.
   d) lifestyle orientation.

27) Which psychological orientation accepts the fact that biology and culture interact in complex ways to form gender roles?
   a) behavioral psychologists
   b) social constructionists
   c) evolutionary psychologists
   d) social psychologists

28) The psychiatrist and researcher who found differences in the ways male and female livers metabolize substances, giving support to anatomical differences in male and female organs, is
   a) Ellen Leibenluft.
   b) Charlotte Williams.
   c) William Masters.
   d) John Money.

29) Males, on average, tend to perform at higher levels on tests of
   a) field independence.
   b) mathematical reasoning.
   c) arithmetic calculation.
   d) mechanical reasoning.

30) A substantial part of establishing masculine and feminine gender roles results from
   a) genetics.
   b) socialization.
   c) anatomical differences.
   d) hormonal differences.

31) Each of the following concepts is part of the psychodynamic approach for explaining gender differentiation *except*
   a) children's first awareness of sex differences.
   b) around age two children begin to recognize differences.
   c) boys experience "penis envy" with their fathers.
   d) boys experience Oedipal wishes and girls experience an Electra complex.

32) As children are socialized, the theory of gender development that proposes that gender roles are perpetuated by each culture and through observation and imitation is
   a) cognitive-development theory.
   b) psychodynamic theory.
   c) psychoanalytic theory.
   d) social learning theory.

33) Children tend to engage in behavior considered appropriate for their gender at relatively young ages, and they will regulate their own behaviors based on self-approval at about
   a) 2 years old.
   b) 3 years old.
   c) 4 years old.
   d) 5 years old.

34) This theory suggests that some children and adults rely heavily on their gender role associations:
   a) gender-schematic
   b) gender-equatic
   c) orientation-aschematic
   d) gender-aschematic

35) Sometimes biological models of gender development have been used to justify social
    a) elitism.
    b) classism.
    c) prejudice and discrimination.
    d) discriminative equality.

36) Adolescent and adult males face harsher consequences for stepping outside of roles that are perceived as
    a) gender-constrained.
    b) culturally gendered.
    c) gender-appropriate.
    d) cross-gendered.

37) Early in their lives, boys develop a sense of self-worth
    a) through power based relationships.
    b) relatively independent of others' responses.
    c) in accordance with the way they are treated by the adults in their lives.
    d) as they learn to work in a group.

38) This researcher, in the mid-1980s, began to study girls aged 6 through 18 and found that young girls seem to feel very good about themselves and care deeply for others.:
    a) Carol Gilligan
    b) Ellen Leibenluft
    c) Sandra Bem
    d) Charlotte Williams

39) Men and women who reject prejudices that imply any inferiority of either gender are referred to as
    a) equalists.
    b) genderists.
    c) socialists.
    d) feminists.

40) All of the following are aspects of traditional male roles that make men uncomfortable *except*
    a) male as competent worker and provider.
    b) male as emotionally controlled stoic.
    c) male as sexual learner.
    d) male as sexual aggressor.

41) In societies with the following characteristics, men are less likely to affirm their masculinity through boastfulness, aggressiveness, or high levels of sexual activity *except*
    a) to maintain close relationships with children.
    b) for more control of property.
    c) when women are less deferential toward men.
    d) when women have more control over property.

GUIDED REVIEW AND STUDY
[Answers are provided at the end of the study guide.]

1) From the time of the ancient Greeks until the end of the 17th century, Western culture embraced a _____ model which was male, and the structures of the female anatomy were seen as inverted or underdeveloped.

2) The American Plains Indians once assigned the social status of _____ to men who did not have the skill or interest for typically masculine, aggressive pursuits.

3) Babies born with _____ genitalia are usually subjected to hormonal and surgical treatments.

4) Public, outward expression of gender is called gender _____.

5) The process by which organisms develop into the different sexes or genders is called sexual _____.

6) Sexual differentiation demonstrates that human beings are _____ _____ in the continuing process of creating a personal idea of gender.

7) Gender roles may become _____ _____.

8) _____ is the term used to define when the chromosomes from both parents are combined.

9) It was once assumed that developing as a female was in a sense the _____ gender of the fetus when SRY was not present.

10) Studies have confirmed that fetal androgen exposure during the second three months of pregnancy is indeed associated with a _____ behavior that cannot be completely explained by social influences.

11) Men who have been exposed to DES before birth have shown a reduction in the separateness of brain _____ _____.

12) Genetic males with androgen insensitivity syndrome typically report desiring _____ sexual partners and having dreamed of raising a family.

13) In a case study with DHT-deficiency syndrome, researchers found the woman almost completely lacking in _____ desire.

14) Except for _____ behavior, there are no behaviors that are either absolutely male or absolutely female.

15) When a boy is born with an undescended testes and an underdeveloped penis that may easily be mistaken for a clitoris, the condition is referred to as a _____ _____.

16) The first stage in preparation of hormonal secretions is referred to as _____, while the more profound hormonal release at puberty is referred to as _____.

17) The levels of sex hormones, particularly _____, in the blood may exert some effect on the strength of the sex drive.

18) Gender identity is confirmed during adolescence through _____ and _____.

19) The _____ model assumes that at least, to some degree, the more masculine people are the less feminine they tend to be and the more feminine, the less masculine.

20) _____ is characterized by greater deference to others, particularly toward men, more acceptance of aggressive sexual behavior, and holding traditional attitudes about the rights and roles of women.

21) Research has suggested that _____ people may be more adaptable and flexible and have higher levels of ego development.

22) _____ may be expressed in a variety of behaviors, ranging from the occasional cross-dressing to being surgically and hormonally reassigned to the other sex.

23) One of the earliest instances of sex change through surgery was the case of Sophia Hedwig in _____, who, with the help of physicians in _____, was transformed into Herman Karl.

24) Research has found average differences between human males and females in a few cognitive and motor functions; differences that can only be true as _____ generalizations.

25) It has been generally accepted that the two _____ hemispheres of the human brain may be responsible for different functions.

26) Research evidence indicates that the gender role _____ of parents seems to have some effect on their children's perceptions of themselves.

27) A unique feature of the cognitive-development theory of gender development is the idea that the child _____ basic male and female values on its own.

28) Gender _____ adults and children pay less attention to socially determined associations.

29) Behavioral genetics attempts to examine the impact of both _____ and _____ on childhood socialization.

30) Boys play groups are much more rough-and-tumble _____.

31) Even well-meaning teachers often are susceptible to gender _____.

32) Researchers have concluded that adolescence is a time of _____ for girls, as they are more hesitant to express feelings.

33) In married couples who both work, over _____ percent of the wives earn more money than their husbands.

34) The year 2002 represents the first time in history when American women earned more _____ than American men at U.S. universities.

35) During the 19th century, women began to liken their position to that of _____ and began to fight for their own rights.

36) Men have been caught up in a vicious cycle of proving their strength, _____, and effectiveness as providers.

ESSAY QUESTIONS
[Answers are provided at the end of the study guide.]

1) Compare and contrast cross-cultural perceptions of intersexuality with Western cultural perceptions of intersexuality.

2) Describe the chromosomal, fetal gonadal, and hormonal factors involving sexual differentiation.

3) Briefly describe the physiological and gender effects of androgen insensitivity syndrome.

4) Describe the continuum of transgenderism, as well as how transgendered individuals are perceived socially and professionally.

5) Compare and contrast the feminist movement and the men's movement as cultural phenomena and initiators of social change in the United States.

CHAPTER RESOURCE REFLECTIONS

How Parents Raise Boys & Girls

In light of what John Colapinto observed in his son, Bruce, and the apparently contrasting information from the "experts," what types of toys and activities will you provide to your male child and to your female child? If in a partnered relationship, discuss these issues with your partner. Do you agree or disagree? If you disagree, how do you see yourselves resolving your disagreement?

Case Study

If you had been in the room when Ricardo "voiced his sentiments" about perceived "anti-male" attitudes from women, what would your reactions have been? Should men expect the retribution of women for the "sins" of our fathers and brothers? Why or why not? Should women be allowed a period of transition through which they express their "frustrations" before society becomes as egalitarian as possible? Why or why not?

Cross-Cultural Perspective

As you read the story of the town of Bassam, how would you react to being invited to partake in this ritual? Would you be able to cross-dress? What would prevent you from doing this activity? Contrastly, why would you engage in this ritual? Could you publicly declare your misdeeds in front of the community and your spouse? What benefit do you believe this ritual has for the people of Bassam? If this ritual were integrated into our culture, what benefit do you believe we could derive from this experience?

Gender Gaps in Problem Solving

After reading through both columns, which tasks do you feel that you would complete with ease? Does your opinion and gender match the gender listed at the top of the column you chose? Have an informal discussion with friends…do their opinions and gender match what the article suggests is true?

Study: Gender Wage Gap Is Widening

After forty years, the research cited in this article suggests that women earn even less on the dollar as compared to their male counterparts. Essentially, no progress has been made to close the wage gap. Does this seem true to you? Do you consider this inequity a sociocultural concern or an issue to be regulated by the government? What is your reaction to the notion that women may never make as much on the dollar as men?? What if the situation continues to not progress and there is a wage gap forty years from now? What are the implications of that?

Self-Evaluation: Masculinity and Femininity in Your Life

The exercise contained in this self-evaluation focuses on our perceptions of gender, of ourselves, of others, and of society. Through our socialization, we often take gender issues for granted, and that we are functioning in some predestined social order. Yet, gender is a socially constructed reality unlike our sex. Carefully examining the influences of others regarding our conceptions of gender is important. To be informed is to provide a foundation from which we can grow. Even if you believe in clear gender differences based on socialization or religious beliefs, you will live in a world that does not uniformly hold those beliefs. Within these parameters, how will you function to the benefit of yourself, your partner, and your family? Take stock of the influences and views you have regarding gender by completing these exercises. As a result of your inquiry, you may contribute to a better world regarding gender issue and dynamics.

Remember that this section of the study guide takes you beyond the text to explore other resources in the field of human sexuality. The experience attempts to expand on at least one concept covered in the chapter.

Access the McGraw-Hill Web pages associated with sexuality at:
        http://www.mhhe.com/socscience/sex

Scroll down and "click" on the hyperlink for "Resource Room."

Scroll down and "click" on the hyperlink for "Web Resources."

Scroll down and "click" on the hyperlink for "Go Ask Alice" or "www.goaskalice.columbia.edu"

For this exercise, you are to ask Alice a question regarding an issue that is relevant to the content of the chapter. Your question can be submitted in any of the relevant areas of this site (i.e., sexuality, sexual health, or relationships). Submit your question and return to the site at a later date to see if a response has been posted. If a response has been posted, what did you learn from the response? Would you use "Go Ask Alice" if you had another question regarding a topic dealing with human sexuality? Why or why not?

CHAPTER 6
SEXUALITY THOUGH THE LIFE CYCLE

CHAPTER OUTLINE

SELF-EVALUATION

Looking Ahead: Sex in Later Years

CHAPTER LEARNING OBJECTIVES

1. Describe, in general terms, the concept of psychosexual development.

2. Describe the concept of "sexual instinct."

3. Describe the influence of sexual instinct theory regarding sexual behavior.

4. Describe the origins and major assumption of psychodynamic theory.

5. Describe how psychodynamic theory views libido including the latency period.

6. Describe the principle of conditioning theory including generalization of this theory.

7. Describe how conditioning theory applies to sexuality.

8. Describe the principles of social learning theory.

9. Describe the principles of developmental theory.

10. List and describe the stages of Erickson's psychological development theory.

11. List and describe the three strands of Bancroft's unified theoretical model.

12. List and describe three labeling stages of sexual development.

13. Describe the principles of sexual script theory.

14. List and describe three different types of sexual scripts.

15. Describe the sexual concept of choice theory as well as two major components of the theory.

16. Describe the principles of social network theory.

17. Describe fetal and infant physiological responses of arousal.

18. Describe the foundations and developmental tasks of infancy.

19. Describe the findings of the UCLA study regarding childhood sexuality.

20. Describe the findings of the Mayo Clinic study regarding childhood sexuality.

21. Describe the influence of parents on childhood sexuality.

22. Describe the lack of concern regarding nudity in the home.

23. Describe the sexual and romantic interests of children.

24. Describe the sexual concept of adolescence including its ambiguous nature in western culture.

25. Describe the physiological changes that early adolescents experience and the impact those changes have on gender.

26. Describe what is known regarding early adolescent ejaculation and orgasm as well as erotic fantasies.

27. Describe the reason for and consequences of engaging in or refraining from sexual activity.

28. Describe the contradictory messages and education sources about sexuality for young people.

29. Describe influences regarding reported first sexual intercourse.

30. Describe life factor influences regarding first sexual experience.

31. Describe the adolescent heterosexual stages of sharing.

32. Describe the gender differences in adolescent masturbation.

33. Describe how the process of social development applies to adolescent relationships and sexual intimacy.

34. Describe the rate of adolescent same-gender sexual activity.

35. Describe social obstacles to sexual development in same-gender orientation adolescents.

36. Describe the social influence and consequence of teenage pregnancy.

37. Describe concerns regarding adolescent sexual activity and sexually transmitted diseases (STDs).

38. Describe characteristics of sexually healthy adolescents.

39. Briefly describe the transition from adolescence to young adulthood.

40. List and describe four steps for promoting sexuality healthy adults.

41. Describe the concept of and gender difference regarding intimacy.

42. List and describe the three stages of coupling.

43. Briefly describe the psychology theory of mate selection.

44. Describe the social network theory of mate selection.

45. Describe three sociobiological assumptions of mate selection.

46. List and describe four evolutionary theory hypotheses regarding mate selection.

47. Briefly describe relational commitment and sexual activity in marriage.

48. List rates of U.S. cohabitation.

49. Describe factors that influence rates of sexual activity in relationships.

50. Briefly describe U.S. perceptions of monogamy.

51. Describe recent findings regarding the rates of sexual infidelity.

52. Describe evolutionary reasons for infidelity.

53. Describe the emotional consequences of infidelity.

54. Describe ages and roles of marriage in the U.S.

55. Describe the rates of, influence of, and social responses to divorce.

56. Describe general concerns about and support for sexuality and aging individuals.

57. List and describe three myths about sexuality and older people.

58. Describe institutional limitations regarding sexual expression of older individuals.

59. Describe physiological factors and surgical procedures that may influence aging sexuality.

60. List and describe factors that impact sexuality in older individuals.

61. Describe perceptions about masturbation and sexual activity in older individuals.

62. Describe sexual influences and responses of same-gender orientated aging individuals.

63. Describe ways to which older individuals can maximize sexual expression.

KEY WORDS

Adolescence: period of emotional, social, and physical transition from childhood to adulthood.

Cohabitation: living together and sharing sex without marrying.

Consensual adultery: permission given to at least one partner within the marital relationship to participate in extramarital sexual activity.

Discrimination: the process by which an individual extinguishes a response to one stimulus while preserving it for other stimuli.

Dyadic withdrawal (die-ADD-ik): the tendency of two people involved in an intimate relationship to withdraw socially for a time from other significant people in their lives.

Erogenous zone (a-RAJ-a-nus): any area of the body that is sensitive to sexual arousal.

Generalization: application of specific learned responses to other, similar situations or experiences.

In loco parentis: a Latin phrase meaning "in the place of the parent."

Latency period: Freudian concept that during middle childhood, sexual energies are dormant; recent research tends to suggest that latency does not exist.

Libido (la-BEED-o or LIB-a-do): a term first used by Freud to define human sexual longing or sex drive.

Monogamous: sharing sexual relations with only one person.

Polyandry (PAH-lee-ann-dree): also referring to being married to more than one spouse, usually refers to a woman having more than one husband. Cross-culturally, it is less common than polygamy.

Polygamy (pah-LIG-a-mee): practice, in some cultures, of being married to more than one spouse, usually referring to a man having more than one wife.

Psychosexual development: factors that form a person's sexual feelings, orientations, and patterns of behavior.

Psychosocial development: the cultural and social influences that help shape human sexual identity.

Reinforcement: in conditioning theory, any influence that helps shape future behavior as a punishment or reward stimulus.

Social script: a complex set of learned responses to a particular situation that is formed by social influences.

SELF-TEST

When responding to the following multiple-choice questions, choose the "best" answer. The "best" answer is the one that corresponds to the information contained in your text.

1) The process by which we refer to our own individualized ways of thinking and feeling about sexuality, along with our own patterns of sexual orientation and behavior, is called
   a) sociosexual development.
   b) psychosocial development.
   c) psychosexual development.
   d) sexual identity development.

2) Theories about inborn sexual drives or instincts led to all of the following assumptions about particular sexual behaviors *except*
   a) naturalness of them.
   b) unnaturalness of them.
   c) sickness of them.
   d) control over them.

3) Libido and unconscious thought are essential elements in the
   a) psychodynamic theory.
   b) conditional and social learning theory.
   c) biopsychological drive/instinct theory.
   d) development theory.

4) Freud believed that, in children, there was a period during which sexual energies were dormant while intellectual and social growth continued. This period is referred to as the
   a) dormancy period.
   b) latency period.
   c) sociointellectual period.
   d) potency period.

5) Generalization and reinforcement are major concepts in
   a) psychodynamic theory.
   b) conditional and social learning theory.
   c) biopsychological drive/instinct theory.
   d) development theory.

6) The researcher/theorist associated with a model of development psychology is
   a) Piaget.
   b) Kohlberg.
   c) Erikson.
   d) Freud.

7) The three stands identified in John Bancroft's unified theory of sexual development include all of the following *except*
   a) gender identity.
   b) sexual abstinence.
   c) understanding one's sexual orientation.
   d) capacity for intimate dyadic relationships.

8) Children will first go through this process where they begin to identify what is expected of them sexually:
   a) self-labeling
   b) prelabeling
   c) social labeling
   d) developmental labeling

9) Sociologists John Gagnon and William Simon are associated with which of the following theories:
   a) psychodynamic
   b) differential association
   c) libidinal
   d) scripting

10) All of the following are types of sexual scripts *except*
   a) intrapersonal.
   b) interpersonal.
   c) cultural.
   d) intrapsychic.

11) Choice theory is borrowed from what discipline?
   a) economics
   b) marketing
   c) communication
   d) education

12) All but one of the following is part of a complex interaction of factors that constitutes the social process of psychosexual development.
   a) scripting theory
   b) choice theory
   c) psychodynamic theory
   d) social network theory

13) All of the following behaviors have been observed in the uterus during fetal development, or seen soon after birth *except*
   a) erection of the penis.
   b) orgasms.
   c) sex flush.
   d) vaginal lubrication.

14) The time when there is a vague awareness of sexual feelings and during which early ranges of sexual responsiveness are established has been referred to as a period of
   a) actualization.
   b) realization.
   c) sexualization.
   d) potentiation.

15) The Mayo Clinic found that the most frequently observed sexual behavior among children aged 2 to 12 was
   a) oral-genital contact.
   b) insertion of fingers in rectum.
   c) self-stimulation.
   d) simulated sexual intercourse.

16) Most professionals agree that when nudity within the home is permitted, there does not seem to be negative consequences providing there is
   a) no sexual abuse.
   b) no pictures taken.
   c) no cross-gender child nudity.
   d) no showering together.

17) Around which ages do girls and boys begin to show a distinct increase in levels of interest toward the other gender and begin to develop more intimate relationships:
   a) 8 to 10
   b) 14 to 15
   c) 11 to 12
   d) 10 to 12

18) Another term for a nocturnal emission is
   a) orgasmic dream.
   b) wet dream.
   c) wet emission.
   d) spontaneous orgasm.

19) Fantasies that accompany masturbation in adolescence can be identified by all but which of the following factors:
   a) they involve only one gender.
   b) they help to acquaint an adolescent with sexual preferences.
   c) they add to the pleasure of the masturbatory experience.
   d) they are quite vivid.

20) In 2001, the percentage of high school students indicating they had experienced intercourse had dropped to
   a) 34.4%.
   b) 45.6%.
   c) 54.1%
   d) 60.5%.

21) All of the following are reasons cited by teenagers for not engaging in sexual intercourse *except*
   a) fear of pregnancy.
   b) fear of disease.
   c) parental disapproval.
   d) partner disapproval.

22) The primary sources of sex information for the majority of young persons are
   a) friends and reading.
   b) friends and parents.
   c) parents and reading.
   d) sex education and reading.

23) During the 1990s, which of the following adolescent groups experienced the most pronounced decline in rates of sexual experience?
   a) Hispanics
   b) Native Americans
   c) Blacks
   d) Whites

24) All of the following factors are associated with initiating sexual experiences *except*
   a) use of drugs and alcohol.
   b) having residential stability.
   c) unconventionality in behavior.
   d) getting into fights.

25) The most prevalent form of sexual activity in adolescence is
   a) sexual intercourse.
   b) masturbation.
   c) mutual masturbation.
   d) oral-genital stimulation.

26) The period of time during which a couple pulls away from other social responsibilities is referred to by social psychologist as
   a) social withdrawal.
   b) mating withdrawal.
   c) sexual withdrawal.
   d) dyadic withdrawal.

27) All of the following risks have been seen in gay, lesbian, and bisexual adolescents *except*
   a) psychological distress.
   b) suicide.
   c) dropping out of school.
   d) academic success.

28) Since 1990, the teen birth rate in the U.S. has
   a) risen 6%.
   b) risen 15%.
   c) fallen by 26%.
   d) fallen by 10%.

29) Young women who are exposed to all but one of the following have a greater risk for teen pregnancy:
   a) abuse
   b) violence
   c) poverty
   d) family strife

30) Risk of a second teen pregnancy is associated with which of the following factors:
   a) financial stability.
   b) motivation to refrain from sexual intercourse.
   c) returning to school.
   d) parental reaction.

31) Declines in teen pregnancy are more likely due to
   a) sexual abstinence.
   b) parental disapproval.
   c) sexual education.
   d) use of birth control.

32) What percentage of 15 to 24 year olds believes their peers are somewhat or very concerned about sexual health issues?
   a) 88
   b) 42
   c) 70
   d) 16

33) All of the following are stages of coupling *except*
   a) expansive.
   b) preresolution.
   c) contraction and betrayal.
   d) resolution.

34) Social psychologists refer to relationships in which people initiate and maintain contacts with others who have similar social characteristics as
   a) bilateral status contacts.
   b) mating status contacts.
   c) equal status contacts.
   d) equalizing status contacts.

35) In selecting a mate, which of the following mate selection theories assumes that human beings use sexual strategies that are advantageous from an evolutionary perspective because they contribute to the survival and perpetuation of the species?
   a) psychological theory
   b) social network theory
   c) psychodynamic theory
   d) sociobiology theory

36) Which of the following theories believes that cross-cultural evidence suggests that the complex decision-making processes involved in choosing a mate are patterned and universal themes built into human psyches and societies?
   a) evolutionary psychologists
   b) social psychologists
   c) cognitive psychologists
   d) socioecological psychologists

37) Although evolutionary psychologists view marriage as a social arrangement within which children will be produced and raised, the National Marriage Project reports that _____ of Americans disagree that the main purpose of marriage is to have children.
   a) 30%
   b) 50%
   c) 70%
   d) 90%

38) To maintain a loving relationship over a long period of time takes all of the following *except*
   a) work.
   b) commitment.
   c) relational space.
   d) communication.

39) The frequency of sexual activity tends to be highest during which period of a relationship?
   a) first few months
   b) second five years
   c) after the first child
   d) first two years

40) More than ever before, women and men are also choosing to be single or to live together in loving and sexual relationships without marrying, a pattern called:
   a) contiguous habitation.
   b) continued habitation.
   c) cohabitation.
   d) consensual habitation.

41) A coupled relationship that allows the partners greater sexual freedom is referred to as
   a) consensual adultery.
   b) consensual monogamy.
   c) consensual polygamy.
   d) monogamous adultery.

42 According to the 2000 census, _____ of children under the age of 18 are living either with a single parent or no parents at all.
   a) 19%
   b) 24%
   c) 31%
   d) 45%

43) What percentage of divorced individuals will remarry?
   a) 20%
   b) 50%
   c) 70%
   d) 100%

44) In 1998, the National Council on Aging confirmed that about half of people in their 60s, 70s, and 80s engaged in sexual activity
   a) once a week.
   b) once a month.
   c) once every two months.
   d) once every six months.

45) Influencing their expression of sexuality, older individuals in institutional care settings often lack the following:
   a) desire
   b) available partners
   c) privacy
   d) free time

46) All of the following are factors that influence sexual potentials in old age *except*
   a) societal values and attitudes.
   b) partner availability.
   c) knowledge about sexuality.
   d) individual and couple sexual history.

47) For many older people who have lost their sexual partners, their sole means of sexual gratification is
   a) sex with prostitutes.
   b) sex with same-gender partners.
   c) use of erotic fantasy.
   d) masturbation.

GUIDED REVIEW AND STUDY
[Answers are provided at the end of the study guide.]

1) It appears that there may well be _____ periods of human development during which a person's stage of biological development interacts with the various processes of socialization.
2) Instinct theory assumes that there is a sexual _____ that causes people to experience a buildup of sexual tension over time.
3) As _____ _____ theory has been called into question, we have had to look to other explanations for psychosexual development.

4) Freud believed that infants were _____ perverse.

5) A _____ _____, according to Freud, is when the sexual energies are said to lie dormant, while intellectual and social growth continues.

6) _____ theory holds that we learn our sexual preferences and behaviors through observational learning.

7) Erikson conceptualized an eight-stage life span of _____ development that extended from birth to old age.

8) The sex orientation labeling of self is subject to _____ by what is known about the society's labels for various sexual orientations and preferences.

9) Choice theory, borrowed from _____, assumes that human beings make choices out of the need to apportion their resources in order to reach certain goals.

10) It has been suggested that the entire surface of the skin of a newborn infant is a single _____ zone.

11) Children's sexual development proceeds along two parallel routes: _____ and

_____ _____ _____ _____.

12) Only a few children seem to have particularly specific preferences, whereas most are apparently _____.

13) _____ to sex play in childhood does not seem to be associated with the level of adjustment in the later teen years.

14) Parental _____ and _____ seem to play a role in determining how children will behave sexually.

15) Children, themselves, may well reach stages in their development when they signal some _____ with being seen naked by other family members.

16) _____ is that period of social, emotional, and cognitive development that moves young people toward adulthood.

17) Most boys experience first ejaculation during _____.

18) Early adolescent girls are particularly prone to having intercourse if their boyfriend is substantially _____.

19) Sexual _____ between males and females is an important step in the development of many adolescents.

20) Many adolescents do not consider _____ to fit under the label of "having sex".

21) Masturbation habits practiced in adolescence generally _____, without decreasing much with age or with partnership status.

22) Adolescents with primarily a same-gender orientation face the task of developing _____ attachments with members of the same sex, while there are many social prohibitions against doing so.

23) Regarding sexual activity among the young, we tend to confuse the _____ _____ public health issues with issues of _____ and punishment.

24) Sexual health issues and ways of approaching them differ between _____ _____ _____.

25) Medical practices that serve adolescents often fail to provide all needed services related to _____ _____ _____ _____, or to offer the kind of _____ that teens need in order to seek those services.

26) _____ is the ability to open oneself to others in a way that permits mutual sharing and caring.

27) During the _____ stage of coupling, there is a burst of romance, sexual attraction, and exploration.

28) Evolutionary theory has often been accused of attempting to find a basis for legitimizing behaviors that many deem to be _____ and inappropriate.

29) In Western culture, _____ love and _____ attraction have become the bases for marriage.

30) Women and men who choose to live together without marrying, often engaging in sexual relations, are said to be living a life of _____.

31) The level of sexual _____ in married couples is strongly correlated with the level of marital _____ they experience

32) In coupled relationships, frequency of _____ should not be construed as a measure of happiness in marriage or cohabitation.

33) _____ refers to the practice that permits men to have more than one wife and _____ refers to a woman who has more that one husband.

34) Marriages between relative young people who do not have children and amass very little joint property are referred to as _____ marriages.

35) There is some evidence that _____ problems in a first marriage reappear in a second marriage.

36) The belief that sex is primarily for procreation negates a spectrum of _____ sexual experiences.

37) In one study, 43% of older people indicated that _____ had affected their sexual functioning.

38) _____ about sex is rampant; this is no less true among seniors than it is among the young.

39) Gay men and lesbians face essentially the same _____ problems of aging as do heterosexuals.

ESSAY QUESTIONS
[Answers are provided at the end of the study guide.]

1)   Describe the major assumptions of psychodynamic theory as well as how this theory views libido and the latency period.

2)   Describe the principles of sexual script theory as well as three different types of sexual scripts.

3)   Briefly discuss the findings of the UCLA and Mayo Clinic studies regarding childhood sexuality.

4)   Describe the social influences regarding premarital adolescent sexual intercourse along with social obstacles to sexual development in same-gender orientated adolescents.

5)   Describe three sociobiological assumptions of mate selection and four evolutionary theory hypotheses regarding mate selection.

CHAPTER RESOURCE REFLECTIONS

Cross-Cultural Perspective

This reading challenges us both individually and culturally to broaden our perspectives regarding the sexuality of adolescents. As you read the various cultural descriptions, what do you believe is important to understand about that cultural experience and why? Also, suspend your "ethnocentric" viewpoints, and describe what our culture and society could learn from each of the other cultural experiences.

Case Study

As you reflect on Ernest's journey to the counseling center, if you, as a young adult, had a concern about an aspect of your sexual behavior, who would you seek professional advice from and why from that person? If you had a child in college and thought he or she might be dealing with a life issue that is sexual in nature, could you encourage him or her to seek professional help through the institutional resources? Why or why not?

Playing the Mating Game

After reading this section and as you examine your own relationships, do you believe that those individuals you have been attracted to or that have found you attractive have done so based on futility attractiveness or relational attractiveness? Why or why not? To begin to understand your perceptions, engage in a discussion with your partner about these issues. What did you learn from this conversation?

Starter Marriage

After reading the information about starter marriages, if you are not presently married and are intending to get married, will a "starter marriage" be in your future? Why or why not? If you are someone who has experienced a "starter marriage," did you benefit from this experience? How or how not? Finally, in light of the facts about marriage presented in the article, why should marriage be considered a lifetime commitment?

New Wrinkle

Should those who manage "Sun City" be concerned about the public sexual behaviors of residents? Why or why not? If you saw one of those acts, would you seek to have the individuals arrested? Why or why not?

Self-Evaluation: Looking Ahead

As you complete this evaluation, be honest with your responses. The sexuality of our grandparents, our parents, and our aging selves is real. A key part of this exercise is reflecting on the reasons why you have the perceptions you do. One challenge we often face is being involved in social or familiar relationships with individuals who do not share our perceptions. In light of your views, how would you deal with a family relation where your views, and consequently actions, were different than your siblings regarding a parent?

MCGRAW-HILL RESOURCES
REFLECTING ON SEXUALTY

Remember that this section of the study guide takes you beyond the text to explore other resources in the field of human sexuality. The experience attempts to expand upon at least one concept covered in the chapter.

Access the McGraw-Hill Web pages associated with sexuality at:
      http://www.mhhe.com/socscience/sex

Scroll down and "click" on the hyperlink for "Resource Room."

Scroll down and "click" on the hyperlink for "Web Resources."

Scroll down and "click" on the hyperlink for "Go Ask Alice," or "www.goaskalicecolubia.edu."

Click on "sexuality" link.

Scroll down to "miscellaneous."

Scroll down to and "click" on the hyperlink for "Men's sex drive and age."

Read Alice's response. (After reading the response text and the article, what are your thoughts and feelings about being sexually active in your life at 45? 55? and 65? On a slightly different note, could you use the information from the article and text in a discussion with your grandparents and parents? Why or why not?)

CHAPTER 7
SEXUAL INDIVIDUALITY AND SEXUAL VALUES

CHAPTER OUTLINE

CHAPTER LEARNING OBJECTIVES

1. Describe Western cultural perceptions of normality and abnormality.

2. Describe cultural influences regarding acceptable sexual behavior.

3. Describe the purpose and limitation of science and scientists.

4. Describe cultural perceptions of masturbation.

5. Describe the terms and labels used by sexologists to explain atypical sexual behaviors.

6. List and describe six "standards" for sexual arousal and behavior.

7. Describe how cultural standards about sexuality influence people's lives.

8. Describe ethnocentricity and the dualistic normal/not normal dichotomy.

9. List and describe four methods of defining normalcy.

10. Describe how sexual orientation labels are not easily culturally applied.

11. Describe the variable associated with describing sexual preferences.

12. List and describe terms used to describe sexual and affectional identities.

13. Describe the origins of sexual individuality.

14. List and describe six generalizations regarding the development of sexual individuality.

15. List the variables of the Klein Sexual Orientation Grid.

16. List and describe the three attitudinal categories discerned from the National Health and Social Life Survey (NHSLS).

17. Briefly describe the influence of attitudinal and demographic variables regarding sexuality.

18. Describe the link between sexual attitudes and behaviors.

19. Describe why homophobia may be an inaccurately used term.

20. Describe the effects of negative attitudes towards homosexuals.

21. Describe the influence of heterosexism on sexual orientation issues.

22. Describe the nature of biphobia.

23. Describe externalized and internalized "phobias."

24. Describe your thoughts in examining influences regarding four relational scenarios.

25. List and describe two perspectives of moral values.

26. List and describe six ethical traditions.

27. Describe Western and Eastern religious influences regarding God and sexuality.

28. Describe two contrasting religious views of world trends.

29. Describe the influences of religious beliefs and denominations regarding sexual behaviors.

30. Briefly describe moral development in humans.

31. List and describe accepted moral principles accepted by society.

32. Describe eight steps for establishing sexual values.

33. Briefly describe barriers to sexuality education.

34. Describe the position of the American Public Health Association regarding sexuality education.

35. Describe four waves of sexuality education.

36. Briefly describe future needs regarding sexuality education.

37. Describe educational needs and efforts regarding sexuality education.

38. Describe the comprehensive sexuality education model

39. Describe the abstinence-only until marriage sexuality education model.

40. Describe eight concerns about abstinence-only sexuality education.

41. Briefly describe the effects of a sexuality education programs.

42. Describe why sexuality education needs to consider issues of cultural diversity.

43. Describe cross-cultural concerns involving sexuality education.

44. Identify Sexuality Information and Education Council of the United States' (SIECUS's) involvement with other nations to develop effective sexuality education programs targeting youth.

45. Describe the need for and limitation of sexuality education for professionals.

46. Describe how disabilities can influence an individual's sexuality.

47. Describe the need for sexuality education for individuals with intellectual or developmental disabilities.

48. Briefly describe the principle of normalization.

49. Describe learning challenges regarding sexuality faced by individuals with visual and auditory disabilities.

50. Describe the capacity of spinal cord injured individuals to engage in sexual behaviors.

51. Describe behavioral and relational challenges faced by individuals with spinal cord injuries (SCI).

52. Describe how various physical and mental disabilities impact sexual functioning.

53. Describe challenges that institutionalized individuals face regarding expressing their sexuality.

KEY WORDS

Abnormal: anything considered not to be normal, that is, not conforming to the subjective standards a social group has established as the norm.

Abstinence-only until mariage education: an approach to educating young people that emphasizes the need to abstain from sexual relations until marriage. It is essentially the "just say no" philosophy.

Affectional: relating to feelings or emotions, such as romantic attachments.

Asceticism (a-SET-a-siz-um): usually characterized by celibacy, this philosophy emphasizes spiritual purity through self-denial and self-discipline.

Biphobia: prejudice, negative attitudes, and misconceptions relating to bisexual people and their lifestyles.

Bisexual: refers to some degree of sexual activity with or attraction to members of both sexes.

Coitus (KO-at-us or ko-EET-us): heterosexual, penis-in-vagina intercourse.

Comprehensive sexuality education: an approach to educating young people about human sexuality that includes information about sexuality but also encourages clarifying values and developing decision-making skills.

Deviation: term applied to behaviors or orientations that do not conform to a society's accepted norms; it often has negative connotations.

Erotocentricity (ee-ROT-oh-sen-TRIS-ih-tee): the application of ethnocentric like judgments to sexual values and behaviors, creating the assumption that our own ways of approaching sexuality are the only "right" ways.

Ethnocentricity (eth-no-sen-TRIS-ih-tee): the tendency of the members of one culture to assume that their values and norms of behavior are the "right" ones in comparison to other cultures.

Facilitated sex: assistance provided to a person with severe physical disabilities in order to enable them to achieve sexual pleasure through masturbation or with a partner.

Foreplay: sexual activities shared in early stages of sexual arousal; the term implying that the activities are leading to a more intense, orgasm-oriented form of activity such as intercourse.

Gay: refers to persons who have a predominantly same-gender sexual orientation and identity; more often applied to males.

Hedonists (HEE-don-ists): people who believe that pleasure is the highest good.

Heterosexism: the biased and discriminatory assumption that people are or should be attracted to members of the other gender.

Heterosexual: attractions or activities between males and females.

Homophobia (ho-mo-FO-bee-a): strongly held negative attitudes and irrational fears relating to gay men and/or lesbians and their lifestyles.

Homosexual: term traditionally applied to affectional and sexual attractions and activities between members of the same gender.

Integrated sexuality education programs: this concept emphasizes the possibility of combining education to prevent pregnancy and the transmission of diseases with realistic approaches to educating young people about sexuality and how to make safer decisions about sex.

Lesbian (LEZ-bee-un): refers to females who have a predominantly same-gender sexual orientation and identity.

Moral values: beliefs associated with ethical issues, or rights and wrongs; they are often a part of sexual decision making.

Normal: a highly subjective term used to describe sexual behaviors and orientations. Standards of normalcy are determined by social, cultural, and historical standards.

Normalization: integration of mentally retarded persons into the social mainstream as much as possible.

Paraphilia (pair-a-FIL-ee-a): a newer term used to describe sexual orientations and behaviors that vary from the norm; it means "a love beside."

Paraplegic: a person paralyzed in the legs, and sometimes pelvic areas, as the result of injury to the spinal cord.

Quadriplegic: a person paralyzed in the upper body, including the arms, and lower body as the result of spinal cord injury.

Self-gratification: giving oneself pleasure, as in masturbation; a term typically used today instead of more negative descriptors.

Self-pleasuring: self-gratification; masturbation.

Sexual individuality: the unique set of sexual needs, orientations, fantasies, feelings, and activities that develops in each human being.

Straight: slang term for heterosexual.

Transvestite: an individual who dresses in clothing and adopts mannerisms considered appropriate for the opposite sex.

Transphobia: negative attitudes, prejudice, and misconceptions toward transgender individuals and lifestyles.

Values: system of beliefs with which people view life and make decisions, including their sexual decisions.

Variation: a less pejorative term to describe nonconformity to accepted norms.

SELF-TEST

When responding to the following multiple-choice questions, choose the "best" answer. The "best" answer is the one that corresponds to the information contained in your text.

1) The job of science, regarding sexuality, is to do all of the following *except*
   a) explain.
   b) understand.
   c) classify.
   d) label.

2) The term that loosely means "a love beside" that is now the preferred term to describe sexual attachment or dependency on some unusual or typically unacceptable stimulus is
   a) variation.
   b) deviation.
   c) paraphilia.
   d) sexophila.

3) All of the following are sociocultural standards for sexual arousal and behavior *except*
   a) coital standard.
   b) genital standard.
   c) orgasmic standard.
   d) romantic standard.

4) Even with the growing emphasis on sexual abstinence as the safest course of action for unmarried people,
   a) significant numbers of young people are choosing to abstain from sex.
   b) no young individuals are choosing to abstain from sex.
   c) only females are choosing to abstain from sex.
   d) significant numbers of young people are not choosing to abstain from sex.

5) Sexual attitudes and values seem to be associated with all but one of the following:
   a) ethnic background
   b) socioeconomic status
   c) sexual abuse history
   d) upbringing in a rural or suburban or urban setting.

6) A type of ethnocentricity that causes us to assume that our own sexual values, standards, and activities are right and best is called
   a) erotocentricity.
   b) socioerotocism.
   c) eroto-cultural-centricity.
   d) eroto-sociocultural-centricity.

7) The increase in acceptance of concepts such as situational morality, reality as a matter of perception, and nonjudgmentalness are components of which form of normalcy:
   a) statistical.
   b) moral.
   c) continuum.
   d) expert opinion.

8) The term that usually represents a distinct and permanent category, a defining characteristic of the person who has been labeled, and implies a great deal beyond some occasional behavior is
   a) bisexual.
   b) homosexual.
   c) heterosexual.
   d) transsexual.

9) The term *heterosexual* can be used to refer to all of the following opposite-gender examples *except*
   a) orientation.
   b) identity.
   c) behavior.
   d) fantasy.

10) Accordingly to 20th century research, it is believed that sexual orientation is largely determined by
   a) early childhood.
   b) young adulthood.
   c) adolescence.
   d) late childhood.

11) The researcher who developed a list of seven variables needed to be considered when describing a person's sexual orientation that resulted in the development of the KSOG SCALE is
   a) Kelly.
   b) Klein.
   c) Kraft von Ebbing.
   d) Masters.

12) All of the following are attitudinal categories developed from the NHSLS *except*
   a) procreational.
   b) traditional.
   c) relational.
   d) recreational.

13) One of the salient findings of the NHSLS was a clear link between which of the following characteristics and sexual behavior:
   a) religious affiliation.
   b) gender.
   c) sexual orientation.
   d) attitudes.

14) Irrational fears of lesbians and gay men have been labeled
   a) homosexualphobia.
   b) same-gender phobia.
   c) homophobia.
   d) heterosexism.

15) One of the occupations that poll respondents were concerned about openly gay people occupying was
   a) classroom teacher.
   b) college professor.
   c) social worker.
   d) police officer.

16) Biphobia and homophobia can be
   a) socialized and internalized.
   b) externalized and socialized.
   c) materialized and categorized.
   d) externalized and internalized.

17) Moral values have been classified into which of the following perspectives:
   a) essentialists and moral constructionists.
   b) essentialists and social constructionists.
   c) social constructionists and moralists.
   d) moralist and essentialists.

18) Sexual morality today tends to be founded in each of the following categories *except*
   a) situation ethics.
   b) adherence to divinely established natural laws.
   c) sexonistic tradition.
   d) hedonistic tradition.

19) In the earliest religious traditions, the emphasis was on which form of power:
   a) masculine.
   b) dualistic.
   c) ritualistic.
   d) feminine.

20) Which of the following traditions has not tended to view sexuality in terms of its creative potential and its power in spiritual development?
   a) Tantric
   b) Muslim
   c) Hindu
   d) Buddhist

21) All of the following are accepted moral principles *except*
   a) the principle of noncoercion.
   b) the principle of nondeceit.
   c) the principle of pleasure.
   d) the principle of treatment of people as ends.

22) One of the major barriers to effective parent-teenager communication regarding sexuality is
   a) parents' lack of comfort with the subject.
   b) parents' lack of knowledge about human sexuality.
   c) teens' level of comfort with sexuality.
   d) parents' and teens' dysfunctional relationships.

23) Which of the following terms has gained in popularity over sex education?
   a) systematic sexuality education.
   b) systematized sex education.
   c) comprehensive sex education.
   d) comprehensive sexuality education.

24) Which of the following education efforts was based largely on the assumption that knowledge about consequences translates to immediate changes in behavior?
   a) comprehensive sexuality education
   b) HIV/AIDS education
   c) abstinence-only education
   d) pregnancy prevention and STD/STI education

25) The "just say no" approaches to sexuality education have evolved into the
   a) abstinence-only programs.
   b) abstinence-based programs.
   c) abstinence-only until-marriage programs.
   d) none of the above.

26) Public opinion polls consistently demonstrate that what percentage of adult Americans favor the teaching of sexuality education in schools:
   a) 50%.
   b) 95%.
   c) 85%.
   d) 25%.

27) As states have mandated sexuality and HIV education programs, it has also become clear that
   a) most are comfortable with the topics of human sexuality.
   b) most attend compulsory training programs.
   c) most lack professional training in the field.
   d) most support legislation for sexuality education.

28) Which of the following views has offended those who oppose comprehensive sexuality education?
   a) sex-positive
   b) sex-negative
   c) pro-sexuality
   d) abstinence

29) The U.S. Congress continues to approve funding for which form of sexuality education:
   a) comprehensive
   b) risk reduction
   c) procreative
   d) abstinence-until-marriage

30) Abstinence-until-marriage curricula implore all but which of the following philosophical strategies?
   a) an emphasis on the unreliability of birth control
   b) lack of discussion about same-gender sexual orientation
   c) an emphasis on the traditional stereotypes of male and female gender roles
   d) medically accurate, fact based information about STIs

31) To date, research seems to indicate what about current sexuality education programs:
   a) they hasten the onset of intercourse
   b) they decrease the use of contraception use
   c) they increase the use of safer sex techniques
   d) they decrease the onset of intercourse

32) To be effective, sexuality educators may need to become:
   a) culturally relevant
   b) culturally competent
   c) socially relevant
   d) socially competent

33) SIECUS has been working with organizations in other countries to develop comprehensive sexuality education. One of the techniques that has been employed in Belize and Peru is to combine education with
   a) drama and dance.
   b) national holiday events.
   c) religious services.
   d) door to door efforts to raise awareness.

34) What percentage of medical schools report requiring core curriculum preparation in sexuality?
   a) 50%
   b) 25%
   c) 74%
   d) 92%

35) The ability of educators, health and counseling professionals, and clergy to perceive sexuality concerns depends on
   a) their ability to communicate.
   b) permission from the ethical standards body of that particular discipline.
   c) their degree of comfort level with the subject of sexuality.
   d) the comfort level of those people seeking support from that professional.

36) Most disabling conditions do not directly affect any of the following *except*
   a) sex organs.
   b) sexual feelings.
   c) need for sex.
   d) view their attractiveness.

37) The process used when working with individuals with intellectual or developmental disabilities to help them adapt to the norms and patterns of mainstream social life is referred to as
   a) stabilization.
   b) norming.
   c) normalization.
   d) resocialization.

38) In addition to the challenge of gaining an understanding of sex and sexuality, individuals with visual or hearing impairments face a second challenge in the
   a) functional process.
   b) socialization process.
   c) integration process.
   d) sexualization process.

39) It is often assumed that people with spinal cord injury are incapable of sexual sensations or response; however, in a particular study, _____ reported having sensation in their genitals.
   a) 5% of males and 35% of females
   b) 10% of males and 40% of females
   c) 15% of males and 45% of females
   d) 25% of males and 50% of females

40) Less than _____ of couples dealing with one partner having a spinal cord injury receive counseling.
   a) 10%
   b) 25%
   c) 35%
   d) 60%

41) Facilitated sex is a term that requires
   a) family approval for those in institutional settings.
   b) notification from that individual's primary care physician.
   c) special sensitivity and training for the aids or facilitators.
   d) certification and state licensure to practice.

42) Institutional settings in which same-gender sexual contacts may occur more frequently are ones that are
   a) socially liberal.
   b) sexually liberal.
   c) segregated.
   d) integrated.

1) To be _____ is to be attracted sexually to members of the opposite sex and to desire penis-in-vagina intercourse; everything else is considered _____.

2) It is important, when examining the findings of researchers, that they are products of their _____ environments.

3) Safe sex standards are reinforced by prevailing cultural _____ and _____.

4) The term _____ is not likely to be used to define a person, behavior, or lifestyle.

5) Definitions of the term *homosexual* have tended to focus only on sexual activity and thus have sometimes ignored the individual's _____ preferences.

6) A man who dresses in women's clothing is often labeled a _____.

7) There does not seem to be a _____ sexual way for human beings or an inborn instinct to guide their sexual behaviors.

8) In the NHSLS, about one-third of the population indicated that their _____ beliefs always guide their sexual behaviors.

9) The _____ are not guided by any religious beliefs and are most accepting regarding attitudinal items within the recreational attitudinal category.

10) _____ people were unlikely to fall into the traditional category, and were more likely to be recreational.

11) Cultural _____ fosters antigay and antilesbian attitudes.

12) _____ values deal with ethics, or rights and wrongs, of life situations.

13) Contemporary writers suggest that it is time to reclaim sexual _____ as part of living comfortably in one's body and/or finding one's playful side.

14) In Christian theology, _____ decided that sexual desire represented the ultimate clash between desire and reason.

15) By the time children are _____ to _____ years old, they are beginning to adapt to the moral codes required of them by their environment.

16) Achieving a healthy sexuality must involve a level of _____ between a person's behaviors and values.

17) Congress has approved funding to support narrowly-defined _____ education.

18) Most of the popular abstinence based education programs are produced by organizations or individuals that represent particular _____ moral frameworks. State departments of education and the courts have begun to restrict abstinence based education programs use in public schools.

19) Research suggests that the abstinence message _____ _____ _____ particularly effective.

20) One of the greatest challenges to sexuality education programs is the need to develop approaches that will be sensitive to _____ differences.

21) Teachers are not required to take courses or earn certification in _____.

22) Sixty-one percent of future physicians were found to have received _____ hours or less of training in human sexuality.

23) The more _____ professionals are about dealing with sexual issues, the less apt they will be to pursue a patient's sexual history.

24) Myths and misperceptions about children with disabilities may lead to _____ in their development as healthy sexual individuals.

25) _____ and _____ disabilities may influence a person's sexuality in many different ways.

26) Most disabling conditions do not directly affect the sex _____ or their ability to _____.

27) Erection of the penis and lubrication of the vagina are also partially controlled by a localized _____ reflex.

28) Many people who experienced a _____ or _____ may be physically debilitated and may worry about how much physical exertion they can withstand during and after their recovery.

29) A variety of _____ conditions, such as multiple sclerosis and muscular dystrophy, can result in gradual loss of body control.

ESSAY QUESTIONS
[Answers are provided at the end of the study guide.]

1) Describe Western cultural perceptions and influences regarding the normality, abnormality, and "acceptability" of sexual behavior.

2) Describe the terms and labels used by sexologists to explain atypical sexual behaviors as well as four methods of defining normalcy of sexual behaviors.

3) Briefly describe how homophobia and biphobia impact individuals, including the dimension of internalized and externalized "phobias."

4) Briefly describe barriers to sexuality education including the controversies surrounding comprehensive and abstinence based sexuality education models.

5) Briefly describe how individuals with spinal cord injuries can engage in sexual behaviors, as well as behavioral and relational challenges faced by these individuals.

CHAPTER RESOURCE REFLECTIONS

Case Study

Maybe after reading Jonathon's story you could not relate to the issues presented. Yet, what if you found someone attractive, both physically and emotionally, and they developed a psychological or psychiatric disorder during your relationship. How would you react to those circumstances? Why would you react in that manner? What if you learned the same information about that individual at the onset of your relationship? Would your reactions be the same? Why or why not?

Survival Sex

As you read Nanette Ecker's reflection, do you support her conclusions regarding the action that needs to be taken to address the "survival sex" concern? Why or why not? Could she be "charged" with being extremely "ethnocentric"? Would that be good or bad? Why or why not?

Sexuality of Persons with Disabilities

After reading the position of SIECUS, do you support this stand? Why or why not? Would you prefer that educational efforts to people with disabilities continue to focus on sexual abuse prevention and to not include education about intercourse and other sexual behaviors? Imagine what might be the concerns of providers of sexual and reproductive healthcare services?

The World Association for Sexology (WAS) developed and adopted a declaration of sexual rights. How is the WAS list different from the SIECUS list (see article in your text)? How might particular cultural values affect an individuals' ability to practice these rights?

Adolescence and Sexuality Education

In the article "A close-to-perfect health class," the student author states that a peer and a book offered her enlightenment with regard to how she could learn this information. Was this similar in your experience in learning about sex? Did you realize that numerous messages from multiple sources were available to you? From which source would you have preferred to learn this information? Could you have learned "too much information" at the "wrong time"?

After reading the article "Teens on Sex…," place yourself in the position of being a parent of a teenager. After reading the information about teen sex, what types of discussion will you have with them about sexuality? Furthermore, what message will you send to your local school board? Why will you send these types of messages to your teen and school board? What would your choices include should you reside in a school district that does not provide the type of sexuality education to which you expect your teen to be exposed?

"Parents need to start listening and talking" suggests that parents are not doing a good job of listening or talking to their teens. Is it a realistic expectation for parents not to react to their teens when the subject of sex is raised? Would you *react* or *respond*? What might be some steps you could take to send a clear message about sex to your teen that would encourage your teen to engage you in conversation?

Facilitated Sex

This article clearly defines a list of items to consider for facilitated sex situations. Would you add anything to the list? Review the items from a personal perspective: could you be a trained facilitator? How would you feel if you were the individual with the disability receiving assistance? How do you think the theory of facilitated sex would be received in a national discussion?

MCGRAW-HILL RESOURCES
REFLECTING ON SEXUALTY

Remember that this section of the study guide takes you beyond the text to explore other resources in the field of human sexuality. The experience attempts to expand upon at least one concept covered in the chapter.

Access the McGraw-Hill Web pages associated with sexuality at:
> http://www.mhhe.com/socscience/sex

Scroll down and "click" on the hyperlink for "Resource Room."

Scroll down and "click" on the hyperlink for "Web Resources."

Scroll down and "click" on the hyperlink for "Feminist against Censorship."

Read the material listed on the home page.

Scroll down and "click on the hyperlink for "FAQ."

Read the responses to "Frequently Asked Questions." Based on your reading in the chapter regarding several attitudes and several choices, which category do you believe best represents the position of this organization? Explain your reasons for making the categorical choice.

CHAPTER 8
SEXUALITY, COMMUNICATION, AND RELATIONSHIPS

CHAPTER OUTLINE

SELF-EVALUATION

    Communicating about Sex

    Working on Communication: An Exercise for Two

CHAPTER LEARNING OBJECTIVES

1. Describe general concerns regarding communicating about sex.

2. List and describe five components of the communication process.

3. Briefly describe cultural influence regarding the meaning and use of sexual words.

4. Describe the use of sexual slang by each gender.

5. List and describe five myths about communication.

6. List and describe three common sexual games people play.

7. List and describe five ground rules for effective communication.

8. List and describe nine ways to make effective communication happen.

9. Describe personality typologies and their relationships to communication.

10. Describe childhood and adult gender differences in communication.

11. List and describe four categories of gender communication generalizations.

12. Consider the differences of communication patterns in the workplace and the influence of gender.

13. Describe the effects of constructive and destructive quarreling.

14. List and describe three types of relationship impasses.

15. Describe both ineffective and effective ways to resolve impasses.

16. Describe the concept of a "shift to mutuality."

17. Describe gender differences regarding fighting.

18. List and describe six findings about loving relationships.

19. List and describe four risks of sex.

20. Describe three global transformations that affect relationships.

21. Describe challenges regarding love and relationships.

22. Describe the benefits and limitations of infatuation.

23. Describe the concept of being in love.

24. List and describe the components of Sternberg's Triangular Theory of Love.

25. Briefly describe two sexual chemical attractants.

26. Briefly describe brain chemicals involved in attraction.

27. List and describe three factors that influence sexual intimacy.

28. Describe how perceptions about love can influence relationships.

29. Describe same-gender similarities and differences regarding same-gender intimate relationship.

30. List and describe three patterns of same-gender intimate relationships.

31. Describe concerns regarding gender and intimate friendship.

32. Briefly describe the nature of computer mediated communication and computer mediated relating.

33. Describe findings and risks concerning computer mediated communication and computer mediated relating.

34. List and describe three styles of emotional bonding.

35. Describe positive and negative aspects of jealousy.

36. List and describe four ways of dealing with a jealous partner.

37. Describe why people need to be open to change in relationships.

38. Describe emotional and social responses to the termination of a relationship.

KEY WORDS

Endorphins (en-DORE-fins): brain secretions that act as natural tranquilizers and pain relievers.

Oxytocin (ox-ee-TOH-sin): a chemical produced by the brain in response to physical intimacy and sexual satisfaction.

Pheromones (FAIR-oh-moans): human chemicals, the scent of which may cause an attraction or behavioral change in other individuals.

SELF-TEST
When responding to the following multiple-choice questions, choose the "best" answer. The "best" answer is the one that corresponds to the information contained in your text.

1) It is assumed that "nice guys"
   a) are insensitive to others needs.
   b) are more sexually experienced.
   c) are not preferred for intimate relationships.
   d) have had fewer sexual partners.

2) Our culture delivers mixed messages about sexuality, including all of the following *except*
   a) saturating our senses with sexy messages.
   b) hinting that sex is spiritual.
   c) hinting that sex is dangerous.
   d) hinting that sex is dirty.

3) Communication works best when
   a) there is a minimal feedback loop.
   b) the partners clarify only some messages.
   c) there is a well-developed feedback system.
   d) there is a perpetual feedback loop.

4) Which of the following has far more terms associated with males than females?
   a) sexual intercourse
   b) relational names
   c) masturbation
   d) anal intercourse

5) For college students, _____ are shaped by the students' social networks.
   a) ideals
   b) norms
   c) feelings
   d) slang

6) All of the following are "myths" associated with communication *except*
   a) having a confident opinion on every issue.
   b) an impressive conversation delivered to dead air.
   c) mapping out strategies ahead of time which makes for better communication.
   d) the rational mind is the only basis for effective communication.

7) Sexual myths stimulate the development of all but one of the following:
   a) games
   b) phone conversation
   c) manipulative sexual seduction
   d) fulfilling relationships

8) When sex is used to express struggles and control over one another, it is referred to as what type of sexual game?
   a) operating by the "rules"
   b) relationship games
   c) communication games
   d) power games

9) All but which of the following are considered sexual game playing techniques?
   a) power
   b) relationship
   c) control
   d) communication

10) The statement "It is important to understand your own heritage as well as someone you might build a relationship with," refers to which of the following communication rules:
   a) knowing your own values
   b) building trust for one another
   c) understanding your cultural differences
   d) keeping yourselves on equal ground

11) All of the following are ways to make the communication process happen *except*
   a) demonstrating an attitude of apathy and all-ness.
   b) listening carefully and really hearing.
   c) avoiding making snap judgments.
   d) demonstrating an attitude of warmth, caring, and respect.

12) Which of the following ways to make the communication process happen is perceived as a "trap"?
   a) don't let silence scare you
   b) I don't want to hurt you
   c) asking for clarification
   d) making all-ness statements

13) Which of the following tests is based on a model that portrays the human personality as a combination of varying balances between four main pairs of traits?
   a) Kinsey Personality Scale
   b) Masters-Briggs Type Indicator
   c) Myers-Briggs Type Indicator
   d) Kiersey Type Indicator

14) Regarding talking over problems,
   a) women are less likely to tell men about difficult feelings.
   b) men are gentler and more emotional.
   c) men feel more obligated to offer solutions to a problem.
   d) women are more demanding in their communication.

15) Research about talking and listening shows
   a) women talk more in public situations.
   b) both men and women talk equally in public situations.
   c) both men and women resist talking in public situations.
   d) men talk more in public situations.

16) It has been found that certain types of quarreling
   a) can destroy all relationship.
   b) can improve relationships.
   c) has no effect on relationships.
   d) make couples miserable.

17) Using "I" messages is a way to
   a) exclusively introduce your opinion without objections.
   b) dominate and control the flow of the conversation.
   c) block interference by a partner interrupting with his/her thoughts.
   d) take responsibility for communicating with a partner.

18) In relationships, women are often what type of managers?
   a) emotional
   b) sexual
   c) communication
   d) relational

19) Each of the following in an impasse that can occur in a relationship *except*
   a) dread/anger impasse.
   b) product/process impasse.
   c) power-over/power-with impasse.
   d) communication/detachment impasse.

20) All of the following are styles for resolving impasses *except*
   a) dominating.
   b) cooperating.
   c) compromising.
   d) obliging.

21) Researcher John Gottman found which of the following qualities might make or break a relationship?
   a) emotionally expressive relationships are not very successful
   b) positive feelings about the future of the relationship are correlated with a higher likelihood of remaining together
   c) volatile relationships can be very long lasting
   d) confronting complaints and differences later in the relationship seems to help

22) All of the following are risks of sex *except*
   a) modeling your sexuality only after external standards.
   b) confusing romantic and sexual attractions.
   c) modeling your sexuality only after internal standards.
   d) not allowing oneself to be vulnerable.

23) Which of the following seem to be primary ingredients that bring people together in intimate relationships?
   a) sex and communication
   b) love and communication
   c) sex and marriage
   d) love and sex

24) Which item below is not one of the three primary human emotion-motivation systems associated with love?
   a) infatuation
   b) lust
   c) attachment
   d) attraction

25) The initial "falling in love" experience causes the object of affection to take on special meaning
    a) usually at the delight of family members.
    b) usually because hormones have triggered this reaction.
    c) usually to the exclusion of anyone else.
    d) usually to the benefit of friends and family members.

26) What provides the motivational component of love?
    a) intimacy
    b) commitment
    c) passion
    d) sex

27) The scents of chemical sex attractants that may play an influential role in romantic attraction are called
    a) sexualmones.
    b) pherostimuli.
    c) pheromones.
    d) andromones.

28) Two chemicals associated with the relational period of attachment are
    a) endorphins and dopamine.
    b) dopamine and oxytocin.
    c) norepinephrine and PEA.
    d) endorphins and oxytocin.

29) The brain chemical associated with causing intrusive or obsessive thinking is
    a) serotonin.
    b) dopamine.
    c) endorphins.
    d) estrogen.

30) All of the following are factors related to intimacy *except*
    a) being an observer.
    b) touching.
    c) relaxation.
    d) being a participant.

31) The confusion over love and sex is best resolved through effective
    a) sexual techniques.
    b) communication methods.
    c) crisis resolution methods.
    d) sociosexual methods.

32) One theory of same-sexed partner attachment suggests that men are drawn into forming a relationship with other males
    a) to achieve a sense of relational completion.
    b) to achieve a self of competition.
    c) to achieve a sense of self completion.
    d) to achieve a sense of emergence.

33) All of the following are components of attachment theory *except*
   a) occupied.
   b) avoidant.
   c) secure.
   d) fearful avoidant.

34) Possessiveness, when jealousy gets out of control, is associated with which style of attachment?
   a) secure
   b) dismissing avoidant
   c) preoccupied
   d) avoidant

35) All of the following are suggested ways for dealing with a partner who is being unreasonably jealous *except*
   a) allowing to be ruled by pity for the other person.
   b) taking a close look at whether this is a relationship that is healthy for you.
   c) encouraging your partner to work on the jealousy with you.
   d) being ruled by self-pity.

GUIDED REVIEW AND STUDY
[Answers are provided at the end of the study guide.]

1) A great many sexual _____ could be prevented or resolved through open, honest _____.

2) Words are _____ and often _____, and their meanings may be interpreted differently by different people.

3) In early 20th century America, the words *leg*, *bull*, and *pregnant* were considered _____ for mixed company because of their presumed sexual connotations.

4) In some contexts, the proper _____ terminology about sex may seem more inappropriate or embarrassing than slang terms.

5) Every relationship will evolve its own _____ for the intimate discussions of sex.

6) Use of any of the myths can form the basis for a surefire prescription to _____ good communication.

7) Sexual games involve developing a _____ that will help a person feel that they can control an outcome.

8) Relationship games result when some men and women bring _____ conflicts and _____ problems with them to their sexual relationships.

9) It is not enough to feel a sense of caring for another person; the feelings need to be _____ or _____ in some way.

10) Often people who appear to be listening are actually _____ _____, formulating their response to what the other person is saying, and thereby not carefully listening or really hearing.

11) How we talk to ourselves can have a profound effect on the ways we relate to other people. This is referred to as _____.

12) _____ people simply tend to draw their energy more from inside themselves.

13) _____ differences in relationships only underscore the need for good communication skills and a commitment to using them.

14) One of the areas of communication that often causes trouble for women and men is how they _____ various _____.

15) In their interactions with other employees, women are often _____ in their communications.

16) Conflicts in communicating may be complicated by differences in communication styles resulting from _____ factors or _____.

17) A key to arguing is whether the mode is _____ or _____.

18) In communication, there comes a point at which couples feel that they are really working together; this is referred to as the shift to _____.

19) Couples sometimes reach a _____, meaning that the process of two people relating has become stuck and unmoving.

20) The best way to resolve relational impasses is to press into the conflict with a sense of _____.

21) Gottman applied _____ models to his relationship data and was able to find some predictive value in those models.

22) _____ is a term that refers to a partner who makes hurtful comments when the other partner is attempting to pull the conversation in a more positive direction

23) There is an increasing belief in the equality of the genders and ethnic groups that is eroding the long-standing _____ _____ and prejudices.

24) _____, _____ and _____ are the three components of Sternberg's Triangular Theory of Love.

25) During attraction, the brain is stimulated by _____.

26) There is evidence that when _____ occurs, the pituitary gland produces _____, a hormone that tends to suppress sexual desire for a time.

27) The confusions over love and sex are best resolved through effective _____ methods.

28) In the 19th century, _____ friendships were apparently common among upper-middle-class women.

29) In gay and lesbian relationships, the _____ model of dating and marriage has one partner adopting more of the traditional masculine functions and the other adopting more of the feminine roles.

30) The pervasive impression created by the media is that the Net promotes _____, _____ relationships, but the realities are far more complex and positive than this.

31) _____, avoidant people hold negative views of both themselves and their partners.

32) The _____ process is almost always a painful one, but it may also represent a viable choice for a failing relationship in which one or both partners lacks the desire and motivation to move to a new level of commitment.

33) Some people rush to put the pain of their loss behind them and may even hurry into a _____ relationship.

ESSAY QUESTIONS
[Answers are provided at the end of the study guide.]

1) Describe four common sexual games people play and some ground rules that can address these games people have in their relationships.

2) Describe gender differences in childhood and adult communication along with four categories of gender communication generalizations.

3) Describe the components of Sternberg's Triangular Theory of Love.

4) Describe similarities and differences in same-gender intimate relationships along with three same-gender patterns of intimate relationships.

5) Describe the impact that Internet dating has had on forming intimate relationships. What are the implications?

CHAPTER RESOURCE REFLECTIONS

Cross-Cultural Perspective

As you read this cross-cultural perspective, imagine yourself living in China. If information about sexuality and sexual behavior was not readily available, how would you learn about sexual types? Although the nonconsummated marriage may be "extreme," what aspects of human sexual behavior have you learned about up to this point in the course? We all can and will continue to learn about human sexuality throughout our lives. Some people simply need to learn more than others.

Dating...Is All but Dead

From your experiences, is dating "all but dead" on your college campus? Do you agree with the reasons for "dead dating" presented in the reading? Why or why not?

Case Study

The case study of Jennifer and Ted reinforces the position that individuals need to understand themselves first, especially their personality characteristics. Then they need to understand the personality characteristics of their partner. Finally, they need to understand how these personality characteristics can impact their relationship. To understand your personality a little better, you might want to visit the counseling center at your college or university. Schedule an appointment to take one of the many personality tests available. After taking the test and reflecting on the results, how can you use the information to make your relationship better? Although you can't mandate that your partner also take the same test, you may want to discuss the personal and relational benefits of the process.

Emotional Infidelity

After reading the article, do you believe friendships with the other sex is being "unfaithful?" Why or why not? What would your response be to your partner if you learned that he or she had been confiding in a friend of the opposite sex?

Internal/External Consistency in Communication

When you read the columns with statements from the man and the woman, do they ring true? Have you experienced these situations? What role does assertive communication play in your relationships?

Cupid's Rendezvous

Where are the romantic hot spots at your campus? What makes a spot hot?

What Goes into Sex Appeal?

Do you consider these people attractive? Look around the classroom; do a majority of your fellow students look like the people depicted in this photo? Do you look like either of the people in the photo? Is that a good thing? How does that make you feel? What do you think is sex appeal? Does that make a person sexy?

Know Your Partner

This activity could create an opportunity for you and your partner to discuss your relationship.

Self-Evaluation: Communicating about Sex

This exercise may be challenging, but certainly worth the effort, as communication is a foundational block of any relationship. If you perceive the communication dynamics in your relationship to be less than desirable, you will definitely need to create a "safe space" for this exercise. Remember that the objective is improving the communication in your relationship as well as the general nature of your relationship. Even if you believe the communication and overall nature of your relationship is good, you may need to create a "safe space" in the event this exercise brings an unknown issue to the surface. Remember the objective is improving your relationship.

MCGRAW-HILL RESOURCES
REFLECTING ON SEXUALTY

Remember that this section of the study guide takes you beyond the text to explore other resources in the field of human sexuality. The experience attempts to expand upon at least one concept covered in the chapter.

Access the McGraw-Hill Web pages associated with sexuality at:
    http://www.mhhe.com/socscience/sex

Scroll down and "click" on the hyperlink for "Resource Room."

Scroll down and "click" on the hyperlink for "Web Resources."

Scroll down and "click" on the hyperlink for "Go Ask Alice," or "www.goaskalice.columbia.edu"

"Click" on the "Relationships" icon.

Scroll down and "click" on the hyperlinks for one of the topics that deal with a communication issue, such as "Asking Someone about Their Sexuality."

After reading the question and response, be capable of discussing which section of the chapter best applies to the dynamics presented in the question or the response (i.e., Communication Process, Communication Myths, Communication Games, etc.).

CHAPTER 9
REPRODUCTION, REPRODUCTIVE TECHNOLOGY, AND BIRTHING

CHAPTER OUTLINE

Learning Objectives

CHAPTER LEARNING OBJECTIVES

1. Briefly describe the structures and chemicals associated with fertilization.

2. Briefly describe rates and causes of twinning.

3. List and describe two types of twins.

4. Describe risk and reduction methods associated with twinning.

5. Describe the structures and processes of embryo development and implementation.

6. List and describe the extraembryonic structures associated with embryonic survival.

7. List and describe changes in the fetus and mother during pregnancy.

8. Briefly describe the status of reproductive and fetal technology.

9. Briefly describe the importance of genes in humans.

10. Briefly describe genetic therapy and gene therapy.

11. Identify how genetic testing and gene therapy can help people.

12. Describe concerns regarding the science and use of genetic research.

13. Describe the process and legal consideration of artificial insemination.

14. Describe the general nature of and legal issues associated with the storage of gametes.

15. Describe the processes used in vitro fertilization (IVF).

16. Describe controversies and rates of success associated with IVF.

17. List and describe seven additional fertilization technologies.

18. Briefly describe how alternative methods of fertilization can be used by older women.

19. Describe the general considerations of choosing the sex of a fetus.

20. Describe concerns about and ethical issues regarding fetal sex determination.

21. Describe two cloning techniques and the results of using these processes.

22. Describe ethical and physiological concerns associated with cloning.

23. Briefly describe the controversy associated with embryo and stem cell research.

24. Describe the process of gestational surrogacy and the controversies surrounding it.

25. List and describe five technologies used in monitoring fetal health.

26. Describe reasons for male and female infertility.

27. Briefly describe the psychological effects of infertility.

28. Describe why prenatal care is important.

29. Briefly describe reasons for birth defects.

30. Briefly describe possible initial signs of pregnancy.

31. Briefly describe concerns regarding pregnancy tests.

32. Briefly describe the influence of alcohol, drugs, and smoking on fetal development.

33. Describe reasons for refraining from or engaging in sex during and after pregnancy.

34. List and describe the stages of the birth process.

35. Describe concerns regarding caesarian sections.

36. List and describe six alternative birthing methods.

37. Briefly describe concerns associated with a newborn.

38. List and describe three pregnancy complications.

39. List and briefly describe three adjustments associated with post partum care.

KEY WORDS

Afterbirth: the tissues expelled after childbirth, including the placenta, the remains of the umbilical cord, and fetal membranes.

Amniocentesis (am-nee-oh-sen-TEE-sis): a process whereby medical problems with a fetus can be determined while it is still in the womb; a needle is inserted into the amniotic sac, amniotic fluid is withdrawn, and fetal cells are examined.

Amnion (AM-nee-on): a thin membrane that forms a closed sac around the embryo; the sac is filled with amniotic fluid which protects and cushions the embryo.

Artificial embryonation: a process in which the developing embryo is flushed from the uterus of the donor woman five days after fertilization and placed in another woman's uterus.

Artificial insemination: injection of the sperm cells of a male into a woman's vagina with the intention of conceiving a child.

Assistive reproductive technology (ART): a collection of laboratory techniques that have been developed to help couples overcome infertility problems and have children, usually through bypassing one of the usual biological pathways to pregnancy or gestation.

Birth canal: term applied to the vagina during the birth process.

Birthing rooms: special areas in the hospital, decorated and furnished in a nonhospital way, set aside for giving birth; the woman remains here to give birth rather than being taken to a separate delivery room.

Blastocyst: the ball of cells, after five days of cell division, that has developed a fluid-filled cavity in its interior; it has entered the uterine cavity.

Bond: the emotional link between parent and child created by cuddling, cooing, and physical and eye contact early in the newborn's life.

Cesarian section: a surgical method of childbirth in which delivery occurs through an incision in the abdominal wall and uterus.

Chorion (KOR-ee-on): the outermost extraembryonic membrane essential in the formation of the placenta.

Chorionic villi sampling (CVS): a technique for diagnosing medical problems in the fetus as early as the eighth week of pregnancy; a sample of the chorionic membrane is removed through the cervix and studied.

Clone: the genetic-duplicate organism produced by the cloning process.

Cloning: a process by which a genetic duplicate of an organism is made either by substituting the chromosomes of a body cell into a donated ovum or by separation of cells in early embryonic development.

Computerized sperm selection: use of computer scanning to identify the most viable sperm which are then extracted to be used for fertilization of an ovum in the laboratory.

Deoxyribonucleic acid (DNA) (dee-AK-see-rye-bow-new-KLEE-ik): the chemical in each cell that carries the genetic code.

Dilation: the gradual opening of the cervical opening of the uterus prior to and during labor.

Ectopic pregnancy (ek-TOP-ik): the implantation of a blastocyst somewhere other than in the uterus, usually in the fallopian tube.

Effacement: the thinning of cervical tissue of the uterus prior to and during labor.

Embryo (EM-bree-o): the term applied to the developing cells when, about a week after fertilization, the blastocyst implants itself in the uterine wall.

Episiotomy (ee-piz-ee-OTT-a-mee): a surgical incision in the vaginal opening made by the clinician or obstetrician to prevent the baby from tearing the opening in the process of being born.

Exocytosis (ex-oh-sye-TOH-sis): the release of genetic material by the sperm cell permitting fertilization to occur.

Fertilin (fer-TILL-in): a chemical in the outer membrane of a sperm that assists in attachment to the egg cell and penetration of the egg's outer membrane.

Fetal alcohol syndrome (FAS): a condition in a fetus characterized by abnormal growth, neurological damage, and facial distortion caused by the mother's heavy alcohol consumption.

Fetal surgery: a surgical procedure performed on the fetus while it is still in the uterus or during a temporary period of removal from the uterus.

Fetus: the term given to the embryo after two months of development in the womb.

Fraternal twins: twins formed from two separate ova that were fertilized by two separate sperm.

Gamete intrafallopian transfer (GIFT): direct placement of ovum and concentrated sperm cells into the woman's fallopian tube to increase the chances of fertilization.

Gene therapy: treatment of genetically caused disorders by substitution of healthy genes.

Genetic engineering: the modification of the gene structure of cells to change cellular functioning.

Gestational surrogacy: implantation of an embryo created by the sperm and ovum of one set of parents into the uterus of another woman who agrees to gestate the fetus and give birth to the child which is then given to the original parents.

Human chorionic gonadotropin (HCG): a hormone detectable in the urine of a pregnant woman.

Identical twins: twins formed by a single ovum that was fertilized by a single sperm before the cell divided in two.

Immature oocyte collection: extraction of immature eggs from undeveloped follicles in an ovary, after which the oocytes are matured through cell culturing methods to be prepared for fertilization.

Infertility: the inability to produce offspring.

Intracytoplasmic sperm injection (ICSI): a technique involving the injection of a single sperm cell directly into an ovum. It is useful in cases where the male has a low sperm count.

In vitro fertilization (IVF): a process whereby the union of the sperm and egg occurs outside the mother's body.

Labor: uterine contractions in a pregnant woman; an indication that the birth process is beginning.

Lamaze method (la-MAHZ): a birthing process based on relaxation techniques practiced by the expectant mother; her partner coaches her throughout the birth.

Microscopic epididymal sperm aspiration (MESA): a procedure in which sperm are removed directly from the epididymis of the male testes.

Midwives: medical professionals, both women and men, trained to assist with the birthing process.

Morula (MOR-yuh-la): a spherical, solid mass of cells formed after three days of embryonic cell division.

Natural childbirth: a birthing process that encourages the mother to take control, thus minimizing medical intervention.

Ovum donation: use of an egg from another woman for conception, with the fertilized ovum then being implanted in the uterus of the woman wanting to become pregnant.

Oxytocin (ox-ee-TOH-sin): a pituitary hormone believed to play a role in initiating the birth process.

Placenta (pla-SEN-ta): the organ that unites the fetus to the mother by bringing their blood vessels closer together; it provides nourishment and removes waste for the developing baby.

Post partum depression: a period of low energy and discouragement that is common for mothers following childbearing. Longer-lasting or severe symptoms should receive medical treatment.

Pregnancy-induced hypertension: a disorder that can occur in the latter half of pregnancy marked by a swelling in the ankles and other parts of the body, high blood pressure, and protein in the urine; can progress to coma and death if not treated.

Preimplantation genetic diagnosis (PGD): examining the chromosomes of an embryo conceived by IVF, prior to implantation in the uterus.

Premature birth: a birth that takes place prior to the 36th week of pregnancy.

Rh incompatibility: condition in which a blood protein of the infant is not the same as the mother's; antibodies formed in the mother can destroy red blood cells in the fetus.

RhoGAM: medication administered to a mother to prevent formation of antibodies when the baby is Rh positive and its mother Rh negative.

Selective reduction: the use of abortion techniques to reduce the number of fetuses when there are more than three in a pregnancy, thus increasing the chances of survival for the remaining fetuses. Also called selective termination.

Sonograms: ultrasonic rays used to project a picture of internal structures such as the fetus; often used in conjunction with amniocentesis or fetal surgery.

Umbilical cord: the tubelike tissues and blood vessels originating at the embryo's navel that connects it to the placenta.

Villi: fingerlike projections of the chorion; they form a major part of the placenta.

Zona pellucida (ZO-nah pe-LOO-sa-da): the transparent, outer membrane of an ovum.

Zygote: an ovum that has been fertilized by a sperm.

Zygote intrafallopian transfer (ZIFT): zygotes resulting from IVF are inserted directly into the fallopian tubes.

SELF TEST

When responding to the following multiple-choice questions, choose the "best" answer. The "best" answer is the one that corresponds to the information contained in your text.

1) Fertilization is most likely to occur, according to the most recent research, when sperm are present
   a) during any of the 3 days of the cycle that end with the day of ovulation.
   b) during any of the 2 days following ovulation.
   c) during any of the 6 days of the cycle that end with the day of ovulation.
   d) during any of the 6 days prior to ovulation.

2) Fertilin is a chemical that is contained in the membrane of the sperm and helps
   a) the adhering and penetration process of the outer layer of the ovum.
   b) the thousands of sperm not stick to each other.
   c) the fertilized ovum move through the fallopian tubes.
   d) the viability of sperm.

3) The process in which the sperm cell opens to allow its chromosomes to be released into the ovum is referred to as
   a) zytotysosis.
   b) exocytosis.
   c) zona pellucida.
   d) zozotysosis.

4) Aborting one or more of the fetuses in large multiple pregnancies is referred to as
   a) selective reduction.
   b) selective abortion.
   c) reductive abortion.
   d) reduction pregnancy.

5) When the fertilized zygote implants on the uterine wall, it is referred to as a
   a) morula.
   b) blastocyst.
   c) fetus.
   d) embryo.

6) Which of the following plays an essential role in the formation of the placenta?
   a) umbilical cord
   b) amnion
   c) chorion
   d) villi

7) Today it is estimated that over 75,000 babies are born as a result of assisted reproductive technology techniques. When was the first "test-tube baby" born?
   a) 1950
   b) 1978
   c) 1850
   d) 1990

8) Heritable traits of human beings are essentially the result of the random combination of
   a) RNA.
   b) DGA.
   c) DNA.
   d) PNA.

9) All of the following are "true" about genetic testing *except*
   a) it may only be available to the social elite.
   b) it may be used to abort fetuses with genetic defects.
   c) it may be used to avoid transmission of a genetic disorder to one's offspring.
   d) it may be used by employers in all states as an employment screening device.

10) Artificial insemination has been available for over
    a) 50 years.
    b) 100 years.
    c) 150 years.
    d) 200 years.

11) The technique in which an ova is fertilized by sperm in a laboratory glassware is referred to as
    a) in vetro fertilization.
    b) in vitro fertilization.
    c) artificial fertilization.
    d) scientific fertilization.

12) PGD, which is used to detect any possible defects in a blastocyst, refers to
    a) preliminary genetic diagnosis.
    b) postfertilization diagnosis.
    c) preimplantation genetic diagnosis.
    d) preimplantation gene diagram.

13) All of the following are fertilization techniques *except*
    a) fallopian gamete aspiration.
    b) gamete intrafallopian transfer.
    c) intracytoplasmic sperm injection.
    d) computerized sperm selection.

14) Which of the following cases raised ethical issues regarding the use of IVF technology?
    a) a 25-year-old woman who used artificial embryonation
    b) a 16-year-old woman who used ovum donation
    c) a 63-year-old woman who used a donated ovum
    d) a 40-year-old man dating a 20-year-old woman

15) The use of sperm sorting can result in the selecting of an infant's sex to about
    a) 10% for girls and 30 percent for boys.
    b) 80% for girls and 65 percent for boys.
    c) 90% for girls and 100 percent for boys.
    d) 50% for both sexes.

16) Which country utilizes chroionic villi sampling, or amniocentesis, to identify the sex of the fetus which results in the termination of the female fetuses?
    a) United States
    b) England
    c) Iran
    d) China

17) All of the following are ethical questions associated with cloning *except*
    a) giving birth to one's own twin.
    b) reproducing a child with exceptional characteristics, just like the parents.
    c) setting aside genetic duplicates to recreate a child who may die.
    d) avoiding the trauma of pregnancy.

18) The National Institute of Health (NIH) has temporarily banned new embryo cloning and stem cell research because that agency received pressure to do such from
    a) other countries, such as France.
    b) the federal government administration and Congress.
    c) conservative religious groups.
    d) the Federal Food and Drug Administration.

19) Surrogate motherhood is also referred to as
    a) gestational pregnancy.
    b) pseudopregnancy.
    c) pregnancy in abstentia.
    d) gestational surrogacy.

20) The procedure used to example fetal chromosomes during the 8th week of pregnancy is referred to as
    a) chorionic villi sampling.
    b) sonograms.
    c) amniocentesis.
    d) fetoscopy.

21) Which of the following technologies was mentioned as being crucial in one of the "newest technological advances," in fetal surgery?
    a) embryoscopy
    b) ultrasound
    c) MRI
    d) CAT Scans

22) Women may be infertile who have all of the following conditions *except*
    a) hypertension.
    b) pelvic inflammatory disease.
    c) sexually transmitted infection.
    d) endometriosis.

23) An over-the-counter test is available in drug stores that measures sperm
  a) viability.
  b) motility.
  c) count.
  d) shape.

24) Women who undertake which of the following actions are more likely to prevent birth defects in their children?
  a) waiting until they are ready to deliver the child to seek medical care
  b) use alternative methods of care throughout their pregnancy
  c) use tobacco and alcohol products during pregnancy
  d) undertake comprehensive prenatal care for the early stages

25) The risk factors associated with pregnancy are significantly higher for women aged _____ or older.
  a) 35
  b) 45
  c) 50
  d) 60

26) Tests for pregnancy involving woman's urine or blood detect the presence of the hormone
  a) human chorionic gonadotrophin.
  b) fetal chorionic gonadotrophin.
  c) uterine chorionic gonadotrophin.
  d) embryonic chorionic gonadotrophin.

27) It is speculated that heavy use of marijuana during pregnancy affects fetal development
  a) in a similar manner as FAS.
  b) in a benign way.
  c) in a manner that can potentially cause miscarriage.
  d) in a manner that can cause a slower rate of growth.

28) Research has shown that sexual intercourse during pregnancy
  a) should not occur at any time.
  b) with few exceptions, should not be prohibited.
  c) should not occur during the first few months.
  d) should not occur during the final month.

29) The surgical procedure that is preformed in order to present the tearing of the vaginal opening is
  a) effacement.
  b) vagiotomy.
  c) episiotomy.
  d) periotomy.

30) All of the following are birthing alternatives *except*
  a) natural childbirth.
  b) the Lamaze Method.
  c) home birth.
  d) birthing hospitals.

31) Midwives are now assisting in about _____ of vaginal deliveries in the United States.
   a) 10%
   b) 20%
   c) 35%
   d) 45%

32) All but which of the following can lead to a premature birth?
   a) bacterial infections
   b) allergic reactions
   c) prenatal vitamins
   d) preterm labor contractions

33) Women who are experiencing low energy levels, feelings of being overwhelmed, and sleep disturbances may be experiencing
   a) post delivery psychosis.
   b) post partum psychosis.
   c) post partum depression.
   d) post birth depression.

GUIDED REVIEW AND STUDY
[Answers are provided at the end of the study guide.]

1) A fertilized ovum is called a _____.
2) Fraternal twins are also called _____, whereas identical twins are sometimes called _____.
3) By the end of the fifth day after fertilization, the sphere, which has developed into a fluid-filled cavity and interior, is referred to as a _____.
4) _____ are increasing in occurrence which is probably due to the use of fertility drugs or increases in stress and STI.
5) Usually after 2 months of development, the embryo is called the _____.
6) _____ _____ techniques are being developed for the treatment of more than 4,000 human disorders that have genetic causes.
7) Scientists have had some success turning the embryonic _____ _____ of mice into both eggs and sperm that can eventually be used for the fertilization process.
8) The process of selecting human traits for improvement of the species is referred to as _____.
9) There has been some evidence over the years that social and _____ factors might affect the sex determination of human offspring.
10) _____ is a process of reproductive technology that allows for duplication of genetic material so that offspring are genetically identical.
11) Despite controversies and because there are potentially significant financial gains, private funding will continue to be used in support of _____ research in the United States.
12) Although some have hailed gestational surrogacy as a significant advance for childless couples, others have argued that it is nothing more than _____ prostitution.
13) _____ is used to detect certain genetic disorders such as Down Syndrome.
14) _____ _____, despite FDA caution about unnecessary exposure, is so popular that it has become a burgeoning business where even online sites encourage postings for contests.
15) Couples are said to have a (an) _____ problem if a successful pregnancy has not occurred after a period of a year or more of intercourse without contraception.

16) Male infertility is usually caused by a low sperm count, which is less than _____ million sperm per cubic centimeter of semen.

17) For many couples, working together on infertility often brings a deepened sense of _____ and _____ to the relationship.

18) Physicians who provide prenatal care and delivery of babies are usually _____.

19) There is growing evidence that _____ and _____ in the environment may damage sperm cells leading to possible damage to the developing fetus.

20) Women who become pregnant after the age of _____ have increased risks with infant mortality and illness; however, that group of women who are first-timers also seem to adjust emotionally quite well

21) About_____ percent of women will still have some menstrual flow even during the early stages of pregnancy.

22) _____ _____ _____ is characterized by abnormal fetal growth, neurological damage, and facial distortions.

23) Sexual activity that could risk exposure to _____ _____ _____ should be avoided during pregnancy.

24) Breast-feeding women tend to have less sexual activity and lower levels of sexual satisfaction, possibly the result of both _____ and _____ factors.

25) The hormone _____, manufactured by the pituitary gland, is believed to play some part in the birthing process.

26) The expelled tissues, following delivery, are collectively called the _____.

27) The _____ method refers to "prepared" childbirth.

28) Trained and licensed _____ may assist with home births.

29) It is believed that parents should be provided, within the first two hours following delivery, a time to _____ with their new infant.

30) The U.S. infant mortality rate continues to be _____ than that of many other industrialized nations.

31) A birth that takes place prior to the 37th week of pregnancy is considered a _____ _____.

32) In the U.S., one out of _____ babies is born prematurely.

33) _____ is a medication administered to mothers to eliminate the risks associated with Rh incompatibility.

34) Breastfed babies are less likely to be _____in early childhood.

ESSAY QUESTIONS
[Answers are provided at the end of the study guide.]

1) Describe the types, causes, risk, and reduction methods associated with twinning.

2) Describe the process of and controversies surrounding in vitro fertilization.

3) Describe general and ethical considerations regarding choosing the sex of the fetus.

4) Briefly discuss the reasons for and psychological effects of infertility.

5) Describe three complications of pregnancy as well as three adjustments associated with post partum care.

CHAPTER RESOURCE REFLECTIONS

What Not to Say to an Infertile Couple

If you were an infertile couple, how would you react to each of the "10 worst things to say?" Looking at the statements from another perspective, have you ever made one of those statements to a childless couple? If you made one of these statements, what was your motivation for the comment?

More Men Ready for Cloning

Does it surprise you that men responded more approvingly than women in all the categories listed? What might encourage men to respond in this way?

Planning for the Future

Were you aware that over 50% of pregnancies are unplanned? Would you add anything to the list suggested for planning for a healthy pregnancy? How easy would it be to adopt these strategies? If you are male, would you consider adopting/maintaining this lifestyle along with your female partner?

Case Study

As you read this brief reading by Betsy Kelly, envision yourself as Betsy or her husband. Could you see yourself, or have your seen yourself, in Betsy's position? Can you identify with those feelings and thoughts? Why or why not?

Cross-Cultural Perspective

The rates of death and debilitating illness and injuries associated with pregnancy and childbirth seem, and are, significant. As you read this information, is there anything you can do to help the women described in this reading? If you believe you can do something, what is keeping you from taking action?

MCGRAW–HILL RESOURCES
REFLECTING ON SEXUALTY

Remember that this section of the study guide takes you beyond the text to explore other resources in the field of human sexuality. The experience attempts to expand on at least one concept covered in the chapter.

Access the McGraw-Hill Web pages associated with sexuality at:
    http://www.mhhe.com/socscience/sex

Scroll down and "click" on the hyperlink for "Resource Room."

Scroll down and "click" on the hyperlink for "Web Resources."

Scroll down and "click" on the hyperlink for "Childbirth.org."

Scroll down and "click" in the hyperlink for "chat room."

Scroll down and "click" on the hyperlink for "Log on to Chat Room 1."

For ethical reasons, once you enter the chat room, introduce yourself as a student in a human sexuality course who is presently learning about pregnancy issues. Explain that you would like to learn more about these issues through on-line chatting. Engage in an on-line chat about issues related to pregnancy (or other related topics that the "members" discuss). Politely thank the individuals who responded to your questions and comments. Now reflect on the experience. What did you learn from the experience that added to your learning from the text or classroom? What information will you use from this experience? Why will you use this information?

CHAPTER 10
DECISION MAKING ABOUT PREGNANCY AND PARENTHOOD

CHAPTER OUTLINE

Learning Objectives

SELF-EVALUATION

Contraceptive Comfort and Confidence Scale

CHAPTER LEARNING OBJECTIVES

1. Describe the historical, medical, mechanical, and social efforts to control birth.

2. Describe the effect of Margaret Sanger on birth control.

3. Describe population projections and factors that influence population growth.

4. Describe considerations (economic, "wrong," and skills) for becoming a parent.

5. Briefly describe cultural comparisons regarding the use of birth control.

6. Briefly describe general considerations about the choice of birth control.

7. Briefly describe ethical and religious influences regarding use of birth control.

8. Describe political factors that influence the availability of birth control.

9. Briefly describe health considerations and concerns with the selection and use of birth control.

10. Describe the influence of negative psychological factors regarding the use of birth control.

11. List and describe five factors to consider and steps to take when choosing birth control.

12. List and describe four factors to consider when choosing a contraceptive.

13. Describe the concepts of theoretical and typical failure rates for contraceptive effectiveness.

14. Describe how each gender and couples can share responsibility for the use of birth control.

15. Describe nonpenetrative and "interruptive" means of controlling births.

16. List and describe two types of oral contraceptives.

17. Identify a relatively new option for birth control pill use that causes women to have a period four times a year.

18. Describe how oral contraceptives work.

19. Briefly describe noncontraceptive benefits of oral contraceptives.

20. Describe medical considerations for choosing and using oral contraceptives.

21. Describe the use and benefits of contraceptive implants.

22. Identify why contraceptive implants are not currently available.

23. Describe the two newest forms of hormonal birth control products.

24. Compare and contrast the use of 3 month injectable (Depo Provera) and 1 month injectable (Lunelle).

25. List and describe three types of chemical methods for controlling births.

26. Describe what the latest research about spermicide has demonstrated.

27. List and describe two types of barrier methods of birth control used by women.

28. Describe the use, effectiveness, and controversies concerning male condoms.

29. Describe the use effectiveness and advantages of female condoms.

30. List and describe the types of IUDs.

31. Describe how IUDs work.

32. List and describe three types of fertility awareness methods used to control births.

33. List and describe male and female types of voluntary surgical contraception.

34. Briefly describe a controversy regarding the use of emergency contraceptive methods.

35. List and describe one new male and one female method for controlling conception.

36. Describe rates of and cultural perceptions about unintended pregnancies.

37. List and describe three alternatives for dealing with an unintended pregnancy.

38. Identify concerns and issues that effect the decision to keep the baby.

39. Identify historical and current issues relating to adoption.

40. List and describe the means of terminating a pregnancy.

41. Describe the cultural and legal controversies regarding terminating pregnancies.

42. List and describe four abortion methods.

43. Briefly describe the benefits and controversies concerning the use of fetal tissue.

44. Briefly describe the psychological effects of having an abortion.

KEY WORDS

Abortifacients: substances that cause termination of pregnancy.

Cervical cap: a device that is shaped like a large thimble and fits over the cervix; not a particularly effective contraceptive because it can dislodge easily during intercourse.

Coitus interruptus (ko-EET-us *or* KO-ut-us): a method of birth control in which the penis is withdrawn from the vagina prior to ejaculation.

Comstock Laws: enacted in the 1870s, this federal legislation prohibited the mailing of information about contraception.

Contraceptive implants: contraceptive method in which hormone-releasing rubber cylinders are surgically inserted under the skin.

Depo-Provera: an injectable form of progestin that can prevent pregnancy for three months.

Diaphragm (DY-a-fram): a latex rubber cup, filled with spermicide, which is fitted to the cervix by a clinician; the woman must learn to insert it properly for full contraceptive effectiveness.

Dilation and curettage (D & C): a method of induced abortion in the second trimester of pregnancy that involves a scraping of the uterine wall.

Dilation and evacuation (D & E): a method of induced abortion in the second trimester of pregnancy; it combines suction with a scraping of the inner wall of the uterus.

Essure transcervical sterilization procedure: a less invasive alternative to tubal ligation in which a small coil is implanted in the fallopian tube through a small abdominal incision. Tissue grows on the coil eventually blocking the ovum.

Female condom: a lubricated polyurethane pouch that is inserted into the vagina for intercourse to collect semen and help prevent disease transmission.

Induced abortion: a termination of pregnancy by artificial means.

Intrauterine devices (IUDs): birth control method involving the insertion of a small plastic device into the uterus.

Laminaria (lam-a-NER-ee-a): dried seaweed sometimes used in dilating the cervical opening prior to vacuum curettage.

Laparoscopy (lap-ar-OSK-uh-pee): simpler procedure than tubal ligation involving the insertion of a small fiber-optic scope into the abdomen, through which the surgeon can see the fallopian tubes and close them off.

Laparotomy (lap-ar-OTT-uh-mee): operation to perform a tubal ligation, or female sterilization, involving an abdominal incision.

Male condom: a sheath worn over the penis during intercourse that collects semen and helps prevent disease transmission.

Mifepristone (RU 486): a progesterone antagonist used as a postcoital contraceptive.

Miscarriage: a natural termination of pregnancy.

National Birth Control League: an organization founded in 1914 by Margaret Sanger to promote use of contraceptives.

Natural family planning/fertility awareness: a natural method of birth control that depends on an awareness of the woman's menstrual/fertility cycle.

Pelvic inflammatory disease (PID): a chronic internal infection of the uterus and other organs.

Prostaglandin - *or saline-induced abortion*: used in the 16th to 24th weeks of pregnancy, prostaglandins, salt solutions, or urea are injected into the amniotic sac, administered intravenously, or inserted into the vagina in suppository form, to induce contractions and fetal delivery.

Spermicidal jelly (cream): sperm-killing chemical in a gel-base or cream used with other contraceptives such as diaphragms.

Spermicides: chemicals that kill sperm; available as foams, creams, jellies, or suppositories.

Sponge: a thick, polyurethane disk that holds a spermicide and fits over the cervix to prevent conception.

Spontaneous abortion: another term for miscarriage.

Suppositories: contraceptive devices designed to distribute their spermicide by melting or foaming in the vagina.

Theoretical failure rate: a measure of how often a birth control method can be expected to fail when used without error or technical problems, sometimes called perfect use failure rate.

Toxic shock syndrome (TSS): an acute disease characterized by fever and sore throat, and caused by normal bacteria in the vagina that are activated if tampons or contraceptive devices, such as diaphragms, are left in for long periods of time.

Tubal ligation (lie-GAY-shun): a surgical cutting and tying of the fallopian tubes to induce permanent female sterilization.

Typical use failure rate: a measure of how often a birth control method can be expected to fail when human error and technical failure are considered.

Vacuum curettage (kyur-a-TAZH): a method of induced abortion performed with a suction pump.

Vasectomy (va-SEK-ta-mee *or* vay-ZEK-ta-mee): a surgical cutting and tying of the vas deferens to induce permanent male sterilization.

Voluntary surgical contraception: sterilization; rendering a person incapable of conceiving with surgical procedures that interrupt the passage of the egg or sperm.

Zero population growth: the point at which the world's population would stabilize, and there would be no further increase in the number of people on Earth. Birthrate and death rate become essentially equal.

SELF TEST

When responding to the following multiple-choice questions, choose the "best" answer. The "best" answer is the one that corresponds to the information contained in your text.

1) Which plant was known to be used for its contraceptive effects as early as the seventh century b.c.?
   a) marigold
   b) cactus
   c) silphium
   d) Queen Anne's lace

2) Who founded the National Birth Control League?
   a) Margaret Sanger
   b) Margaret Smith
   c) Alfred Kinsey
   d) Virginia Johnson

3) Which U.S. Supreme Court decision gave married couples the right to buy and use contraceptives?
   a) *Eisenstadt* v. *Bird*
   b) *Griswold* v. *Connecticut*
   c) *Eisenstadt* v. *Connecticut*
   d) *Griswold* v. *Bird*

4) Japan instituted a program to offer incentives for having babies. That program is called
   a) One Plus One Plan.
   b) One Plus Plan
   c) Two Plus Plan.
   d) Plus One Plan.

5) Regarding global population, what percent of new births are living in economically and ecologically impoverished areas?
   a) 45
   b) 60
   c) 75
   d) 90

6) All of the following are wrong reasons to become a parent *except*
   a) to give parents grandchildren.
   b) as part of a healthy relationship.
   c) to have something to love.
   d) to fill emotional gaps.

7) Most parents have found that which of the following has changed markedly with pregnancy and the birth of a child?
   a) strength of relationship
   b) lack of work needed in the relationship
   c) their sexual lives
   d) general relationship satisfaction

8) The World Health Organization estimates that _____ of all pregnancies worldwide are unwanted:
   a) 75%
   b) 33%
   c) 25%
   d) 5%

9) Women typically select their form of contraceptive for all of the following reasons *except*
   a) cost.
   b) effectiveness.
   c) health concerns.
   d) potential effects.

10) Which of the world's major religious groups are opposed to efforts that encourage use of birth control or abortion?
   a) Jewish and Christian groups
   b) Roman Catholic and Christian groups
   c) Jewish and Christian groups
   d) Roman Catholic and fundamentalist Muslim groups

11) All are political factions that can play a significant role in determining the availability of contraceptive methods *except*
    a) Japanese sexual morals.
    b) pregnancy and family planning services for children.
    c) family planning clinics.
    d) managed health care.

12) What percentage of teens indicated that they would discontinue using contraceptive services if their parent were going to be notified?
    a) +80%
    b) +50%
    c) +30%
    d) +20%

13) Which of the following groups promotes popularized research studies to stimulate the use of contraceptives that have not fully met rigorous evaluative standards?
    a) Public Health Departments
    b) CDC
    c) Pharmaceutical companies
    d) Religious denominations

14) The key issue is making sure that the chosen contraceptive method is/has
    a) available for use 24 hours a day and 7 days a week.
    b) fully understood by the user.
    c) affordable.
    d) the highest effectiveness rate possible.

15) Which of the following does not often interfere, in a negative manner, with the ability to plan for the potential consequences of sex?
    a) guilt
    b) fear
    c) anxiety
    d) happiness

16) All of the following are necessary factors to consider or steps to take in becoming an effective user of birth control *except*
    a) social concerns.
    b) health concerns.
    c) ethical and moral values.
    d) attitude about your own sexual feelings.

17) Methods of contraception are changed most often because of
    a) partner complaints.
    b) cost continuing to increase and methods becoming less affordable.
    c) concerns about effectiveness or health risks.
    d) aging.

18) The "perfect" or "lowest observed" failure rate is referred to as the
   a) typical use failure rate.
   b) the normative failure rate.
   c) the statistical failure rate.
   d) the theoretical failure rate.

19) Which form of male birth control is generally considered an option only in the later stages of the male's life?
   a) the male condom
   b) vasectomy
   c) abstinence
   d) birth control pills

20) Couples can share in the use of birth control by all of the following *except*
   a) the female placing a diaphragm on the male partner.
   b) the male inserting spermicidal foam in the female.
   c) the male inserting a female condom in his partner.
   d) the female placing a condom on the male partner.

21) The birth control method sometimes used among couples who have not yet obtained a safer method and by 20% of college students is
   a) abstinence.
   b) condoms.
   c) coitus interruptus.
   d) coitus nonconceptus.

22) The most widely used birth control pill is
   a) progestin-only pills.
   b) minipills.
   c) estrogen-only pills.
   d) combined oral contraceptive.

23) Seasonale brand birth control pills are taken in a manner that allows for a period once every
   a) 3 weeks.
   b) 6 weeks.
   c) 3 months
   d) 6 months.

24) All of the following are noncontraceptive benefits of oral contraceptives *except*
   a) lighter menstrual periods.
   b) stable rates of heart disease.
   c) decreased incidence of breast cysts.
   d) increasing bone mass.

25) The period of effectiveness for contraceptive implants is generally
   a) 1 year.
   b) 10 years.
   c) 5 years.
   d) 6 months.

26) Contraceptive implants were taken off of the market due to all but one of the following:
   a) cost
   b) unpleasant side effects during the first year
   c) introduction of other hormonal options
   d) effectiveness rates were low

27) Injectible methods of contraception are designed to be effective in a woman's body for
   a) 3 weeks or 10 weeks.
   b) 4 weeks or 11 weeks.
   c) 4 weeks or 12 weeks.
   d) 5 weeks or 13 weeks.

28) Most spermicides, sponges, and suppositories contain which substance:
   a) pregoxynol
   b) nonpregnosol
   c) octoxynol-9
   d) nonoxynol-9

29) Suppositories are designed to melt and require
   a) a water source to make them effective.
   b) 10 to 30 minutes to become effective.
   c) staying in the body for 1 hour past last act of intercourse to be effective.
   d) the addition of foam to get the best rate of effectiveness.

30) Diaphragms and cervical caps may increase the risk of
   a) unintended pregnancy.
   b) birth defects.
   c) toxic shock syndrome.
   d) acquired immune deficiency syndrome.

31) All of the following are forms of condoms *except*
   a) polyurethane.
   b) latex.
   c) skin.
   d) plastic.

32) Errors with condom use can be explained by all but one of the following:
   a) female partners putting condoms on their male partners.
   b) using a colored condom.
   c) putting the condom on after starting sex.
   d) not leaving space at the tip.

33) Among young people, what increases the likelihood of condom use during sexual activity?
   a) parent-teenager discussion about sexuality
   b) peer-group discussion about sexuality
   c) educational system condom presentation
   d) community based sex education programs

34) What is an obvious advantage for female use of the vaginal pouch?
    a) men assume responsibility for its use
    b) it affords minimal protection against HIV
    c) the female can take full responsibility for protection
    d) responsibility for protection can be shared

35) All of the following are forms of intrauterine devices *except*
    a) ParaGard.
    b) TCu 380A.
    c) LNG-IUS.
    d) Vagisil T.

36) Natural family planning or fertility awareness was once referred to as
    a) systematic method.
    b) rhythm method.
    c) basal body temperature method.
    d) PID method.

37) All of the following are fertility awareness methods *except*
    a) calendar method.
    b) basal body temperature.
    c) mucus method.
    d) cervical dilation method.

38) These pregnancies occur earlier than desired or expected:
    a) unwanted
    b) unplanned
    c) mistimed
    d) accidental

39) The percentage of young adults who favor women having the right to choose abortion:
    a) 66%.
    b) 75%.
    c) 60%.
    d) 25%.

40) What percentage of present-day mothers plan on relinquishing their babies for adoption?
    a) 85%
    b) 50%
    c) 5%
    d) 33%

41) If a woman chooses to seek the termination of her pregnancy, it is referred to as
    a) a miscarriage.
    b) a spontaneous abortion.
    c) a conscious abortion.
    d) an induced abortion.

42) The method of abortion most often used in the first 12 weeks is
    a) dilation and evacuation.
    b) vacuum curettage.
    c) dilation and curettage.
    d) prostaglandin-induced abortion.

43) As long as abortion is legal, researchers say that the use of _____ should still be allowed.
    a) partial birth abortions.
    b) aborted fetuses.
    c) fetal tissue.
    d) D & Cs.

GUIDED REVIEW AND STUDY
[Answers are provided at the end of the study guide.]

1) Although there are often family and social pressures to procreate, especially for married couples, there is not a particularly close association between _____ and _____ among humans.

2) _____ is a general and more encompassing term that refers to any practice, procedure, or device that reduces or eliminates the chances of a birth taking place.

3) By the _____, medical training no longer included information on contraceptive methods.

4) In the 1870s, federal regulations known as the _____ prohibited the mailing of contraceptive information.

5) If population growth rates would reach a steady state where births equal deaths by the year 2030, the world population would have reached what is called _____.

6) Every stage of child development place demands on parents and requires the exercise of appropriate _____ skills.

7) _____ tend to be more skeptical about the effectiveness of birth control methods.

8) There are several methods of contraception that, if used consistently and properly, will mean that less than _____ in 100 will conceive over the course of a year.

9) It is often wise to consult a _____ or family planning specialist to determine which method(s) of contraceptives will be most effective for a particular couple.

10) Regarding the purpose of sex, some insist that sexual intercourse is meant to be a _____ function, the primary objective of which is _____.

11) A thorough _____ history must be taken and a careful evaluation made of any potential health risks when using the IUD, pill, or hormonal implants.

12) In choosing a contraceptive method, you should know the _____ involved.

13) Contraceptive failure rates are measurable, whereas actual rates of _____ are somewhat more elusive.

14) Clinical trials of contraceptive methods tend to generate lower failure rates, probably because the participants are carefully chosen and _____.

15) In choosing a contraceptive method, women tend to place the highest priority on _____, whereas men are more likely to consider _____.

16) The reality of various forms of _____ is that people do change their minds and it clearly fails quite frequently.

17) Oral contraceptives create changes in the menstrual cycle that interrupt normal patterns of _____ and _____, thus preventing pregnancy.

18) Failure of the pill is uncommon when taken correctly; however, it is slightly more likely to fail in women who are significantly _____.

19) One of the newest hormonal methods of contraception is Ortho Evra and comes in the form of a _____.

20) Recent research has demonstrated that _____ can cause vaginal irritation which may in fact increase the risks of being infected by HIV or other STI.

21) Research indicates that continued use of the female condom depends on careful _____ about insertion and placement.

22) A _____ is a latex rubber cap with a flexible rim that is placed in the vagina in such as way as to cover the cervix.

23) The IUD represents an extremely effective method that lasts _____years, and is comparatively inexpensive, requires practically no user maintenance and is reversible.

24) For the first three weeks after the insertion of an IUD, women are at a slightly greater risk of an infection called _____.

25) Male sterilization, called _____, is a simple procedure in which a small incision is made in the side of the scrotum and each vas deferens is cut and tied.

26) The newest, least invasive surgical method of contraception is _____.

27) The hormonal method of emergency contraception, also known as Plan B, should be administered within ____ hours of the unprotected sex, and studies show that it can be effective for up to _____ days afterward.

28) Two new birth control techniques for men currently being studied are _____ and _____.

29) The historic _____ v. _____ decision in 1973 legalized a woman's right to obtain an abortion from a qualified physician.

30) All studies have indicated that legal medical abortions have _____ to the woman than carrying a pregnancy to full term and giving birth.

31) The psychological effects of abortion for a woman depend a great deal on her own _____ and _____ and the degree of care with which she has made her decision.

ESSAY QUESTIONS

[Answers are provided at the end of the study guide.]

1) Describe ethical, religious, and political considerations or influences regarding the use or availability of birth control.

2) Describe the concepts and significance of knowing the theoretical and typical failure rates for contraceptive effectiveness.

3) Describe two types of oral contraceptives and how these oral contraceptives work.

4) Describe the use, effectiveness, controversies, and advantages of male and female condoms.

5) Describe the safety, risks, and psychological effects associated with an abortion.

CHAPTER RESOURCE REFLECTIONS

Father Volunteers

If male hormonal contraceptives were reliable and available, would you take them or request that your male partner take them? Why or why not? What would it take for you or your male partner to be completely comfortable with a new method of male contraception? Should males assume more responsibility for preventative contraception? Why or why not?

Margaret Sanger

As you read this portion of Margaret Sanger's autobiography, place yourself in the position of three individuals. First, read the story from the position of Mrs. Sachs. Next, read it from the position of Mr. Sachs. Finally, read the story from the position of Mrs. Sanger. How does your view of abortion, both illegal and legalized, change from each vantage point?

Childless Couples

The article states that one out of four women rejected motherhood by choice. If female, what reasons would you give for remaining childless? If male, how would you respond to a female partner who wanted to remain childless? Why do you believe you would respond in that manner? What are some social implications for not having children?

Case Study

After reading the case of Joanne and Arthur and knowing that the effectiveness of female condom is incomplete, would you make the same decision? Why would you make that decision?

Cheat Sheet - Contraceptives

Patch
Ring
Injection
IUD

Is the information on these methods of birth control new to you? How did you first hear about the patch and the ring? Does the fact that the injection lasts 4 weeks inspire confidence or concern? What have you heard historically speaking about the IUD?

Case Study

Place yourself in either the position of Millie or Max. What decision would make if you were facing this unexpected pregnancy? Why did you make that decision? Since men are held accountable for impregnating a female, should not women have to carry a fetus to birth if the male wishes to become a parent or it violates the couple's religious views? Why or why not?

Cross-Cultural Perspective

If you found yourself in one of the more restrictive countries, concerning birth control, how would your deal with a desire to obtain an abortion? How did you respond to the requirement in Japan that the husband or partner is required to give consent? Why did you respond that way?

After reading this article, what are your immediate reactions? Are you surprised at the various countries' legislation of abortion? Do you feel validated in your beliefs? If not, what would you do to effect change? If so, what would you do to offer support for the status quo?

Self-Evaluation: Contraceptive Comfort and Confidence Scale

If you found yourself with a number of "yes" answers, what decisions do you need to make regarding your use of contraceptives?

MCGRAW-HILL RESOURCES
REFLECTING ON SEXUALTY

Remember that this section of the study guide takes you beyond the text to explore other resources in the field of human sexuality. The experience attempts to expand on at least one concept covered in the chapter.

Access the McGraw-Hill Web pages associated with sexuality at:
 http://www.mhhe.com/socscience/sex

Scroll down and "click" on the hyperlink for "Resource Room."

Scroll down and "click" on the hyperlink for "Web Resources."

Scroll down and "click" on the hyperlink for "Planned Parenthood."

Scroll down and "click" on the hyperlink for "Research & Media."

Scroll down and "click" on the hyperlink for "Articles."

Scroll down and "click" on the hyperlink for one of the articles dealing with a contraceptive issue such as "What most American women don't know about an IUD."

Read the article.

After reading your chosen article, be able to summarize its content. Also, be able to compare and contrast the information contained in the article with that presented in the text and lectures. If the information in the text is not the same as found in the article , which information would you believe and why?

CHAPTER 11
SOLITARY SEX AND SHARED SEX

CHAPTER OUTLINE

CHAPTER LEARNING OBJECTIVES

1. Briefly describe concerns regarding the use of research and sexual behaviors.

2. Briefly describe gender differences regarding the private world of sex.

3. Briefly describe an historical perceptive of masturbation.

4. Describe rates of masturbation.

5. Describe methods of female masturbation.

6. Describe methods of male masturbation

7. Briefly describe how pictures and fantasy are used during masturbation.

8. List and describe 10 facts about masturbation.

9. Briefly describe the association of guilt with masturbation.

10. Briefly describe the moral implications of masturbation.

11. Describe the general dynamics of shared sexual behaviors.

12. Briefly describe the intimate nature of nongenital oral stimulation.

13. Describe the range of stimulation of erogenous zones.

14. List and describe two types of oral sex as well as rates for each.

15. Describe ways to reduce risks associated with oral sex.

16. Briefly describe the process of mutual masturbation and perceptions about this behavior.

17. Briefly describe forms of nonvaginal and penile intercourse.

18. Describe the rates and concerns associated with anal intercourse.

19. Briefly describe the relationship of vibrators, pornography, and fantasy with sexual behaviors.

20. Describe the risks and benefits associated with using aphrodisiacs.

21. Describe how the period after sexual activity can impact a relationship.

22. Describe the range of male same-gender sexual behavior.

23. Describe the range of female same-gender sexual behaviors.

24. Briefly describe general perceptions about sexual intercourse.

25. Briefly describe HIV risks associated with sexual intercourse.

26. Describe the process of and concerns associated with intromission.

27. Describe the process of intercourse and ways in which couples can change and enhance the experience.

28. List and describe three general "position" categories for intercourse.

29. List and describe three reclining face-to-face positions for intercourse.

30. List and describe three face-to-face variations for sexual intercourse.

31. List and describe four rear vaginal entry positions for intercourse.

32. Describe cross-cultural views of intercourse within marriage.

KEY WORDS

Anal intercourse: insertion of the penis into the rectum of a partner.

Aphrodisiacs (af-ro-DEE-zee-aks): foods or chemicals purported to foster sexual arousal; they are believed to be more myth than fact.

Autofellatio (fe-LAY-she-o): a male providing oral stimulation to his own penis, an act most males do not have the physical agility to perform.

Cantharides (kan-THAR-a-deez): a chemical extracted from a beetle that, when taken internally, creates irritation of blood vessels in the genital region; it can cause physical harm.

Cunnilingus (kun-a-LEAN-gus): oral stimulation of the clitoris, vaginal opening, or other parts of the vulva.

Fellatio: oral stimulation of the penis.

Onanism (O-na-niz-um): a term sometimes used to describe masturbation, it comes from the biblical story of Onan who practiced coitus interruptus and "spilled his seed on the ground."

Rubber dam: a piece of rubber material, such as used in dental work, placed over the vulva during cunnilingus.

SELF TEST

When responding to the following multiple-choice questions, choose the "best" answer. The "best" answer is the one that corresponds to the information contained in your text.

1) Which of the following research studies provided the more reliable statistics on the types and frequencies of sexual behavior among people in the United States?
   a) Kinsey study
   b) National Sexuality Survey
   c) Masters and Johnson Survey
   d) National Health and Social Life Survey

2) What are the two distinct worlds of human sexual experience?
   a) social and societal
   b) social and private
   c) private and intrapersonal
   d) social and interpersonal

3) According to the National Health and Social Life Survey (NHSLS), people who engage in all but one of the following tend to have the most active sexual lives with partners as well:
   a) thinking about sex.
   b) pursuing erotic materials for their own use
   c) engaging in sexual behaviors with a partner beginning in their 20's
   d) masturbating

4) Very few people appear to use masturbation
   a) to avoid getting someone pregnant.
   b) because they do not have a sexual partner
   c) to help them relax.
   d) to avoid HIV infection.

5) All of the following are ways in which men generally masturbate *except*
   a) stroking the shaft of the penis.
   b) rubbing the scrotum and perineum exclusively.
   c) pulling at the penile glans.
   d) touching the corona.

6) All of the following are facts about masturbation *except*
   a) masturbation can be done excessively.
   b) masturbation is not confined to childhood.
   c) masturbation can be as physically satisfying as shared sex.
   d) masturbation can be shared.

7) Which of the following is a factually incorrect statement?
   a) males can deplete their libidinal energy
   b) masturbation helps us to learn about sexual feelings
   c) men only produce a certain amount of semen in their lives
   d) masturbation does not lead to same-gender orientation

8) All of the following religious groups are predominantly antimasturbation *except*
   a) Jewish.
   b) Hindu.
   c) Christian.
   d) Muslim.

9) According to the NHSLS, what is the second most popular sexual activity after sexual intercourse?
   a) oral sex
   b) anal sex
   c) watching partner masturbate
   d) watching partner undress

10) Many individuals derive intense genital pleasure from being orally stimulated partly because
   a) it is a taboo behavior.
   b) of localized stimulation.
   c) there is little concern for a pregnancy.
   d) oral sex condoms taste good.

11) What nongenital sexual behavior is not practiced in a few societies and is frowned upon in a few others?
   a) kissing
   b) licking ears
   c) nibbling at the neck
   d) rubbing the abdomen

12) Therapy programs typically encourage couples to spend time together doing all of the following *except*
   a) fondling each other.
   b) being nude with each other.
   c) having sexual intercourse.
   d) exploring each other's body.

13) When partners perform oral sex with another simultaneously, the position is sometimes referred to as
   a) thirty-three.
   b) sixty-nine.
   c) ninety-nine.
   d) fifty-fifty.

14) Oral sex is much less common in which of the following groups?
   a) Highly educated Blacks
   b) Under educated Hispanics
   c) Under educated Blacks
   d) Under educated Whites

15) More than _____ of college students reported having masturbated while another person watched.
   a) 1/3
   b) 1/2
   c) 2/3
   d) 1/4

16) Which of the following behaviors is unsafe to do to either the penis or vagina?
   a) blow on or into either
   b) nibble on or at either
   c) suck on either
   d) lick on or at either

17) What form of nonvaginal intercourse may result in pregnancy?
   a) anal intercourse
   b) intermammary intercourse
   c) intromissionary intercourse
   d) interfemoral intercourse

18) It appears that men achieve sexual arousal fastest through the use of
   a) a video alone.
   b) a vibrator alone.
   c) a video and vibrator together.
   d) through the use of none of the above.

19) Substances that create erotic stimulation are referred to as
   a) aphrodisiacs.
   b) erotodisiacs.
   c) pseudo-stimulants.
   d) sexual-stimulants.

20) One study showed that the aphrodisiac deer horn powder had absolutely no effect on all but one of the following:
   a) performance
   b) arousal
   c) desire
   d) ejaculation

21) Use of amyl nitrate and isobutyl nitrate has been associated with which serious health condition?
   a) heart attacks
   b) fatal cerebral hemorrhages
   c) fatal blood clots
   d) "nervous breakdowns"

22) What percentage of women and men, respectively, report always having an orgasm in their sexual activities?
   a) 75 % of women; 100 % of men
   b) 10 % of women; 50 % of men
   c) 25 % of women; 50 % of men
   d) 29 % of women; 75 % of men

23) Some gay men participate in intentional unprotected anal sex popularly called
    a) stonewalling.
    b) barebacking.
    c) hardballing.
    d) hardjacking.

24) When individuals place the hand of one partner into the rectum of the other, producing an intense sexual experience, it is referred to as
    a) hardballing.
    b) anioporctic activity.
    c) fisting.
    d) fistballing.

25) Women involved in a sexual encounter usually spend a longer period of time than male couples
    a) in penetrative sexual activities.
    b) in gentle and affectionate foreplay.
    c) giving more direct genital stimulation.
    d) in rough sexual pleasuring.

26) All of the following are reasons given for regulating sexual intercourse *except*
    a) regulating the ratio of male to female births.
    b) regulating which heterosexual couples have babies.
    c) preventing people from enjoying bodily pleasures.
    d) regulating pleasures some consider sinful.

27) Another term for male-female intercourse is
    a) penilmission.
    b) genital insertion.
    c) intromission.
    d) coital insertion.

28) What is not a crucial factor for women regarding sexual pleasure?
    a) time spent during intromission
    b) stimulation of their breasts
    c) stimulation of the clitoris
    d) size of the male penis

29) All of the following, but one, are indicators that help determine the most enjoyable, comfortable and mangeable intercourse behaviors:
    a) body size
    b) location of sex behaviors
    c) diameter of the erect penis
    d) body weight

30) Which sexual position is recommended for use with the treatment of sexual dysfunctions?
    a) side-by-side
    b) woman on top, man supine
    c) both partners seated
    d) man on top, woman supine

31) What sexual position is used by most mammals to copulate?
   a) male of species on top
   b) side by side
   c) rear vaginal entry
   d) rear anal entry

32) Which sexual activity is preferred by most married individuals?
   a) fellatio
   b) vaginal sexual intercourse
   c) extended genital stimulation
   d) anal intercourse

GUIDED REVIEW AND STUDY
[Answers are provided at the end of the study guide.]

1) There is new legitimacy being given to the concept of sexual _____.
2) College women are likely to feel _____ about a _____ masturbation.
3) In comparison studies, during a 30 year period, men and especially women began to masturbate _____ and that behavior became more accepted as being _____ in its own right.
4) Just as in men, the tissues of the _____ _____ are apparently too sensitive for any prolonged direct stimulation.
5) Kinsey reported that a significant proportion of men attempt _____ at one time or another.
6) Most common sexual fantasies seem to be about sexual activity with a _____ _____.
7) From a purely physical standpoint, _____ can offer full sexual satisfaction for some people.
8) _____ does not seem to affect the frequency of masturbation in males, but it is sometimes associated with less-frequent masturbation in females.
9) Pursuing somewhat casual sexual encounters with acquaintances is collectively called _____ _____.
10) If touching a particular part of a person's body leads to sexual arousal, the area is called an/a _____ _____.
11) _____ involves kissing, licking, or sucking the clitoris, labia, and vaginal opening.
12) To reduce the possible transmission of HIV, the safest practice is for a condom to be worn during fellatio or a _____ _____ placed over the vulva during cunnilingus.
13) Masturbation is usually a very _____ experience, and sharing it often represents a level of _____ even deeper than some other forms of sexual sharing.
14) Anal intercourse is slightly more prevalent among _____ and _____.
15) It has long been recognized that _____ can be an integral part of sexual experiences, and that it can induce sexual arousal.
16) Although ____ _____ and _____ can lead to relaxation and lowered inhibitions, larger amounts actually inhibit sexual desire and arousal.
17) A widely touted aphrodisiac is "Spanish fly," the slang name for _____, a chemical extracted from a certain species of southern European beetle.
18) Talking out _____ feelings while they are fresh in an atmosphere of mutual warmth, caring, and reassurance can often be a strengthening influence on any relationship.
19) Lesbians tend not to use _____ or engage in _____ _____.

20) If the _____ is still present at the opening of the vagina, prodding by the penis may be necessary to rupture it; the female should expect some discomfort or pain.

21) Rapid, forceful movements of the penis generally bring males to orgasm quite quickly, and the amount of _____ stimulation also plays and important role.

22) Coital positions in which both partners _____ are generally the most difficult to manage and sustain.

23) The social mores related to sexual intercourse are often intimately associated with a particular society's _____ customs.

24) There is no doubt that in North America, _____ is perceived as a significant part of marriage.

ESSAY QUESTIONS

[Answers are provided at the end of the study guide.]

1) Describe the association of guilt, as well as the moral implications associated with masturbation.

2) Briefly describe the types of risks and risk reduction techniques associated with oral sex.

3) Describe the relationship of vibrators, pornography, fantasy, and aphrodisiacs to sexual behavior.

4) Describe general perceptions associated with sexual intercourse along with the risk of HIV infection involved with this behavior.

5) Describe three general "position" categories for intercourse as well one specific position from each of the general categories.

CHAPTER RESOURCE REFLECTIONS

Knowing Thyself

What reactions did you have to the historical perspectives of masturbation? Although you may perceive some of these responses as humorous, what perceptions about contemporary sexuality do you believe might be perceived as humorous to future generations?

Girls Ordered to Avoid Sex

Do you believe the King's approach to reducing HIV infections will be effective? Why or why not? Isn't our abstinence-only until marriage sexuality education program similar to the King's approach? Why or why not?

Case Study

After reading the story of Sybil and Carl, do you believe Carl is being insensitive? Why or why not? Is Sybil being insensitive since most of the behaviors Carl wishes to engage in are viewed as acceptable by many individuals? Why or why not? Since Carl wants to engage in anal intercourse, should Sybil suggest he experience it first with a "strap-on" worn by Sybil? Why or why not?

Learning About Sex from the Past

This article offers a reality based approach to some of the challenges involved with achieving great sex. Reread the section that begins with, "There isn't a feeling in the entire…" and consider how it makes you feel. Should sex positive messages and techniques be a more commonplace discussion in our culture?

MCGRAW-HILL RESOURCES
REFLECTING ON SEXUALTY

Remember that this section of the study guide takes you beyond the text to explore other resources in the field of human sexuality. The experience attempts to expand on at least one concept covered in the chapter.

Access the McGraw-Hill Web pages associated with sexuality at:
    http://www.mhhe.com/socscience/sex

Scroll down and "click" on the hyperlink for "Resource Room."

Scroll down and "click" on the hyperlink for "Web Resources."

Scroll down and "click" on the hyperlink for "American Sexual Behavior."

To access this document, you will need a program that can read/access PDF formatted documents such as Acrobat Reader. Do not read the entire document, but rather compare and contrast the reported rates of various behaviors discussed in the text and lectures with the information in the report. Because the report is somewhat comprehensive, look for facts or rates of behavior that "challenge" the general perceptions regarding that behavior. You should be able to offer a reason why there may be these differences.

CHAPTER 12
SAME-GENDER ORIENTATION AND BEHAVIOR

CHAPTER OUTLINE

Learning Objectives

CHAPTER LEARNING OBJECTIVES

1. Briefly describe the general views of same-gender orientation.

2. Describe the Kinsey scale and its benefits and limitations for explaining sexual orientation.

3. Describe reported roles of same-gender sexual behavior prior to the National Health and Social Life Survey (NHSLS).

4. Describe the NHSLS concerns regarding same-gender orientation classifications.

5. List three aspects of same-gender orientation studied in the NHSLS.

6. Describe the NHSLS aspects of desire and self-identification as well as rates for each.

7. Describe how the NHSLS supports the position that same-gender sexuality is multidimensional.

8. Briefly describe how age and geography influence same-gender sexuality.

9. Describe cross-cultural rates of same-gender sexual behavior.

10. Describe cross-cultural reactions to same-gender sexual behavior.

11. Describe the effects of professional corporate responses to homophobia.

12. Describe historical and contemporary religious views of same-gender sexual behavior.

13. Briefly describe how views about same-gender sexually orientation are socially constructed.

14. Describe how psychodynamic theory views same-gender orientation.

15. Describe the result of two studies that influenced how same-gender orientation is seen within a normal variant model.

16. List and describe five conclusions about sexual orientation from the Bell et al. study.

17. Briefly describe how a biological position could be supported by the Bell et al. research.

18. Describe perceived hormonal influences concerning gender and sexual orientation.

19. Describe genetic explanations of same-gender sexual orientation.

20. Briefly describe heritability as related to same-gender sexual orientation.

21. Describe the perceived relationship of the X chromosome to same-gender sexual orientation.

22. Describe other biological factors and gender trait differences seen in same-gender orientated individuals.

23. Describe the dynamics of the multifactorial model of sexual orientation.

24. Describe how therapists personally and professionally address same-gender orientation.

25. Briefly describe effeminacy and any relationship to sexual orientation.

26. Describe how self-perception is related to same-gender orientation.

27. Briefly describe limitations of the Cass model of sexual identity formation.

28. List and describe the six stages of Cass's model of sexual identify formation.

29. Describe male same-gender identity formation.

30. Describe female same-gender identity formation.

31. Describe challenges faced in developing a bisexual identity.

32. Describe bisexuality identity formation.

33. Briefly describe geographic factors related to the homosexual culture.

34. Describe cultural dimensions of the homosexual culture.

35. Describe the functions of the homosexual community.

36. Describe three controversies associated with same-gender couples/relationships.

37. Describe responses of gay men to HIV/AIDS.

38. Briefly describe ways for reducing HIV transmission.

39. Briefly describe the emotional impact of HIV on the homosexual community.

40. Describe historical and contemporary vs. military positions regarding sexual orientation.

41. Briefly describe the reasons same-gender orientated individuals marry opposite-gender partners.

42. Describe government positions regarding same-gender relationships.

KEYS WORDS

Coming out: to acknowledge to oneself and others that one is lesbian, gay, or bisexual

SELF-TEST

When responding to the following multiple-choice questions, choose the "best" answer. The "best" answer is the one that corresponds to the information contained in your text.

1) Social scientists, during Kinsey's time, had not given much consideration to making distinctions among
   a) behaviors, orientations, attractions, and identities.
   b) behaviors, preferences, attractions, and personality.
   c) orientations, preferences, identities, and actions.
   d) orientations, attractions, personality, and actions.

2) On the Kinsey scale of rating sexual behavior, the category that represents exclusively homosexual is
   a) category one.
   b) category five.
   c) category three.
   d) category six.

3) To be exclusively same-gender oriented in behavior, some research has suggested that attraction, fantasies, and falling in love may actually be
   a) impossible.
   b) highly unlikely.
   c) relatively rare.
   d) undoable.

4) According to the National Health and Social Life Survey (NHSLS), all of the following were aspects of studying about same gender orientation *except*
   a) desire.
   b) social identification.
   c) behavior.
   d) self-identification.

5) According to the NHSLS, in the 12 largest cities in the United States what percentage of men and women respectively identify themselves as gay or bisexual or lesbian or bisexual respectively?
   a) 20% and 10%
   b) 30% and 5%
   c) 9% and 3%
   d) 9% and 10%

6) European studies of same-gender behavior, in contrast to the findings of the NHSLS, have found
   a) slightly lower rates of same-gender behavior.
   b) slightly higher rates of same-gender behavior.
   c) significantly higher rates of same-gender behavior.
   d) no differences in rates of same-gender behavior.

7) From a cross-cultural perspective, which of the following concepts potentially contributes to gay males in Brazil apparently fearing for their safety?
   a) the religious nature of Brazil
   b) the machismo mentality of Brazilian men
   c) the sexist mentality of Brazilian men against women
   d) the secret nature of the Brazilian gay subculture

8) What is a leading cause of death among young people who see themselves as part of some sexual minority?
   a) HIV disease
   b) Gay bashing
   c) Suicide
   d) none of the above

9) All of the following religious denominations have sought to judge or regulate various forms of sexual behavior, including same gender behavior *except*
   a) Jewish.
   b) Muslim.
   c) Buddhist.
   d) Christian.

10) Gay and lesbian people have called for a new religious and moral ethic that would allow for all but which of the following?
   a) human diversity
   b) acknowledgment of variant sexual orientations
   c) limitation of sexual expression
   d) affirmation of the freedom to grow and change

11) What individual is associated with the notion that homosexuality is a sexual function produced by arrested sexual development?
   a) Kraft von Ebing
   b) Trissot
   c) Kinsey
   d) Freud

12) The U.S. Supreme Court upheld the right of which organization to exclude homosexual youth and adults:
   a) Boy Scouts of Canada
   b) Boys and Girls Club
   c) Boy Scouts of America
   d) Girl Scouts of America

13) Research has determined that sexual orientation appears to be largely determined
   a) after marriage.
   b) prior to birth.
   c) prior to adolescence.
   d) many times throughout life.

14) Studies of biological determinants have involved all of the following *except*
   a) examining behavioral differences.
   b) examining hormonal differences.
   c) detecting genetic factors.
   d) examining anatomical differences.

15) Although there is no clearly demonstrated relationship between prenatal factors and the development of sexual orientation in humans, which condition supports the contention of a possible relationship?
   a) transsexuality
   b) hermaphroditism
   c) congenital adrenal hyperplasia
   d) congenital estrogen hyperplasia

16) Recent research has begun to suggest some interesting genetic links to sexual orientation.
   a) same-gender orientation tends to run in families
   b) same-gender orientation tends to run in the mother's side of the family.
   c) gay males have a higher likelihood of having a gay brother, uncle, or male cousin.
   d) lesbians have a higher likelihood of having a lesbian or bisexual sister,.

17) Some research has indicated that same gender orientation may be likened to
   a) the Y chromosome.
   b) the X chromosome.
   c) both the X and Y chromosome.
   d) neither of the chromosomes.

18) Body differences such as_____ have been studied as a determinant of orientation.
   a) ear lobes
   b) toes
   c) fingers
   d) tongues

19) What part of the brain has been shown to be related to human sexuality and to have a potential relationship with same-gender orientation?
   a) anterior hypothalamus
   b) cerebral cortex
   c) posterior hypothalamus
   d) medulla

20) There are research studies that are now focusing on the correlation of orientation and
   a) education levels.
   b) sex preferences.
   c) sex practices.
   d) masculinity and femininity.

21) In same-gender psychotherapy, being "cured" usually means
   a) being asexual.
   b) to stop participating in heterosexual sexual activities.
   c) to stop participating in pedophilic sexual activities.
   d) to begin functioning sexually with members of the opposite sex.

22) A recently published study about "reparative therapy" allowed feedback from experts that offered all but one of the following responses:
    a) thinking that "ex-gays" were deceiving themselves and others.
    b) support for finding out more about why and how people might change.
    c) criticisms of the research ethics methodology.
    d) a therapy strategy that would be popular for gays and lesbians.

23) There is some evidence indicating that among children and adolescents who have a greater likelihood of same-gender attractions and behaviors later in life, these children and adolescents have previously engaged in
    a) early sexual experiences.
    b) later sexual experiences.
    c) gender nonconformity.
    d) sexual nonconformity.

24) The psychologist who developed a model of same-gender orientation was
    a) Cass.
    b) Kaplan.
    c) Masters.
    d) Johnson.

25) During which stage of the same-gender orientation model is it speculated that individuals with a same gender orientation may "come out?"
    a) Identity Confusion
    b) Identity Tolerance
    c) Identity Comparison
    d) Identity Socialization

26) During which stage of the same-gender orientation model is the realization that the world is not divided into us and them?
    a) Identity Confusion
    b) Identity Comparison
    c) Identity Socialization
    d) Identity Synthesis

27) Individuals who engage in both heterosexual and same-gender sexual behaviors may experience
    a) heterophobia.
    b) homophobia.
    c) biphobia.
    d) heterosexism.

28) Which model is associated with bisexual identity, personal growth, and a wider range of possibilities for fulfillment?
    a) flexibility model
    b) transference model
    c) subliminal model
    d) biphillic model

29) The estimated number of gay men in the United States who are battered or physically abused by their partners each year is
   a) 10,000 to 50,000.
   b) 1 to 2 million.
   c) 750,000.
   d) 330,000 to 650,000.

30) Alcohol and drug use seems to increase the likelihood of unsafe sexual practices among all groups of people as well as in people with
   a) sexual disorders.
   b) physical disorders.
   c) personality disorders.
   d) none of the above.

31) In the first decade of the "don't ask, don't tell" policy, _____ members of the armed forces were discharged for being gay.
   a) 1500
   b) 4500
   c) 8000
   d) 10,000

32) Studies of the military have tended to demonstrate that which of the following notions is unfounded?
   a) the compatibility of military service and same-gender orientated individuals
   b) the incompatibility of military service and bisexually orientated individuals
   c) the incompatibility of military service and same-gender orientated individuals
   d) the compatibility of military service and heterosexually orientated individuals

33) The U.S. Congress passed which of the following acts that allow states not to recognize same gender marriages?
   a) Defense of Marriage Act
   b) Saving the Marriage Act
   c) Antihomosexual Marriage Act
   d) The Antifornication Marriage Act

GUIDED REVIEW AND STUDY
[Answers are provided at the end of the study guide.]

1) Instead of conceptualizing masculinity and femininity as polarized entities in themselves, we now see them as representing _____ of relatively independent traits.
2) Kinsey's scale of rating sexual behaviors has been called a "stroke of _____ genius," because it seemed to resolve issues that had been troubling researchers for many years.
3) Across people's life spans, there may be changes and discontinuities in sexual _____ _____ and _____.
4) Researchers have recognized that because of the _____ and _____ associated with same-gender sexual orientation, some people might be reluctant to say much about such attractions or behaviors.
5) Desire issues were measured by two questions, indicated by the _____ and _____ scales on the graph.

6) Some cultures, such as Mediterranean regions and in some non-industrialized societies and developing countries, orientation categories are not based on the _____ of the sexual partner, but instead on the _____ assumed in the sexual act.

7) The research data also show that people who identify themselves as lesbian, gay, or bisexual tend to be more highly _____ and of _____ or _____ socioeconomic status.

8) The _____ tradition among American Plains Indians is an example of gender-reversed orientation.

9) In 1973, the American Psychiatric Association's board of trustees voted unanimously to remove _____ from its list of mental illnesses, declaring that it does not constitute a _____ _____.

10) Around 400 B.C., Christianity began to introduce a new sexual code that focused on maintaining _____ and equated some sexual behaviors with the _____ state of the human soul.

11) Between 1880 and 1900, same-gender orientation was _____ and defined as a _____.

12) Theories and models of the origin of sexual orientation have focused on _____, _____ and _____ factors.

13) Many recent psychodynamic theorists now integrate some of the newer findings about possible _____ and _____ _____ on sexual orientation.

14) _____ _____ was one of the most influential researchers to propose that same-gender sexual orientation and behavior are normal variants.

15) Some recent studies have found a greater incidence of _____ and _____ among gay people, especially gay men.

16) The findings of genetics could indicate some sort of _____ connection in the development of sexual orientation.

17) Much same-gender orientation research has focused on _____.

18) One study found that a part of the brain that governs daily rhythms, the _____ nucleus, is twice as large in gay men as it is in heterosexual men.

19) Unusual _____ levels present at some critical period in brain growth may affect the development of susceptible areas of the brain.

20) The _____ suggests that there could be many shades of sexual orientation, the origins of which are more complex and subtle than the either/or approach could accommodate.

21) To "cure" or change gay or lesbian people into heterosexuals is referred to as _____ _____.

22) People with a same-gender orientation are generally _____ from heterosexual people.

23) As people who have same-gender orientation function in a society with mostly _____ assumptions, at some point in their lives they begin to perceive themselves as member of a _____.

24) Whether individuals move to the final stage of sexual identity formation is often determined by the reaction of _____ _____ to the disclosure of their orientation.

25) There is a common myth that if gay men or lesbians were exposed to a happy _____ encounter with a good lover, they would realize "what they are missing."

26) Lesbians are less likely to use _____ stimulation as a route into same-gender sexual identity formation process.

27) Heterosexual women tend to perceive _____ less favorably than heterosexual men.

28) _____ is a term that has sometimes been used to describe identity recognition mechanisms that gay people use to identify one another.

29) For gay men who are not infected with HIV, there is sometimes a feeling of _____ about being able to enjoy aspects of life.

30) The state of _____ passed a law confirming civil rights and allowing legalized "civil unions.".

ESSAY QUESTIONS
[Answers are provided at the end of the study guide.]

1) Describe the Kinsey scale for explaining sexual orientation, as well as its benefits and limitations.

2) Describe how age, geography, and cross-cultural perceptions influence same-gender sexual behavior.

3) Describe both hormonal and genetic influences and explanations regarding same-gender orientation.

4) Describe both male and female same-gender identity formation.

5) Describe military and governmental positions regarding same-gender orientation and relationships.

CHAPTER RESOURCE REFLECTIONS

Gay Navajos Walk Tightrope between Two Cultures

Were you aware of the "nadleeh" prior to reading this article? Speculate about why or why not? Can you imagine not having a clear image of who you are in relation to your culture? Do you think that the Beauty Rainbow Project should exist?

Riddle Homophobia Scale

When assessing your personal values about homosexuality, what category do you fit in? Are you content with that label? Speculate about what a gay or lesbian person might feel if all the people in their life fit into the Repulsion category? The Nurturance category? If you are gay or lesbian, which category do you fit in?

Times Change, and So Do Absolutes

What is your initial reaction to this article? Do you find the author's perception to ring true? What are your thoughts about the author citing significant civil rights issues in history in an article about gay and lesbian marriage?

Case Study

After reading Nancy's plight, how would you deal with the challenge of sharing your same-gender attraction and lifestyle with your parents? Other than Nancy's concerns about how her parents may react, pondering a similar response like her brother, what other concerns might Nancy have about revealing this aspect of her life with her parents?

James Dale comments that the torch needs to be passed to someone else, a torch representing the acceptance of homosexuality in society. Do you believe minority populations and movements need "torch bearers?" Why or why not? Who are the current National, State, and Local torchbearers (from your state and local perspectives)? What are their current concerns? Do you perceived these concerns as legitimate? Why or why not?

MCGRAW-HILL RESOURCES
REFLECTING ON SEXUALTY

Remember that this section of the study guide takes you beyond the text to explore other resources in the field of human sexuality. The experience attempts to expand on at least one concept covered in the chapter.

Access the McGraw-Hill Web pages associated with sexuality at:
http://www.mhhe.com/socscience/sex

Scroll down and "click" on the hyperlink for "Resource Room."

Scroll down and "click" on the hyperlink for "Web Resources."

Scroll down and "click" on the hyperlink for "The Gay and Lesbian Alliance against Defamation."

Scroll down and "click" on the hyperlink for "Publications & Resources."

Scroll down and "click" on a hyperlink of your choosing. You might want to select one of the "publications." After choosing a "publication", "news pop," or "op-ed", read the information from the perspective of a same-gender orientated individual. Why is this issue of importance to this group of people?

CHAPTER 13
THE SPECTURM OF HUMAN SEXUAL BEHAVIOR

CHAPTER OUTLINE

CHAPTER OBJECTIVES

1. Describe the general cultural and scientific perceptions of sexual expression.

2. Describe sexologists' use of the terms *variant* and *paraphilia*.

3. Describe erotophilia and erotophobia.

4. Describe hypersexuality and hyposexuality.

5. Describe promiscuity and culturally positive and negative implications.

6. Briefly describe two forms of hypersexuality.

7. Describe reasons why individuals may be celibate.

8. Describe the perceptions of why men express more variability of sexual behavior.

9. Describe general and specific forms of transvestism.

10. Briefly describe rates of cross-dressing.

11. Briefly describe characteristics and rates of the transvestite subculture.

12. Describe transgenderism.

13. Describe autogynephilia and the potential conflict with heterosexuality.

14. Describe transexualism and cultural, ethical, and hormonal concerns associated with this variance.

15. Briefly describe the surgical procedures involved with sex change surgery.

16. Briefly describe the evidence that sexual orientation is independent of a transsexual identity.

17. Briefly describe the relationship of transgenderism and sexual orientation.

18. Briefly describe gender identity disorder treatment concerns.

19. Describe criteria for and concerns about diagnoses of gender identity disorder.

20. Briefly describe general considerations involving sexual arousal.

21. Describe rates and use of erotic/pornographic materials for arousal.

22. Describe the use of sexual enhancement devices in women and men.

23. Describe rates, onset, and use of sexual fantasies.

24. Briefly list and describe four types of sexual fantasies.

25. Describe general and extreme fetishism.

26. Briefly describe cultural influences of multiple partnered sex.

27. Briefly describe two forms of group sex.

28. Briefly describe concerns about group sex.

29. Briefly list and describe three types of male prostitutes.

30. Briefly list and describe three types of female prostitutes.

31. Briefly describe the victimless controversy associated with sex workers.

32. List and describe three types of sex associated with phones/technology.

33. Briefly describe two forms of sexual variances involving touching.

34. Describe forms of exhibitionism.

35. Describe motivations for and reactions to exhibitionism.

36. Describe rates and degrees of voyeurism.

37. Describe sadomasochism and two roles associated with this practice.

38. Describe the rates of sadomasochism, including its dangerous variants.

39. Describe rates of and theoretical explanations for sadomasochism.

40. Describe rates of, reasons for, and concerns about bestiality.

41. Briefly describe concerns about necrophilia.

42. Describe the emerging concept of pansexualism.

KEY WORDS

Asexuality: a condition characterized by a low interest in sex.

Autoerotic asphyxiation: accidental death from pressure placed around the neck during masturbatory behavior.

Autogynephilia (otto-guy-nuh-FEEL-ee-ah): a tendency found in some males to become sexually aroused by obsessive thoughts and images of being females and having female attributes, or even female sex organs.

Bestiality (beest-ee-AL-i-tee): a human being's having sexual contact with an animal.

Bondage: tying, restraining, or applying pressure to body parts as part of sexual arousal.

Brothels: houses of prostitution.

Call boys: highly paid male prostitutes.

Call girls: highly paid female prostitutes who work by appointment with an exclusive clientele.

Celibacy (SELL-a-ba-see): choosing not to share sexual activity with others.

Coprophilia: sexual arousal connected with feces.

Erotomania (air-aht-oh-MAY-nee-ah): a very rare form of mental illness characterized by a highly compulsive need for sex.

Erotophilia (air-aht-oh-FEEL-i-ah): consistent positive responding to sexual cues.

Erotophobia (air-aht-oh-FOBE-i-ah): consistent negative responding to sexual cues.

Exhibitionism: exposing the genitals to others for sexual pleasure.

Fetishism (FEH-tish-i-zum): sexual arousal triggered by objects or materials not usually considered to be sexual.

Frotteur: one who practices frotteurism.

Frotteurism (frah-TOUR-izm): gaining sexual gratification from anonymously pressing or rubbing one's genitals against others, usually in crowded settings.

Hookers: street name for female prostitutes.

Hustlers: male street prostitutes.

Hypersexuality: unusually high level of interest in and drive for sex.

Hyposexuality: an especially low level of sexual interest and drive.

Hypoxphilia: creating pressure around the neck during sexual activity to enhance sexual pleasure.

Kleptomania: extreme form of fetishism in which sexual arousal is generated by stealing.

Masochist: the individual in a sadomasochistic sexual relationship who takes the submissive role.

Massage parlors: places where women can be hired to perform sexual acts under the guise of giving a massage.

Ménage à trois (may-NAZH-ah-TRWAH): troilism.

Necrophilia (nek-ro-FILL-ee-a): having sexual activity with a dead body.

Nymphomania (nim-fa-MAY-nee-a): a term sometimes used to describe erotomania in women.

Orgy (OR-jee): group sex.

Pansexual: lacking highly specific sexual orientations or preferences; open to a range of sexual activities.

Pimps: men who have female prostitutes working for them.

Promiscuity (prah-mis-KIU-i-tee): sharing casual sexual activity with many different partners.

Pyromania: sexual arousal generated by setting fires.

Sadist: the individual in a sadomasochistic sexual relationship who takes the dominant role.

Sadomasochism (sade-o-MASS-o-kiz-um): refers to sexual themes or activities involving bondage, pain, domination, or humiliation of one's partner by the other.

Satyriasis (sate-a-RYE-a-sus): a term sometimes used to describe erotomania in men.

Streetwalkers: female prostitutes who work on the streets.

Toucherism: gaining sexual gratification from the touching of an unknown person's body, such as on the buttocks or breasts.

Troilism (TROY-i-liz-um): sexual activity shared by three people.

Urophilia: sexual arousal connected with urine or urination.

Voyeurism (VOYE-yur-i-zum): sexual gratification from viewing others who are nude or who are engaging in sexual activities.

Zoophilia (zoo-a-FILL-ee-a): bestiality.

SELF-TEST

When responding to the following multiple-choice questions, choose the "best" answer. The "best" answer is the one that corresponds to the information contained in your text.

1) Kinsey based his understandings of sexual expression on a concept of total sexual outlet, or what was termed
   a) the biologically driven theory of sex.
   b) the exhausting theory of sex.
   c) the hydraulic theory of sex.
   d) the dynamic theory of sex.

2) Erotic plasticity refers to the concept that
   a) stretching exercises, especially in the genital area, can increase sexual pleasure.
   b) the sex industry thrives on people spending money.
   c) sexuality is changeable so sexual needs/behaviors may be modified by daily life circumstance.
   d) certain substances are used to manufacture sex toys and aids.

3) The subjective erotic experience includes
   a) desire.
   b) drive.
   c) sexuality.
   d) performance.

4) Which term is more often used to describe sexual preferences and behaviors that are viewed within a framework that considers them to be pathological or antisocial?
   a) variant
   b) deviant
   c) sexiophilia
   d) paraphilia

5) Consistently responding positively to sexual cues is called
   a) eurocentric.
   b) erotophilia.
   c) erotophobia.
   d) eroticism.

6) Erotomania in men is more generally known as
   a) nymphomania.
   b) erotocentrism.
   c) satyriasis.
   d) satomania.

7) Which of the following may represent normal asexuality characterized by a very low interest in sex, or it may be a conscious choice?
   a) chastity
   b) non-sexualism
   c) asexualphobia
   d) celibacy

8) What may cause male sexual behavior to exhibit greater diversity?
   a) inborn biological propensities
   b) developed biological propensities
   c) inborn socialized propensities
   d) developed socialized propensities

9) The term applied to anyone who cross-dresses or wears clothes of the opposite sex, for any reason is
   a) transsexual.
   b) homosexual.
   c) transvestite.
   d) transgenderist.

10) Cross-dressers, while escaping their usual gender roles, feel a greater sense of
    a) shame.
    b) intensity.
    c) sexual arousal.
    d) relaxation.

11) A transsexual desiring sex reassignment surgery must have psychiatric treatment that includes living all aspects of life as the gender they aspire to be for up to
    a) 6 months.
    b) 12 months.
    c) 1.5 years.
    d) 2 years.

12) Most high-intensity female-to-male transsexuals choose the more complex and expensive surgical procedure called
   a) metoidioplasty.
   b) penoplasty.
   c) vaginoplasty.
   d) phalloplasty.

13) Post surgical transsexuals cannot do any of the following *except*
   a) reproduce.
   b) ejaculate.
   c) experience an orgasm.
   d) menstruate.

14) All are DSM-IV guidelines for determining if a child has a gender identity disorder *except*
   a) minimal identification with the opposite sex.
   b) desire to cross-dress.
   c) behaving in cross-gender roles.
   d) preferring playmates of the opposite gender.

15) There is evidence that, at least in males, continued exposure to the same pornographic material results in
   a) fixated deviancy.
   b) saturation.
   c) habituation.
   d) pervision.

16) Dildos, made of everything from ivory to clay, have existed for at least
   a) 500 years.
   b) 1,000 years.
   c) 2,000 years.
   d) 2,500 years.

17) Sexual fantasies have been categorized into the following categories *except*
   a) exploratory.
   b) intimate.
   c) impersonal.
   d) relational.

18) The kinds of sexual fantasies people experience, and their length and degree of explicitness, seem to be determined to a large degree by
   a) the amount of pleasure they experience about sex.
   b) the amount of guilt they experience about sex.
   c) the amount of sexual behaviors that follow the fantasies.
   d) the use of sexual toys during the fantasies.

19) Kleptomania and pyromania are both considered
   a) form of positive paraphilias.
   b) forms of maniaisms.
   c) forms of fetishism.
   d) none of the above

20) Another term for ménage à trois is
    a) twosomes.
    b) foursomes.
    c) orgies.
    d) troilism.

21) All of the following can be elements of group sex *except*
    a) relational group commitment.
    b) exhibitionism.
    c) voyeurism.
    d) same-gender sexual interaction.

22) In recent years, there has been a prevalent attitude that prostitution represents an
    a) exploitation and victimization primarily of women.
    b) opportunity for a woman to raise her socioeconomic status.
    c) issue of great social concern that causes harm to society.
    d) opportunity for the spread of disease.

23) Male sex workers who service older affluent men are referred to as
    a) escorts.
    b) hustlers.
    c) call boys.
    d) mangolos.

24) According to an Australian study, the men who use services of prostitutes stated that all of the following were reasons they paid for sex except
    a) to satisfy sexual needs.
    b) their steady partners wouldn't engage is sex as much as they wanted.
    c) it was easier and less complicated.
    d) it was entertaining.

25) All are risks for girls that make them susceptible to become sex workers *except*
    a) having a poor self-image.
    b) having run away from home.
    c) seeking independence from an adult.
    d) having friends who are already prostitutes.

26) Another term for obscene phone calls is
    a) telephone sex play.
    b) telephone talkalogia.
    c) telephone scatalogia.
    d) telephone sex talk.

27) Gaining sexual enjoyment from pressing or rubbing one's genitals against another is called
    a) toucherism.
    b) voyeurism.
    c) exhibitionism.
    d) frotteurism.

28) Exhibitionism is not a common sexual offense for which men are arrested in
   a) Africa.
   b) Europe.
   c) Canada.
   d) the United States.

29) Voyeurs tend to be all of the following *except*
   a) younger males.
   b) usually married.
   c) separated.
   d) none of the above

30) Practitioners of BDSM sometimes refer to more conventional sexual interests as being
   a) cherry.
   b) boring.
   c) vanilla.
   d) non-stimulating.

31) Which is the least understood of the relatively common routes to sexual arousal and connection?
   a) urophilia
   b) coprophilia
   c) sadomasochism
   d) exhibitionism

32) Sadomasochism seems to fit into each of the following themes *except*
   a) hypermasculainty.
   b) administration or receipt of pain.
   c) physical restraint.
   d) hypomasculity.

33) When individuals attempt to restrict oxygen flow to their brain when engaging in sexual self stimulation, they are practicing a bondage theme referred to as
   a) autoerotic hypoxphilia.
   b) hypoxphilia asphyxiation.
   c) hypoxphilia.
   d) autoerotic strangulation.

34) Having sex with animals is referred to as
   a) bestiality or animalphilia.
   b) zoophilia or animlaphilia.
   c) bestiality or zoophilia.
   d) animalphilia.

35) The sexual behavior that generally stirs the most negative reactions is
   a) bestiality.
   b) sadomasochism.
   c) pedophilia.
   d) necrophilia.

GUIDED REVIEW AND STUDY
[Answers are provided at the end of the study guide.]

1) It has been hypothesized that women have greater _____ plasticity than men.
2) Subjective eroticism also includes what has been termed sensuosity or _____, referring to the inner enjoyment of the whole sensual experience of sex, not just orgasm.
3) Women with high levels of sexual interest tend to be seen in a more _____ light than men with such interests.
4) _____ is the term that is applied to the behavior of those who have sexual contact with several different partners on a relatively emotionally uninvolved, casual basis.
5) HIV+ people may choose celibacy in their later years, partly because they do not wish to risk infecting others, but also because of feelings of _____ or _____.
6) For whatever social or political reason, a _____ _____, with regard to sexual behavior, has persisted in our culture.
7) A study of 1,032 male cross-dressers found that 87% described themselves as _____.
8) _____ is a male who identifies as heterosexual and fantasizes about being a woman, having a woman's body or having woman's sexual organs.
9) For transsexuals, one recognized form of rehabilitative therapy has been the _____ and _____ transformation of the individual's external features into a form resembling the anatomy of the other sex.
10) In a recent study of postoperative male to female transsexuals, _____ of the patients expressed _____ about having undergone reassignment.
11) One of the difficulties in diagnosing children with gender identity disorders is that there are not clearly defined lines of _____ gender behavior.
12) Being a sexual human being, expressing that sexuality, and experiencing sexual responsiveness involve far more than our _____ _____.
13) Women, on average seem to be relatively _____ or even mildly _____ concerning pornography viewing by their intimate partners.
14) _____ are probably the most common of the sexual aids, providing an intense vibration to the genitals or other sensitive body parts.
15) Men's fantasies tend to be more active, _____, and visually oriented, whereas women's fantasy themes are generally more passive and _____.
16) _____ is usually defined as finding sexual excitement in objects, articles of clothing, or the textures of particular materials that are not usually considered to be sex-related.
17) A _____ is an intense fetish where the individual excludes other forms of sex and may be exhibiting signs of emotional insecurity or stress worthy of professional consultation.
18) Group sex may also accompany mate swapping, swinging, and other variations on _____ sex.
19) Both male and female prostitutes, now often called _____ _____, participate in sexual activity for money.
20) It has been claimed that a relatively small amount of disease transmission actually comes from prostitution, and that this would be reduced if prostitution were _____ and _____.
21) Men who have strong feelings of _____ and _____ have a tendency to engage in obscene telephone calls.
22) Anonymity on the internet allows for people to feel more _____ and _____ than they tend to feel in face-to-face situations.
23) _____ refers to the intimate touching of an unknown person's body, typically on the buttocks or breasts.
24) Nudity is obviously a form of exhibitionism, although it may have few, if any, _____ connotations.

25) The _____ is the partner who derives sexual pleasure from being in a dominant role, while the _____ is the individual who is aroused by being in the submissive, receiving role.

26) A study of men involved in heterosexual dominance found that unlike what the researchers had predicted, the men did not have _____ ,nor were they high in _____ attitudes.

27) The _____ tradition carries strong prohibitions about humans having sex with animals.

28) The term _____ has been used to describe individuals who see their sexual capacities as transcending particular human objects of attraction.

ESSAY QUESTIONS
[Answers are provided at the end of the study guide.]

1) Briefly describe erotophilia, erotophobia, hyposexuality, and hypersexuality as well as two forms of hypersexuality.

2) Describe transgenderism as well as general and specific forms of transvestitism.

3) Describe the use of erotic/pornographic materials and sexual enhancement devices for arousal in men and women.

4) Briefly describe forms and concerns about group sex.

5) Describe the term pansexual and offer examples of pansexualism.

CHAPTER RESOURCE REFLECTIONS

Sex-Trade Trafficking Laws

Why should the United States be concerned with the trafficking of humans in other countries? Shouldn't these governments be free to establish their own laws, as well as being free from American pseudoimperialism? Why or why not? Should governments establish witness protection programs for cases linked to trafficking?

Case Study

Imagine living in Vincent's dorm or attending his college. Having learned about the nature of transgenderism from the chapter and class presentations, how would you personally respond to an encounter with Vincent? How would you react to others who ridiculed him? Why would you respond in that manner?

Case Study

Imagine that you are M.J.'s parents. He shares with you the information shared with the counselor. Would you support him emotionally, economically, and socially? For each category, why or why not,? When you read the above reference to "him", what was your reaction? Why did you react in that manner?

Some Notes on My Transgenderness

You are a classmate of Mr. Arrowsmith, living in the same dorm; we will make it co-ed for this reflection. What are your reactions to learning about and living with Mr. Arrowsmith? Why do you believe you had those reactions? If you were Mr. Arrowsmith, how would you feel about having to "pass" and "pack?" Consider the expenses involved with accommodating a male body vs. a female body.

Case Study

Let's change Craig's scenario just a little. Suppose Craig had not previously discussed his fetish with his fiancée. If you were his fiancée, how do you believe you might react? Why might you react that way? Now let's make it a little more personal. What if your future spouse came to you and explained they had a fetish. How do you believe you would respond? Would the type of fetish matter? Why or why not?

Q & A with Dr. Sandor Gardos

Were you familiar with frottage prior to this course? Can you recall times, perhaps during holiday shopping trips or at concert events, where you may have been violated? As Dr. Gardos points out, frottage is an illegal activity. Touching without consent is wrong. What can you do to keep yourself safe from this behavior?

Zoophile Fails to Wow Legislators with His Story of Love

What do you think about the intensity of Mr. Buble's feelings for Lady? Were the legislators' comments insightful or not appropriate?

Self-Evaluation: Your Sexual Fantasies

Fantasies, for most people, are just fantasies and most fantasies, if transferred into real-life experiences, do not harm anyone providing they are in a consensual relationship or sexual encounter. Therefore, the understanding of our fantasies or exploring our fantasies may enhance the erotic nature of our sexual experiences. Take the time to complete this self-evaluation. What did you learn about your fantasies? How might you change or use your fantasy life to improve your personal and relational sex life?

MCGRAW-HILL RESOURCES
REFLECTING ON SEXUALTY

Remember that this section of the study guide takes you beyond the text to explore other resources in the field of human sexuality. The experience attempts to expand on at least one concept covered in the chapter.

Access the McGraw-Hill Web pages associated with sexuality at:
    http://www.mhhe.com/socscience/sex

Scroll down and "click" on the hyperlink for "Resource Room."

Scroll down and "click" on the hyperlink for "Web Resources."

Scroll down and "click" on the hyperlink for "Transgender Forum."

Scroll down and "click" on the hyperlink for "TG Forum-Free." "Click" on the hyperlink for "photos."

Scroll down and read the descriptions next to each photo. "Click" on the hyperlink for a few of the individuals. (You will see a larger photo.)

What are your reactions to the personal descriptions next to each photo? What are your reactions to the photo? The most important aspect of this exercise is examining the reasons for your reactions, especially if your reactions were not accepting/affirming. Transgendered individuals are engaging in, or living out, a personally fulfilling consensual gender identity, just like you. If you had difficulty extending the same level of personal acceptance as you desire, why did that occur? Most importantly, what are you going to do about it?

CHAPTER 14
SEX, ART, THE MEDIA, AND THE LAW

CHAPTER OUTLINE

CHAPTER LEARNING OBJECTIVES

1. Describe three terms used to describe sexuality in visual or literary portrayals.

2. Describe historical, cultural, and educational uses of erotic art.

3. Briefly describe the roots of and reactions toward "modern" sexually explicit materials.

4. Describe the tension between governmental and social support for erotic art.

5. Briefly describe the influence of ancient Greek culture on sexuality in literature.

6. Briefly describe pre- and post- 19th century influences on sexuality in literature.

7. Briefly describe two 20th century literary works that created controversies.

8. Describe the prevalent expansion and censorship of erotic materials.

9. Describe the contemporary historical roots of erotic magazines.

10. Briefly describe emerging trends in magazines addressing sexuality.

11. Briefly describe historical and religious influences on sexuality in films.

12. List and describe the sexual impact of seven films.

13. List and describe the film rating system.

14. Briefly describe the "negative" sexual portrayal of women in film.

15. Describe historical and contemporary views of same-gender relationships in film.

16. Describe how gender identity and romantic themes are portrayed in film.

17. Describe the evolutionary process regarding the availability of pornographic media.

18. Briefly describe concerns regarding use of explicit videos.

19. Describe how computers and multimedia are used for positive and abusive sexual purposes.

20. Briefly describe the efforts of television to portray sexual themes.

21. Briefly describe research findings about television and sexuality.

22. Describe the sexuality connotation of advertising.

23. Describe concerns about and controversies involving child pornography.

24. Briefly describe two theories concerning the potential of sexuality explicit materials.

25. Briefly describe the findings of the <u>Presidential Commission on Obscenity and Pornography (1970)</u>.

26. Describe the findings of and politics involved with the <u>Unites States Attorney General's Commission on Pornography (1986)</u>.

27. Briefly describe challenges faced when making conclusions about exposure to sexually explicit materials.

28. Identify two researchers associated with and the form of communication associated with explaining the impact of sexually explicit materials.

29. Describe the effects of arousal and emotional reactions to sexually explicit materials.

30. Briefly describe the two-path process that attempts to explain attitudinal effects of viewing sexually explicit material.

31. Briefly describe attitudinal effects of viewing pornography.

32. Briefly describe the behavioral impacts of viewing aggressive and nonaggressive sexually explicit materials, including sexual behaviors within 24 hours following exposure.

33. Describe findings about exposure to sexually explicit materials in institutionalized sex offenders and child molesters.

34. Briefly describe the findings concerning depictions of coercive sex or rape.

35. Briefly describe two censorship arguments concerning pornography.

36. Describe the evolution of the definition of obscenity.

37. Briefly describe controversies associated with legislative attempts to regulate pornography.

38. Briefly describe two philosophical legal views concerning sexual behavior.

39. Describe how states use law to limit behaviors.

40. List and describe four constitutional principles used to address sexual issues/behavior.

41. Describe legal, religious, and governmental influences/effects regarding sexuality education.

42. Briefly describe historical and evolving views of sexual assault in marriage.

43. Briefly describe legislative and law enforcement efforts to address rape.

44. List and describe two types of laws used to control prostitution.

45. Briefly describe reasons for the decriminalization of prostitution.

46. Briefly describe court rulings regarding nudity.

47. Describe the range of state and court actions regarding reproductive rights.

48. Describe how HIV/AIDS has impacted the legal dimensions of sexual behavior.

KEY WORDS

Catharsis theory: suggests that viewing pornography provides a release for sexual tension, thus preventing antisocial behavior.

Erotica: artistic representations of nudity or sexual activity.

Hard-core pornography: pornography that makes use of highly explicit depictions of sexual activity or shows lengthy scenes of genitals.

Kiddie porn: term used to describe the distribution and sale of photographs and films of children or younger teenagers engaging in some form of sexual activity

Modeling theory: suggests that people will copy behavior they view in pornography.

Obscenity: depiction of sexual activity in a repulsive or disgusting manner.

Pornography: photographs, films, or literature intended to be sexually arousing through explicit depictions of sexual activity.

Shunga: ancient scrolls used in Japan to instruct couples in sexual practices through the use of paintings.

Sodomy laws: laws in some states that prohibit a variety of sexual behaviors, often described as deviate sexual intercourse. These laws are often enforced discriminatorily against particular groups such as gay males.

SELF-TEST
When responding to the following multiple-choice questions, choose the "best" answer. The "best" answer is the one that corresponds to the information contained in your text.

1) Which term is used to describe sexually explicit materials that are not offensive?
   a) erotica
   b) pornography
   c) obscenity
   d) hard-core pornography

2) Many Greek and Etruscan paintings show all of the following except
   a) sexual intercourse.
   b) fellatio.
   c) bestiality.
   d) pedophilic behavior

3) In Japan, "shunga" refers to
   a) groom scrolls.
   b) marriage scrolls.
   c) instructional scrolls.
   d) bride scrolls.

4) The George Pompidou Center in Paris exhibited 500 works of the 20ᵗʰ century art for several months. The exhibition explored all but one of the sexual themes listed below:
   a) masturbation
   b) transgenderism
   c) voyeurism
   d) sadomasochism

5) Ancient Greek writers utilized the eroticism of the fertility rites of the festivals of the
   a) Etrusans.
   b) Petronians.
   c) Dionysians.
   d) Erotysians.

6) The 19ᵗʰ century brought a rise in prudery, nevertheless,
   a) explicit sexual references were still made.
   b) sexual attitudes were open and varied.
   c) erotic literature flourished.
   d) sexual feelings were discussed.

7) Which James Joyce book was not allowed into the United States until Woolsey wrote a landmark decision that redefined the limits of pornography?
   a) *Lady Chatterley's Lover*
   b) *Ulysses*
   c) *Forever*
   d) *Sex and the Single Girl*

8) During the 1990s, libraries faced challenges regarding materials that contained erotic themes, which is viewed as
   a) censorship.
   b) erotophobia.
   c) pornophobia.
   d) censorphobia.

9) After suffering major declines in their circulation rates due to competition from the Internet, which two erotic magazines went bankrupt?
   a) *Screw* and *Cherry*
   b) *Oui* and *Screw*
   c) *Penthouse* and *Oui*
   d) *Screw* and *Penthouse*

10) One of the emerging trends in contemporary magazines is that they are including more articles about
   a) homoeroticism.
   b) heterosexual eroticism.
   c) sexuality.
   d) transsexualism.

11) Research studies confirm that sexually explicit films and videos produce in viewers higher levels of
   a) endorphins.
   b) arousal response.
   c) serotonin.
   d) respiration.

12) In 1934, the Roman Catholic Church instituted this organization to establish standards for films, standards that were adopted by Hollywood producers:
   a) Anti-Sex Legion.
   b) Legion of Anti-Pornography in Film.
   c) Legion of Anti-Decency.
   d) Legion of Decency.

13) The first film to show bare female breasts was
   a) *Midnight Cowboy*
   b) *Boogie Nights.*
   c) *The Pawnbroker.*
   d) *The Graduate.*

14) Women have been frequently portrayed in films in all of the following manners *except*
   a) self-destructive.
   b) manipulative.
   c) sexually seductive.
   d) self-assured.

15) During which decade did Hollywood become less hesitant about portraying same-gender themes in film?
   a) 1980s
   b) 1960s
   c) 1990s
   d) 1970s

16) All of the following have been used to describe films whose main purpose is to show lengthy scenes of genitals and/or persons engaging in sexual activities *except*
   a) erotica.
   b) blue movies.
   c) stag movies.
   d) hard-core pornography.

17) The earliest "adult films" were made by professionals before
    a) 1900.
    b) 1925.
    c) 1950.
    d) 1965.

18) Sexologists have made recommendations to video stores that include all of the following
    except
    a) children not being portrayed sexually.
    b) sex not being associated with blood or violence.
    c) not regulating positive sexual messages.
    d) regulating positive sexual messages.

19) Which of the following themes is not commonly noted in sexually explicit videos?
    a) high levels of sexual desire
    b) focus on oral and vaginal sex
    c) many sexual partners readily available
    d) pleasure as the purpose sexual activity

20) Models performing, for a fee, sexual acts for viewers via the internet constitutes a form of
    long-distance
    a) cyber-porn.
    b) cyber-sex.
    c) cyber-relationship.
    d) cyber-prostitution.

21) The combination of these characteristics can conspire to cause some individuals to become
    compulsive regarding use of computers to access sexually explicit materials:
    a) easy access, technological speed, and confidentiality.
    b) easy access, affordability, and confidentiality.
    c) affordability, anonymity, and minimal cost.
    d) affordability, anonymity, and easy access.

22) Shows featuring teenagers in sexual situation that deal with sexuality in a frank fashion
    include all except
    a) *Dawson's Creek.*
    b) *The OC.*
    c) *Will and Grace.*
    d) *Boston Public.*

23) The basic idea behind using sex to sell a product is referred to as
    a) imprinting.
    b) identification.
    c) embedding.
    d) sublimation.

24) Why have condom ads not become more mainstream in the media since other sex-related messages are so prevalent?
   a) Condom companies are not willing to sell on television
   b) A message can not be structured that would pass the local obscenity committees
   c) Television shows are not willing to risk being boycotted due to a condom commercial.
   d) publishers and broadcasters claim they are worried that the public will disapprove

25) Child pornography may involve any of the following *except*
   a) children simply posing nude.
   b) children posing with suggestive movement.
   c) children simply posing with each other.
   d) children engaging in sexual activity with each other.

26) The theory that maintains that use of pornography actually prevents violence or unconventional behavior is
   a) catharsis theory.
   b) modeling theory.
   c) psychodynamic theory.
   d) transference theory.

27) Which national commission on pornography worked to contain the spread of pornography?
   a) Presidential Commission on Obscenity and Pornography
   b) Vice Presidential Commission on Obscenity and Pornography
   c) United States Attorney General's Commission on Pornography
   d) Presidential Commission on Pornography

28) There is support for the existence of an association between sexually aggressive behaviors and frequent use of violent pornography among men who have
   a) lower intelligence and are social.
   b) higher intelligence and are antisocial.
   c) higher intelligence and are aggressive.
   d) lower intelligence and are antisocial.

29) The two attitudinal processing routes for how sexually explicit materials are viewed are
   a) central and bilateral.
   b) central and peripheral.
   c) peripheral and bilateral.
   d) central and bihemispheric.

30) Most individuals report an increase in sexual behavior after exposure to sexually explicit materials:
   a) within 12 hours.
   b) within 1 hour.
   c) within 36 hours.
   d) within 24 hours.

31) Psychologists refer to portrayals of women who become aroused and participate willingly in coercive sex as
   a) the rape syndrome.
   b) the assaultive myth.
   c) the rape myth.
   d) the coercive myth.

32) Although its constitutionality continues to be challenged, this law would penalize Internet pornographers if they fail to restrict access to children:
   a) No Access to Pornography for Children Act.
   b) Child Online Protection Act.
   c) Limit Child Access to Pornography Act.
   d) Child Internet Protection Act.

33) The year of a landmark decision in Massachusetts in which a man was convicted of raping his wife was
   a) 1998.
   b) 1979.
   c) 1958.
   d) 1969.

GUIDED REVIEW AND STUDY
[Answers are provided at the end of the study guide.]

1) The term *sexually explicit material* is sometimes used to describe _____.
2) _____ are those who test the limits of moral values and sexual tolerance.
3) _____ often relied on sexual fantasy and free association borrowed from psychoanalysis.
4) Sumerian love songs written about 4,000 years ago contain verses that are _____ _____ than love songs of today.
5) _____ _____ is sometimes considered the originator of European pornography.
6) D. H. Lawrence's work, _____ _____ _____, stirred controversy with its sexual explicitness for decades.
7) For adolescents, _____ has long been one of the most important means of sexual expression.
8) The _____ approach was adopted by a large number of magazines for men.
9) Analysis of the photographs in Maxim and Stuff concluded that they tended to portray women as _____ sex objects much more often than they did men.
10) In 1971, there were only _____ scientific journals relating to sexuality and today there are more than _____.
11) When comparing male and female roles in films from 1927 through the late 1980s, women's roles were generally rather rigidly _____.
12) As society became more _____ of lesbian and gay relationships, these themes have been depicted in a variety of ways in films.
13) In the award-winning U.S. film _____ _____ _____, a woman who lived as a man was depicted and was eventually murdered by intolerant men.
14) Women particularly enjoy _____ themes in movies, whereas men tend to be more focused on _____ behavior.
15) Over time, research has found that there has been decrease in the number and proportion of sexually _____ scenes in sexually explicit videos.

16) Some _____ have used computer networks to make contact with young people.

17) There are a number of controls that can prevent minors from accessing _____ sexual material on the Net; these filters may also block _____ information such as sites on breast cancer and reproductive health.

18) The soaps tend to reflect _____ content that is true to society's _____ related themes.

19) Advertisers may use the technique of _____ to subliminally hide emotionally or sexually charged words or pictures.

20) Courts in the United States continue to support the contention that child pornography lies outside of the _____.

21) People may be reluctant to admit they are _____ by reading or seeing pornographic material, or have some degree of _____ about their reactions.

22) It is clear that government commissions investigating pornography serve mainly to fulfill the _____ agendas of particular administrations.

23) One study of adult pedophiles who were attracted to boys found that viewing erotica involving nudity and sexual acts of boys _____ _____ _____ to cause them to commit sexual acts with boys.

24) Seventy to 90 percent of both men and women have measurable _____ arousal in response to sexually explicit material.

25) Men who have historically had more exposure to sexually explicit materials may in fact be more gender _____ in their attitudes.

26) Males who are exposed to _____ pornography are no more likely to aggress against females than controls who have been exposed to neutral, or nonexplicit, material.

27) Researchers have found the child molesters had in fact been significantly _____ when first exposed to pornography than control groups.

28) The pornography issue is intimately associated with the principles of freedom of _____ and freedom of the _____.

29) The two types of sexual behavior that are usually not potentially subject to criminal prosecution as long as they are practiced in private: _____ masturbation and _____ between married individuals.

30) Those who are in favor of legal reforms argue that laws prohibiting sexual behavior between consenting adults are attempts to impose specific moral and _____ standards on citizens.

31) In 2003, the U.S. Supreme Court overturned a Texas sodomy law stating that the law was _____ to gay people and that the government has no authority to regulate the sexual conduct of _____ _____ _____ _____ _____.

32) The U.S. Supreme Court struck down the _____ state measure on constitutional grounds of being discriminatory and hostile toward a particular group of people, in this case gays and lesbians.

33) Although there are controversies surrounding sexuality education in schools, nearly all states mandate teaching about _____ at some level of the educational structure.

34) Historically forced sex was viewed not as a crime against the female victim, but as a _____ crime against the man who "owned" her.

35) The basic philosophy behind laws dealing with sex workers and nude dancing is the regulation of _____ morality.

36) The Supreme Court did not declare bans on the use of contraceptives to be unconstitutional until the mid-_____.

37) State laws have not generally been aggressive in passing laws that protect the _____ of persons who have positive HIV tests, thereby compromising privacy and creating a disincentive to be tested.

1) Describe historical, cultural, and educational uses of erotica as well as the prevalent expansion and censorship of erotic materials.

2) Describe the film rating system and the evolutionary process regarding the availability of pornographic media.

3) Compare and contrast the findings of the *Presidential Commission on Obscenity and Pornography* with the *United States Attorney General's Commission on Pornography*.

4) Describe the behavioral impacts of viewing aggressive and nonaggressive sexual explicit materials as well as the findings about institutionalized sex offenders' exposure to sexually explicit materials.

5) Describe how states use laws to limit sexual behaviors as well as four Constitutional principles also used to address sexual issues/behaviors.

CHAPTER RESOURCE REFLECTIONS

Cross-Cultural Perspective

This brief reading reminds us of the cultural and social pressures and restraints that limit an individual's actual and perceptual freedoms of self-expression. What role do you believe government should play in regulating the perceived sexuality of clothing? Why do you take this position? What makes certain styles of underwear sexier than others?

Censuring the Library

Should libraries be forced to comply with the "Children's Internet Protection Act?" Why or why not? If taxpayers should utilize libraries for information, including academics, should adults not have free reign to conduct research at public libraries regarding pornography? Why or why not?

Case Study

The story of "The Cave" T-shirt reminds us of the symbolic nature of how individuals present themselves. Have you ever worn a T-shirt that was potentially offensive to someone else? What were your motivations for wearing that T-shirt? Conversely, have you ever been offended by seeing a T-shirt worn by someone else? What was offensive about the T-shirt? How should school systems, both K through 12 and postsecondary, respond to this issue?

Porn: Bad Time for Pizza Boy's Return?

What do you think about the wearing of condoms in adult erotica and pornography? Would it make the scene sexier or less sexy? What do you think about the gay porn industry mandating condom usage while the straight porn industry does not?

Fan Swapping: Gay, Straight, Up Late

What about this article strikes you as most interesting? What do you think about the statement, "It may be that TV portrays the lives we aspire to, rather than the lives we lead"?

Young Lover May Be 'Criminal' at 18

What is an appropriate age to start dating and potentially engage in sexual activity? What do you think about the parents in this article who changed their minds about their daughters' relationship and prosecuted her boyfriend? Is it appropriate that the law regulate control over the young man registering as a sex offender for the rest of his life?

MCGRAW-HILL RESOURCES
REFLECTING ON SEXUALTY

Remember that this section of the study guide takes you beyond the text to explore other resources in the field of human sexuality. The experience attempts to expand on at least one concept covered in the chapter.

Access the McGraw-Hill Web pages associated with sexuality at:
    http://www.mhhe.com/socscience/sex

Scroll down and "click" on the hyperlink for "Resource Room."

Scroll down and "click" on the hyperlink for "Web Resources."

Scroll down and "click" on the hyperlink for "Women's Studies Resources."

"Click" on the hyperlink for "Gender Issues."

Scroll down and "click" on hyperlink for "Sexual Harassment."

Scroll down and "click" on the hyperlink for "Q and A about Sexual Harassment" and read the posting.

Based on the reading, do you believe that definitions and criteria for determining if someone has been sexually harassed are "legally fair?" Why or why not?

CHAPTER 15
SEXUAL COERCION, RAPE, AND ABUSE

CHAPTER OUTLINE

Learning about Sex

Knowing How to Communicate

Having Realistic Expectations

Being Cautious and Responsible

SELF-EVALUATION

Your Sexual Concerns and Problems

CHAPTER LEARNING OBJECTIVES

1. Describe how sexual problems are socially constructed.

2. Describe rates and characteristics of negative self-attitudes regarding bodies and sexual needs.

3. Briefly describe how coercion is involved in sexual behaviors.

4. Briefly describe how prejudice impacts individuals sexually.

5. Identify two roots of sexual dysfunction.

6. Describe the diagnosis, classification, and treatment of paraphilias.

7. Describe how sex can be considered an addiction and controversies associated with this position.

8. Define sexual harassment as well as reported rates of and gender perceptions about harassment.

9. List and describe four bases for a claim of sexual harassment.

10. Describe factors associated with increased rates of harassment.

11. Describe rates of sexual harassment in schools and colleges.

12. Briefly describe sexual harassment concerns within academia.

13. Describe rates of and concerns about sexual harassment in the military.

14. Briefly describe rates of and company responses to sexual harassment.

15. List the legislative acts used to address sexual harassment.

16. List and describe five steps for individuals to take to address sexual harassment.

17. Briefly describe general concerns regarding abuse by professionals.

18. Describe perceived causes, effects, and corrective measures regarding abuse of female clients.

19. Briefly describe the continuum for conceptualizing coercive sexual behavior.

20. Briefly compare/contrast sexual coercion in Sweden and the U.S.

21. Describe controversies regarding the legal definition of rape.

22. Describe developmental and social factors associated with coercive and abusive individuals.

23. Describe seven warning signals of potential sexual aggression.

24. List incidence rates of forced sex.

25. Briefly describe rates of and social factors associated with acquaintance rape.

26. Describe relational and communication concerns involving acquaintance rape.

27. Briefly describe social circumstances that may increase and decrease the risk of acquaintance rape.

28. Describe the concept of marital rape and the challenges faced by women victimized in this manner.

29. List rates and reactions of male sexual assault victims.

30. List and describe the two phases of rape trauma syndrome.

31. Describe the two phases of treatment for sexual assault.

32. Describe six criteria that indicate a successful resolution of a forced sexual event.

33. Describe police and court responses to sexual assault.

34. Briefly describe treatment efforts for victims of sexual assault.

35. List rates of child molestation.

36. Describe considerations for evaluating potentially abusive situations involving sexuality and children.

37. Describe general characteristics of adult sexual abusers.

38. Describe characteristics of male and female sexual abusers.

39. Describe the characteristics of adolescent sexual abusers.

40. Briefly describe parental reactions to a male child's victimization.

41. List and describe four categories of ill effects resulting from sexual abuse toward children.

42. Briefly describe physiological and psychological effects of sexual abuse.

43. Describe the long-term effects of sexual abuse of boys and women.

44. Describe challenges faced when treating children and adult victims of child sexual abuse.

45. Describe methods of treatment for sexual offenders.

46. Describe rates and cultural definitions of incest.

47. Describe familial factors and child responses to incest.

48. Briefly describe treatment goals and options for victims of incest.

49. Describe perceptions and controversies about recovered and false memories of sexual abuse.

50. List and describe five general ways of preventing and dealing with problematic sex.

51. List and describe seven considerations when consulting therapy

KEY WORDS

Acquaintance (date) rape: a sexual encounter forced by someone who is known to the victim

Child molesting: sexual abuse of a child by an adult.

Hebephilia (eh-FEE-bo-fil-ee-a): a term being used to describe the sexual abuse of adolescents.

Incest (IN-sest): sexual activity between closely related family members.

Incest taboo: cultural prohibitions against incest, typical of most societies.

Marital rape: a woman being forced by her husband to have sex.

Paraphile (Paraphiliac): person who is drawn to one or more of the paraphilias.

Pedophilia (pee-da-FIL-ee-a): another term for child sexual abuse.

Quid pro quo: something gained from something given.

Rape trauma syndrome: the predictable sequence of reactions that a victim experiences following a rape.

Sex addiction: inability to regulate sexual behavior.

Sexual harassment: unwanted sexual advances or coercion that can occur in the workplace or academic settings.

Statutory rape: a legal term used to indicate sexual activity when one partner is under the age of consent; in most states that age is 18.

SELF-TEST

When responding to the following multiple-choice questions, choose the "best" answer. The "best" answer is the one that corresponds to the information contained in your text.

1) Sexual activity is a serious problem if it includes any of the following *except*
   a) coercion.
   b) assault.
   c) exploitation.
   d) resistance.

2) Research supports the fact that people who tend not to feel good about themselves after having sex or report not being comfortable during sex have an elevated risk of
   a) sexual abuse.
   b) acquiring an STI.
   c) not reaching orgasm.
   d) low self-esteem.

3) Emotional blackmail might involve
   a) hinting that a relationship will end if sex does not improve.
   b) hinting that a relationship will get better if sex does not improve
   c) saying "You would have sex with me if you didn't love me."
   d) hinting that if sex is engaged, nothing will change.

4) This social reality grows out of exaggerated stereotypes and lack of information:
   a) discrimination
   b) prejudice
   c) acceptance
   d) nonacceptance

5) This diagnosis has been implicated as a cause of many sexual dysfunctions and a correlation found between men with sexual function difficulties and drug abuse.
   a) Borderline Personality
   b) Bi-Polar disorder
   c) Anti-social personality disorder
   d) Depression

6) Paraphilias are characterized by all but one of the following:
   a) intimacy.
   b) sexual arousal to objects or situations that are not normative patterns of arousal.
   c) victimizing aspects.
   d) self-destruction.

7) Research indicates that individuals with paraphilias
   a) lack specific controls over behaviors.
   b) have specific controls over behaviors.
   c) lack general controls over behaviors.
   d) have general controls over behaviors.

8) The sex addiction model has been criticized for all of the following reasons except:
   a) It is oversimplified for some people.
   b) Treatment programs have not been developed.
   c) It is confusing regarding some behaviors perceived as signs of addiction when, instead, they are normal.
   d) It is misleading, because it may prevent people from getting appropriate treatment.

9) Estimates suggest that about what percentage of women are victims of some form of sexual harassment, mostly the "hands-off" type?
   a) 50%
   b) 25%
   c) 75%
   d) 69%

10) All of the following are bases for complaints about sexual harassment *except*
   a) quid pro quo.
   b) quid hara quo.
   c) hostile environment.
   d) third-party effects.

11) A study of college students found that men tend to do all of the following except
   a) be more tolerant of sexual harassment
   b) see heterosexual relationships in adversarial terms
   c) believe myths about rape
   d) deny that they might not be sexually aggressive in some circumstances

12) A central issue in academia regarding even consensual relationships between faculty and students is
   a) the balance of power.
   b) the equality of their adult status.
   c) the imbalance of power.
   d) the equality of power.

13) The General Accounting Office reports that this percentage of female students at the national military academies experience some form of sexual harassment:
   a)   60%.
   b)   90%.
   c)   80%.
   d)   50%.

14) Court cases have indicated that American companies
   a)   need to develop hostile work environments.
   b)   need not modify their actions.
   c)   need to prevent hostile work environments.
   d)   need to affirm positive coworker relationships.

15) All of the following are steps that can be taken by an individual to respond to a situation involving sexual harassment *except*
   a)   write a letter explaining his or her role in the incident.
   b)   consider making use of mediation services.
   c)   seek sources of personal support.
   d)   find out which authorities or administrators are designated for the reporting of such activities.

16) A 2004 report by the U.S. Conference of Catholic Bishops reported that between 1950 and 2002 in the U.S., nearly_____ Roman Catholic priests were accused of sexually molesting children.
   a)   2,500
   b)   4,500
   c)   6,500
   d)   8,500

17) In cases of sexual abuse or sexual harassment by a professional, they are situations in which there is a
   a)   therapeutic boundary utilization.
   b)   therapeutic violation.
   c)   therapeutic transference.
   d)   boundary violation.

18) Research indicates that certain feelings arise for victims of abuse by a professional that make it difficult for the victims to take charge of the situation. All but one of those feelings are
   a)   lack of self-esteem.
   b)   helplessness.
   c)   wanted and cared for.
   d)   shame.

19) According to a study of college students, all of the tactics were used to get another person sexually involved *except*:
   a)   emotional manipulation.
   b)   exploitation of the intoxicated.
   c)   physical touch to elicit sexual arousal.
   d)   offering money as compensation for a "deal."

20) Sexual offenders usually exhibit all but one of the following characteristics:
   a) insecurity and fearful attachments in their relationships.
   b) difficulty maintaining social relationships.
   c) flexibility with meeting others needs.
   d) a propensity toward depression and loneliness.

21) In many states, rape is defined as
   a) vaginal penetration by fingers.
   b) anal penetration by fingers.
   c) vaginal and anal penetration by an object.
   d) vaginal penetration by the penis.

22) All are warning signals of potential sexual abuse *except*
   a) a tendency to use medicines heavily and to get abused when under the influence.
   b) a tendency to drink heavily and to get abusive when drunk.
   c) lack of respect for women, generally by not listening.
   d) a tendency to become more physically involved and invasive.

23) The percentage of women who reported being forced to do something sexual in the National Health and Social Life Survey (NHSLS) is:
   a) 66%.
   b) 22%.
   c) 90%.
   d) 10%.

24) Sexual victimization on college campuses has been associated with
   a) female and male athletes.
   b) students of sexuality courses.
   c) male athletes and fraternity members.
   d) male athletes and male students.

25) Although acquaintance rape cannot always be prevented, there are several ways to reduce the risks:
   a) develop a relationship based on mutual trust and respect
   b) training sessions for men where empathy for women is encouraged
   c) develop a relationship where understanding is the goal
   d) not being open or sharing too much when communicating with a new partner

26) All of the following are factors related to marital rape *except*
   a) an immediate disagreement.
   b) continued disagreement.
   c) nonsexual violence.
   d) alcohol and drug abuse.

27) Males generally appear to react to sexual coercion and violence by
   a) feeling empowered in their primary sexual relationship.
   b) feeling empowered in their new sexual relationships.
   c) feeling a tremendous loss of control.
   d) feeling a tremendous loss of sexual identity.

28) The two phases associated with rape trauma syndrome are
    a) acute and disruptive phases.
    b) disruptive and nonaccute phases.
    c) pre- and posttraumatic phases.
    d) acute and recovery phases.

29) The most common forms of treatment for victims of sexual assault are
    a) group and computer therapy.
    b) group and individual therapy.
    c) individual and computer therapy.
    d) computer and telephone therapy.

30) Pregnancy results in an estimated
    a) 3% of female rapes.
    b) 5% of female rapes.
    c) 7% of female rapes.
    d) 10% of female rapes.

31) This category of sex offender targets adolescents to abuse:
    a) pedophile.
    b) hebephile.
    c) child molester.
    d) adolescephile.

32) Adolescent sexual abusers display all of the following characteristics *except*
    a) symptoms of depression.
    b) serious developmental difficulties.
    c) they come from functional families.
    d) they are generally male.

33) The most frequent reactions seen by therapists when initially treating abused children is
    a) guilt.
    b) anger.
    c) depression.
    d) neglect.

34) All but one of the following are ill effects of sex abuse on children and adolescents:
    a) traumatic sexualization.
    b) a sense of empowerment at overcoming the abuse.
    c) a sense of betrayal.
    d) stigmatization.

35) Based on adult clients exhibiting symptoms of sexual abuse, some counselors and therapists pursued exploration of the client's history looking for memories and employing this controversial theory:
    a) false memories.
    b) newly recovered memories.
    c) untrue memories.
    d) recovered memories.

1) Eating disorders are particularly common in women who have difficulties perceiving their _____ qualities in positive ways.
2) Society has generally perpetuated some rather specific _____ of sexual attractiveness through popular myths and advertising.
3) When there are discrepancies between what a person perceives as the actual and the ideal in their bodies and sexual lives, they are more likely to have _____ _____ and to be _____ _____.
4) Stigmatization of people's sexual identities may easily lead to _____ and _____.
5) The offenders of sexual coercion or abuse often use various forms of _____ to justify his or her coercive or abusive behaviors.
6) Although sexual dysfunctions have physical roots, most often they are caused by _____ blocks and stresses.
7) Use of _____ is often involved in regrettable sexual decision-making and higher risk sexual activities.
8) _____ _____ generally involves unwanted sexual advances, suggestiveness, sexually motivated physical contact, or requests for sexual favors.
9) Studies of college students demonstrate that _____ tend to be more tolerant of sexual harassment
10) If a person's school or work environment is made uncomfortable because of sexual innuendoes, suggestive remarks or pictures, and uninvited advances, this is viewed as creating a _____ _____.
11) Schools that have policies regarding sexual harassment need to provide for _____ procedures, so that an individual who feels unfairly charged will be offered an opportunity for defense.
12) The military even considers _____ sex between persons of different ranks to be inappropriate, as it can lead to a breakdown of discipline and _____ of the units.
13) It is critical that training about sexual harassment be given to workers and that harassment _____ be _____ regualarly.
14) In 1993, the U.S. Supreme Court ruled unanimously that victims need not have suffered severe _____ damage in order to claim that they have been sexually harassed.
15) One common reaction of many victims of sexual harassment is to feel _____ for having somehow precipitated the sexual advances.
16) Several states have enacted legislation providing _____ and _____ penalties for professionals who violate ethical standards.
17) It has become increasingly clear that _____ sexual exploitation often has disastrous consequences.
18) Women who have previously been physically abused are more likely _____ _____ _____ _____.
19) In general usage, the term _____ refers to any form of sex in which one person forces the other person to participate.
20) _____ rape is a legal term used in a situation where an adult or adolescent has sexual intercourse with a younger partner who is under the age of consent.
21) Misunderstandings and a lack of _____ between partners are crucial issues in acquaintance rape.
22) It was once assumed that it was a wife's _____ to submit to her husband's sexual desires.
23) In 1995, _____ delegates to the United Nations mustered enough support to eliminate marital rape from a resolution on violence against women.

24) Most typical forms of coercion for assault against men were: employing tactics of _____, getting the man _____, and threatening to withdraw _____.

25) _____ forcing men to have sex has received little attention in the sexological literature.

26) The majority of victims of forced sex report feeling permanently _____ by the experience.

27) The acute phase of rape trauma syndrome is characterized by what is commonly called _____ stress disorder.

28) Police officers have been trained to interview victims of sexual assault in a sensitive manner that minimizes their _____ and discomfort.

29) The partners of assault victims often become _____ survivors themselves, experienced as a whole range of emotional reactions and posttraumatic symptoms.

30) The majority of sexually abused victims are molested by a _____ _____ or someone _____ to the child.

31) Children are often reluctant to report sexual abuse, or they may lack the _____ development to explain clearly what happened.

32) Adult male sexual abusers tend to report high levels of _____ _____ and difficulties with _____ and _____.

33) It is quite typical for juvenile sex abusers to have been subjected to _____ abuse themselves, and sometimes to _____ abuse.

34) _____ intervention may be the first line of action in treating child sexual abuse cases.

35) It has been suggested that when offenders also have a sexual dysfunction, treating the dysfunction may improve the individual's quality of life and _____ _____ _____.

36) A society's strong prohibition against sexual relationships within families is often called the _____ _____.

37) Abuse of boys by their mothers occurs more often when the mother is overreliant on the son for _____ support.

38) Incest survivors are sometimes _____ at work who tend to suffer from depression and suicide attempts.

39) Children need to understand the concepts of appropriate and inappropriate _____.

40) _____ is fundamental to a continuing, healthy sexual relationship.

ESSAY QUESTIONS
[Answers are provided at the end of the study guide.]

1) Describe how coercion and prejudice impact sexual behaviors and sexuality.

2) Describe the nature of sexual harassment and the four bases for a sexual harassment claim.

3) Describe social, relational, and communication factors associated with acquaintance rape.

4) Describe the controversy in treating offenders and identify two approaches.

5) Describe the controversy surrounding the recovered memory and false memory debate.

CHAPTER RESOURCE REFLECTIONS

Cross-Cultural Perspective

Bob Herbert's piece reminds us of the exploitability of children, in this case in Thailand. What were your reactions to the story? Bring the story home and think about the street kids in major U.S. cities, and even smaller cities, who are selling their bodies to "survive." What should be done to address this exploitation of children in both Thailand and the United States?

How Men Can Tell

After reading and responding to the questions, did you find yourself potentially engaging in behavior that was offensive and that might constitute sexual harassment? The important lesson from this reflection is to change potentially offensive behaviors. What behavior are you going to change?

Acquaintance Rape

Review the suggestions made to both women and men regarding acquaintance rape. Are these suggestions realistic and able to be practiced? Summarize, in a few words, what you believe woman and men should learn from this reflection.

Case Study

After reading the story about Barbara, do you believe she was raped? Why or why not? How could both Charlie and Barbara have made different, and possibly better, decisions? If you were Barbara, would you have Charlie arrested? Why or why not?

Case Study

You are Tony. Based on the facts in the case study, what might you do differently with regard to the present (not the past)? Why would you take these actions?

Unwanted Sex

After reading this piece, what responsibilities do both women and men have regarding the ambiguous nature of communicating about one's sexual intentions? Do you agree with the supporters of rape-law reform in wanting to set aside the empirical findings? Why or why not?

Case Study

Sidney's story reminds us of the need to revisit our past sexual experiences, especially those in which we have harmed someone or through which we have been harmed. Are there any events in your life that need to be worked on? If yes, how do you plan on addressing these issues? Contacting your college or university counseling center might be a good place to start.

Ten Reasons to Obtain

If you were a student at Antioch College, what are your reactions to the verbal consent policy? Do you agree with the "why it makes sense to ask" statements? Why or why not?

The instructions for this exercise indicate that if you are "fully comfortable," you may want to save the questionnaire. As an alternative, everyone should consider completing this self-evaluation. Even though we may perceive ourselves "fully comfortable," often completing an exercise provides us with insights into our perceptions. Our perceptions may be rightly reinforced or our perceptions may be challenged. After completing the self-evaluation, what happened to your perceptions?

MCGRAW-HILL RESOURCES
REFLECTING ON SEXUALTY

Remember that this section of the study guide takes you beyond the text to explore other resources in the field of human sexuality. The experience attempts to expand upon at least one concept covered in the chapter.

Access the McGraw-Hill Web pages associated with sexuality at:
        http://www.mhhe.com/socscience/sex

Scroll down and "click" on the hyperlink for "Resource Room."

Scroll down and "click" on the hyperlink for "Web Resources."

Scroll down and "click" on the hyperlink for "Feminist.com." (page should reload)

In the "search this section" box, type "sexual assault."

"Click on the hyperlink for "Sexual Assault."

Read the article. What reactions did you have as you read the article? Why do you believe you had those reactions? What do you perceive are the most significant issues faced by someone that has been sexually assaulted? Why do you perceive these to be the most significant issues?

CHAPTER 16
SEXUALLY TRANSMITTED DISEASES AND OTHER PHYSICAL PROBLEMS

CHAPTER OUTLINE

CHAPTER LEARNING OBJECTIVES

1. Briefly describe the difference between a STD and a STI.

2. Describe historical and cultural perceptions of STDs.

3. Briefly describe findings of a teen STD knowledge survey.

4. Describe difficulties associated with reporting the incidence of STDs.

5. Describe the National Health and Social Life Survey (NHSLS) findings regarding rates and profile of STD infection.

6. Briefly describe reasons why individuals do not seek treatment.

7. List and describe the epidemiology, symptoms, diagnosis, and treatment of gonorrhea.

8. List and describe the epidemiology, symptoms, diagnosis, and treatment of syphilis.

9. List and describe the epidemiology, symptoms, diagnosis, and treatment of chlamydia.

10. Describe the causes, symptoms, and treatments for nonspecific urethritis (NSU).

11. Briefly describe vulvovaginitis and its symptoms.

12. List and describe four types of vulvovaginitis.

13. Briefly describe methods to prevent vulvovaginal infection.

14. Describe the epidemiology, symptoms, diagnosis, and treatment of genital herpes.

15. Describe the epidemiology, symptoms, and treatment of genital warts (HPV).

16. Describe the epidemiology, symptoms, and treatment for hepatitis B (HBV) and hepatitis C (HCV).

17. Describe the epidemiology, symptoms, and treatment for pubic lice.

18. List and briefly describe three STDs associated with tropical climates.

19. List and describe seven suggestions for minimizing the risks of getting and transmitting a STD.

20. Briefly describe legal considerations associated with STDs.

21. Describe how physical or psychological health conditions, including treatments, can impact sexual functioning.

KEY WORDS

Chancroid (SHAN-kroyd): an STD caused by the bacterium *Hemophilus ducreyi* and characterized by sores on the genitals which, if left untreated, could result in pain and rupture of the sores.

Chlamydia (kluh-MID-ee-uh): now known to be a common STD, this organism is a major cause of urethritis in males; in females it often presents no symptoms.

Genital herpes (HER-peez): viral STD characterized by painful sores on the sex organs.

Genital warts: small lesions on genital skin caused by papillomavirus; this STD increases later risks of certain malignancies.

Gonorrhea (gon-uh-REE-uh): bacterial STD causing urethral pain and discharge in males; often no initial symptoms in females.

Granuloma inguinale (gran-ya-LOW-ma in-gwa-NAL-ee *or* -NALE): STD characterized by ulcerations and granulations beginning in the groin and spreading to the buttocks and genitals.

Hepatitis B virus (HBV): liver infection that is frequently sexually transmitted.

Hepatitis C virus (HCV): liver infection that may occasionally be sexually transmitted.

Lymphogranuloma venereum (LGV) (lim-foe-gran-yu-LOW-ma va-NEAR-ee-um): contagious STD caused by several strains of *Chlamydia* and marked by swelling and ulceration of lymph nodes in the groin.

Molluscum contagiosum (ma-LUS-kum kan-taje-ee-O-sum): a skin disease transmitted by direct bodily contact, not necessarily sexual, that is characterized by eruptions on the skin that appear similar to whiteheads with a hard seedlike core.

Nonspecific urethritis (NSU) (yur-i-THRYT-us): infection or irritation in the male urethra caused by bacteria or local irritants.

Perineal area (pair-a-NEE-al): the sensitive skin between the genitals and the anus.

Pubic lice: small insects that can infect skin in the pubic area causing a rash and severe itching.

Scabies (SKAY-beez): a skin disease caused by a mite that burrows under the skin to lay its eggs causing redness and itching; transmitted by bodily contact that may or may not be sexual.

Syphilis (SIF-uh-lus): sexually transmitted disease (STD) characterized by four stages, beginning with the appearance of a chancre.

Trichomoniasis (trik-uh-ma-NEE-uh-sis): a vaginal infection caused by the *Trichomonas* organism.

Vulvovaginitis (vaj-uh-NITE-us): general term for inflammation of the vulva and/or vagina.

Yeast infection: a type of vaginitis caused by an overgrowth of a fungus normally found in an inactive state in the vagina.

SELF-TEST

When responding to the following multiple-choice questions, choose the "best" answer. The "best" answer is the one that corresponds to the information contained in your text.

1) The French soldiers garrisoned in Naples in the winter of 1495 suffered from
   a) gonorrhea.
   b) hepatitis.
   c) syphilis.
   d) herpes.

2) What contributed to the perception in the late 1940s that VD had finally been conquered?
   a) use of condoms
   b) abstinence
   c) antibiotics
   d) sexual revolution

3) According to one study of adolescents who had received sexuality education,
   a) 91% identified HIV as a major STD.
   b) 2% could identify all eight major STDs.
   c) few could distinguish between the curable and incurable diseases.
   d) all of the above

4) Each year, what percentage of new STD cases are diagnosed among those aged 15 - 24?
   a) 25%
   b) 36%
   c) 48%
   d) 54%

5) The concern about gathering data on reportable diseases is
   a) that medical professionals do not agree on the definition of some STIs.
   b) that the CDC may not get the data from all 50 states.
   c) that many private physicians do not consistently report their occurrence.
   d) that public clinics do not have data gathering technology and human error is prevalent.

6) All of the following are particularly known for the inconspicuousness of their symptoms in the early stages *except*
   a) gonorrhea.
   b) genital warts.
   c) syphilis.
   d) chlamydia.

7) If someone has the "clap" or "the drip," they have
   a) syphilis.
   b) gonorrhea.
   c) chlamydia.
   d) AIDS.

8) In men, gonorrhea may affect
   a) the bladder, prostate, kidneys or epididymis.
   b) the bladder, Cowper's glands and seminal vesicles.
   c) the prostate, kidneys or liver.
   d) the prostate, epididymis, Cowper's glands and testis.

9) Which STI infection often coexists with gonorrhea?
   a) syphilis
   b) genital warts
   c) chlamydia
   d) none of the above

10) The spiral-shaped organism, or spirochete, causes
   a) gonorrhea.
   b) HIV.
   c) syphilis.
   d) genital warts.

11) This stage of syphilis indicates that it can no longer be cured nor transmitted to others:
   a) auxiliary stage.
   b) tertiary stage.
   c) primary stage.
   d) secondary stage.

12) This form of syphilis refers to an unborn fetus being infected by the disease from its mother's bloodstream while in the womb:
   a) latent syphilis.
   b) utero-syphilis.
   c) fetal syphilis.
   d) congenital syphilis.

13) Syphilis infection is also associated with a higher risk of infection with
   a) HIV.
   b) gonorrhea.
   c) chlamydia.
   d) tertiary syphilis.

14) In the later stages of chlamydia, the disease may cause
   a) cervical cancer.
   b) pelvic inflammatory disease.
   c) strokes.
   d) AIDS.

15) The most common cause of Nonspecific Urethritis (NSU) is
   a) gonorrhea.
   b) chlamydia.
   c) HIV.
   d) syphilis.

16) Vulvovaginitis infections are not necessarily related to sexual activity, but
   a) increase the likelihood for HIV.
   b) increase the likelihood for infection.
   c) are easy to diagnose because symptoms are painful and quick to occur .
   d) are easy to diagnose because symptoms cause an intense abdominal ache.

17) One of the best ways to prevent sexually transmitted vaginosis is for the male to
   a) use a spermicidal lubricant on their penis.
   b) have the female use a contraceptive foam.
   c) use a condom during oral sex.
   d) use a condom during vaginal intercourse.

18) Trichomoniasis is an infection caused by a one-celled organism called a
   a) protozoan.
   b) bacterium.
   c) parasite.
   d) spirochete.

19) When an individual has an outbreak of genital herpes, it is advisable to avoid sexual contact, or any direct skin contract, for how many days?
   a) 2 days
   b) 5 days
   c) 10 days
   d) none of the above

20) Women who have had genital herpes
   a) have higher rates of only cervical cancer.
   b) have higher rates of both cervical and vulval cancer.
   c) have higher rates of only vulval cancer.
   d) have no difference in rates of cervical or vulval cancer.

21) Genital warts occur more frequently in people who display the following characteristics *except*
   a) sexual activity early in their lives.
   b) multiple sexual partners.
   c) beginning sexual activity later in their lives.
   d) having casual sexual relationships.

22) Scientists are working on a vaccine that would provide immunity for
   a) HIV.
   b) HSV.
   c) HCV.
   d) HPV.

23) What is the most common blood borne infection in the United States?
   a) HCV
   b) HBV
   c) HAV
   d) HIV

24) About 5,000 people a year in the U.S. die from chronic liver disease caused by
    a) HPV and HBV.
    b) HBV and HCV.
    c) HIV and HBV.
    d) HIV and HCV.

25) All of the following are STDs from tropical climates *except*
    a) granuloma inguinale.
    b) tertiary syphilis.
    c) chancroid.
    d) lymphogranuloma venereum.

26) Which STD is caused by a tiny mite that burrows under the skin to lay its eggs?
    a) pubic lice
    b) vaginal lice
    c) dust mites
    d) scabies

27) This chemical provides a barrier that actually kills or disables disease germs:
    a) germicides.
    b) labialocides.
    c) microbicides.
    d) fungicides.

28) All of the following are specific suggestions for minimizing the chances of getting or transmitting a sexually transmitted disease *except*
    a) recognize that abstinence from sex is a rational choice.
    b) take responsibility for the protection of only your partner
    c) use condoms, vaginal pouches, and spermicides
    d) avoid multiple partners.

29) You should seek medical advice if, in the genital area or urinary tract, you have
    a) suspicious or uncomfortable symptoms.
    b) no symptoms, but suspect an infection.
    c) a "gut feeling" that something is wrong.
    d) no uncomfortable symptoms, but have excess urination.

30) What should be part of the integral health care of individuals with chronic illnesses or acute illnesses that create debilitating effects?
    a) counseling to decrease sexual activity
    b) minimal sexual assessment as sex is not an issue in these conditions
    c) careful sexual assessment
    d) none of the above

31) Who of the following is often concerned about the amount of physical exertion that is safe for them during sexual activity?
    a) only cardiac patients
    b) only stroke patients
    c) only cancer patients
    d) both cardiac and stroke patients

32) All of the following are reasons why patients with mental illness use masturbation *except*
    a) to control anxiety.
    b) to affirm relationships with others.
    c) to affirm the existence of their bodies.
    d) to safely act out their sexual fantasies.

GUIDED REVIEW AND STUDY
[Answers are provided at the end of the study guide.]

1) STIs were feared and often assumed to represent _____ from the gods.
2) It seems likely that gonorrhea and syphilis might well have been completely eliminated if our culture had taken a less _____ stance on sexually transmitted disease.
3) Many STDs lack clear _____ and therefore may go undetected.
4) People who have negative emotions about having sex in the first place, are _____ _____ to use protection than those who feel positively about it.
5) _____ is the second most commonly reported communicable disease.
6) Left untreated in either sex, gonorrhea can cause _____ in women.
7) _____ has been considered a scourge throughout history and in fact, dropped to its lowest rate in the U.S. in 2000 only to increase the next year.
8) _____, an inflammation of the eye, can be contracted at birth as the baby passes through the vagina or birth canal.
9) Chlamydia is a particularly common infection on _____ _____.
10) Treating vulvovaginal infections may _____ the women's risk of contracting _____ _____.
11) Yeast infection in the vagina is caused by an overgrowth of the fungus _____ *albicans*.
12) Exposure of the _____ to the herpes virus is particularly dangerous because a severe infection called herpes keratitis may develop that can cause serious damage.
13) Genital herpes is usually diagnosed by direct observation of the _____.
14) The risk of HPV leading to cervical cancer rises if the woman is also infected with _____.
15) Some strains of HPV have been increasingly associated with a high incidence of _____ and _____ cells in the cervix.
16) The STD commonly called "crabs" is caused by a tiny _____ louse with the scientific name *Phthirus pubis*.
17) The best medication to treat "crabs" is a 1 percent _____ lotion or cream.
18) _____ _____ is a pox virus that causes small papules to appear on the skin.
19) The pharmaceutical industry has been encouraged to work on the development of a vaginal _____ that could be used by women to reduce the risks of sexually transmitted infections.
20) Most of the serious STDs are transmitted by _____ involving mingling of _____ secretions.
21) Whenever there is a risk of a STD infection, male _____ or female condoms or a _____ can reduce the chances of transmission.
22) Condom manufacturers are no longer using _____ in lubricants.
23) The law expects people to be _____ in their sexual behaviors.
24) _____ is known to cause some physical problems with having an erection in men and some degree of vaginal dryness and discomfort in women.

ESSAY QUESTIONS
[Answers are provided at the end of the study guide.]

1) Describe historical and cultural perceptions of STDs and the difficulties associated with reporting the incidence of STDs.

2) Describe the symptoms for and types of vulvovaginitis.

3) Describe the epidemiology, symptoms, diagnosis, and treatment for one of the following: gonorrhea, syphilis, or chlamydia.

4) Describe the ways that an individual can minimize their risk for getting and transmitting a STD.

5) Briefly describe the legal considerations associated with STDs.

CHAPTER RESOURCE REFLECTIONS

Case Study

Place yourself in Carolyn's position. How would you have reacted to the news of your sexually transmitted infection? How would you respond to your partner? Why would you respond in that manner? Would you attempt to seek counseling for yourself? For you and your partner?

The Syphilis Mystery

Is it important to determine if Columbus brought syphilis to the Old World from the New World or for that matter from where the disease originated? Why or why not?

Cross-Cultural Perspective

If you were a woman in one of the restrictive cultures, how could this issue of STIs be addressed? If you were a male in one of those countries, should you change your behaviors? Why or why not? On a more global perspective, how should other coutnries respond to these issues?

A Lover's Checklist

Do you believe the use of the "Lover's Checklist" is realistic? Why or why not? At what point in a relationship would you incorporate it? Why at this particular point? How would you react or respond if a potential partner approached you with this checklist?

Self-Evaluation: Examining Your Attitudes toward STDs

Reflect on your responses to this instrument. Pay particular attention to the total and subscale scores. Briefly describe what you learned from your reflection on entire scale, and then your belief, feeling, and intention subscales.

Remember that this section of the study guide takes you beyond the text to explore other resources in the field of human sexuality. The experience attempts to expand upon at least one concept covered in the chapter.

Access the McGraw-Hill Web pages associated with sexuality at:
    http://www.mhhe.com/socscience/sex

Scroll down and "click" on the hyperlink for "Resource Room."

Scroll down and "click" on the hyperlink for "Web Resources."

Scroll down and "click" on the hyperlink for "Go Ask Alice," or "www.goaskalice.Columbia.edu."

Scroll down and "click" on a hyperlink for a question regarding a sexually transmitted disease (other than HIV) such as "How to ask someone…"

Read the question and respond. What information did you learn from the question/answer? How will you incorporate that information into your personal and sexual life?

CHAPTER 17
THE HIV/AIDS CRISIS AND SEXUAL DECISIONS

CHAPTER OUTLINE

CHAPTER LEARNING OBJECTIVES

1. Describe the historical roots of Human Immunodeficiency virus (HIV).

2. Briefly describe the epidemiology of HIV.

3. List and describe three nonsexual means of transmitting HIV.

4. List estimates of world and U.S. college rates of HIV infection

5. List and describe five populations and rates of HIV infection.

6. Describe demographic and cultural variables that affect rates of HIV transmission.

7. List and describe the stages of HIV infection/disease.

8. Briefly describe the RNA/DNA relationship of HIV.

9. Briefly describe the immune system responses to HIV infection.

10. List the typical fluids and routes involved with the transmission of HIV.

11. Describe the risks of HIV infection associated with oral sex, kissing, and casual contact.

12. List and describe two HIV blood tests.

13. Briefly describe the newest type of HIV testing.

14. Describe social and legal controversies over HIV testing.

15. List six Centers for Disease Control (CDC) recommendations for HIV testing.

16. Describe three concerns regarding HIV testing.

17. Identify the latest strategy regarding microbicides and HIV prevention.

18. Describe treatments for HIV infection/disease.

19. Describe four complications with developing a vaccine for HIV.

20. Describe HIV therapeutic and preventative vaccines.

21. Describe the social tensions surrounding disease, including HIV, regarding individual freedom vs. public health.

22. List and describe three ethical issues involving HIV/AIDS.

23. Briefly describe controversies about HIV education.

24. Describe reasons why people are not using condoms.

25. Briefly describe efforts at making condoms available to students.

26. List and describe five psychological or social factors that influence practicing safer sex.

27. List and describe six methods for reducing the risk of contracting HIV.

KEY WORDS

Acquired immunodeficiency syndrome (AIDS): fatal disease caused by a virus that is transmitted through the exchange of bodily fluids, primarily in sexual activity and intravenous drug use.

ELISA: the primary test used to determine the presence of HIV in humans.

Epidemiology (e-pe-dee-mee-A-la-jee): the branch of medical science that deals with the incidence, distribution, and control of disease in a population.

Hemophiliac (hee-mo-FIL-ee-ak): someone with the hereditary blood defect hemophilia, primarily affecting males and characterized by difficulty in clotting.

Human immunodeficiency virus (HIV): the virus that initially attacks the human immune system, causing HIV disease and eventually AIDS.

Opportunistic infection: a disease resulting from lowered resistance of a weakened immune system.

Perinatal: a term used to describe things related to pregnancy, birth, or the period immediately following the birth.

Retrovirus (RET-ro-vi-rus): a class of viruses that reproduces with the aid of the enzyme reverse transcriptase, which allows the virus to integrate its genetic code into that of the host cell, thus establishing permanent infection.

Rubber dam: small square sheet of latex used to cover the vulva, vagina, or anus to help prevent transmission of HIV during sexual activity.

Syndrome (SIN-drome): a group of signs or symptoms that occur together and characterize a given condition.

Thrush: a disease caused by a fungus and characterized by white patches in the oral cavity.

Western blot: the test used to verify the presence of HIV antibodies already detected by the ELISA.

When responding to the following multiple-choice questions, choose the "best" answer. The "best" answer is the one that corresponds to the information contained in your text.

1) The virus that can eventually produce AIDS when it infects humans is called
   a) gay related immunodeficiency syndrome.
   b) human papolovirus.
   c) human immunodeficiency virus.
   d) simean immunodeficiency virus.

2) Theory about the origin of HIV suggests that chimpanzees had the virus that diversified and began infecting humans around the year
   a) 1860.
   b) 1930.
   c) 1970.
   d) 1980.

3) It was estimated in 2003 that in North America, there are currently _____ living with HIV or AIDS.
   a) 1.2 million
   b) 1.4 million
   c) 1.6 million
   d) 1.8 million

4) Children who become infected with HIV in the womb, during the birth process, or soon after birth are said to have become positive
   a) perinatally.
   b) prenatally.
   c) postnatally.
   d) in utero.

5) All of the following are associated with high-risk sex *except*
   a) alcohol consumption.
   b) use of noninjectable drugs.
   c) women who voluntarily engaged in sex as children.
   d) low self-esteem.

6) Which of the following conditions was proposed by the National Health and Social Life Survey (NHSLS) research as one of the conditions that needed to be met in order for HIV to become an epidemic in the general population?
   a) frequent use of condoms
   b) a sustained "bridge"
   c) frequent sex
   d) needle sharing in the general population

7) The duration of the HIV infection varies depending on
   a) how quickly treatment is begun.
   b) the individual's health and behavior.
   c) diet, stress level, and predisposition to colds and flu.
   d) the strength of the individual's immune system.

8) During which phase of HIV disease does an individual become increasing vulnerable to opportunistic infections?
   a) chronic symptomatic disease
   b) chronic asymptomatic disease
   c) primary HIV disease
   d) HIV latency disease

9) HIV belongs to a class of viruses called
   a) RNA-DNA viruses.
   b) invetro-viruses.
   c) retroviruses.
   d) integrative-viruses.

10) To reproduce itself and multiply in the body, HIV destroys the very cells that are essential in helping the body produce immunity to all disease. These cells are know as
   a) B-lymphocytes.
   b) CD8s.
   c) CD2s.
   d) T-lymphocytes.

11) All of the following are routes of HIV transmission *except*
   a) oral-genital sexual activity.
   b) contact with saliva, tears, or urine.
   c) contact with infected blood.
   d) the transfer from mother to child.

12) None of the following are routes of HIV transmission *except*
   a) hot tubs.
   b) shared drinking or eating utensils.
   c) needles and syringes shared by people getting tattooed.
   d) toilet seats.

13) Generally speaking, antibodies that are tested for the presence of HIV are detectable, following infection, within
   a) 4 weeks.
   b) 6 weeks.
   c) 4 months.
   d) 6 months.

14) The two most popular blood tests for HIV are given in the following order:
   a) ELISA and Westernblot
   b) Westernblot and LIZA
   c) Westernblot and LISAA
   d) ELEESA and Westernblot

15) The CDC recommends that the following individuals should be tested annually for HIV, chlamydia, gonorrhea and syphilis::
   a) gays and lesbians
   b) bisexual women and lesbians
   c) gay and bisexual men
   d) heterosexuals

16) Unfortunately, this population tends not to return to clinic testing sites for the results:
   a) gay and bisexual men
   b) heterosexuals
   c) at -risk youth
   d) African-American males

17) The newest strategy being developed to help prevent the spread of HIV in the future is
   a) cocktail therapy.
   b) AZT.
   c) protease inhibitors.
   d) topical microbicides.

18) Treatment of HIV is most effective
   a) when chemical cocktails are utilized.
   b) when it is begun as soon as possible after infection.
   c) when the positive person is very careful about exposure to opportunistic infections.
   d) when a wide variety of drugs are used to control symptomology.

19) All of the following are major complications that make the search for a vaccine difficult *except*
   a) HIV hides in cells.
   b) There is a lack of a good animal model for the disease.
   c) It's been found that HIV infection, in light of treatments, is not dangerous for vaccine testing.
   d) There are ethical problems in conducting vaccine trials in less-industrialized nations.

20) All of the following are "other" ethical issues associated with HIV *except*
   a) issues of confidentiality.
   b) social ramifications of HIV/AIDS.
   c) costs of caring for HIV-infected patients.
   d) legal ramifications of HIV/AIDS.

21) All of the following are strategies in changing behavior regarding potential HIV infection *except*
   a) minimal media messages so as not to call attention to the problem.
   b) person-to-person discussions with parents.
   c) increasing availability of condoms.
   d) political climate that enables open discussion about HIV.

22) Some experts recommend beginning HIV/AIDS education at what age:
   a) 5–7 year olds
   b) 15–17 year olds
   c) over 18 years old
   d) 9–11 year olds

23) The fear of condemnation from parents, religious leaders, and society has often made it difficult for young people to
   a) overcome peer pressure.
   b) be prepared for sex.
   c) not accept the struggles of establishing sexual identity.
   d) none of the above

24) The best form of protection from HIV is
   a) use of a skin condom throughout a sexual encounter.
   b) use of an IUD throughout a sexual encounter.
   c) use of a polyurethane condom throughout a sexual encounter.
   d) use of a latex condom at the beginning of a sexual encounter.

GUIDED REVIEW AND STUDY
[Answers are provided at the end of the study guide.]

1) _____ treatments have been delaying the onset of certain disease symptoms of HIV but not curing the disease.
2) Because of advances in treatment, more people who were infected at birth are living to the ages when they are becoming _____ _____ and _____, creating a new generation of infected children
3) Worldwide, AIDS has become the _____ largest cause of human death.
4) Sharing _____ intercourse is especially risky behavior for HIV transmission, although the number of males engaging in this behavior has been on the decline.
5) Since the HIV epidemic began, the actual number of infections transmitted by _____ contact has been rising steadily.
6) Some evidence suggests that HIV may be transmitted to the fetus from the mother's _____ system or during the _____ _____.
7) _____ areas continue to represent the epicenter of the epidemic, and it is beginning to concentrate more in _____ neighborhoods.
8) The incidence of HIV infection has increased in _____ _____.
9) _____ _____ is when disease-causing organisms normally present in the environment become able to attack the person by taking advantage of the weakened resistance.
10) One of the most common infections in the third stage of HIV disease is a yeast infection of the mouth called _____.
11) When a retrovirus attacks a cell, a chemical orders the cell's _____ to translate the genetic blueprints of the virus into the cell's _____.
12) _____ are not effective against viral infections, although they may be extremely useful in combating bacterial opportunistic infections.
13) About half of adults in the U.S. have had an HIV test, but for those who turn out to be positive, the testing often has occurred _____ in the onset of their infection.
14) The _____ test for HIV antibodies tends to give a high percentage of false positives.
15) It is recognized that many potentially infected persons are avoiding testing because of embarrassment or lack of _____.
16) Some people donate blood because they know they will be _____ if they are _____.
17) Many clinics provide _____ testing, in which the patient is assigned a number for obtaining the test results.

18) There is still concern that HIV may eventually become _____ to drugs; that the _____ effects will eventually become toxic for the patients; or the virus may be able to _____ _____ in various cells of the body to reappear later on.

19) Viral disease can sometimes be prevented or brought under control by _____.

20) _____ of various degrees of various severity were imposed for certain infectious diseases.

21) As ethical problems multiply, the _____ system is increasingly being called upon to resolve disputes revolving around HIV and AIDS.

22) National and international activist groups have called for increased _____ _____, as once-promising national task forces and committees have gradually disbanded.

23) The federal HIPAA regulations require that patients be given thorough information about how their _____ may be protected.

24) HIV+ people who want to reproduce now have techniques available such as _____ the semen of the infected male, and pregnant women can take various _____ to reduce the chances of transmitting HIV to their babies.

25) There is evidence that as educational efforts _____, the incidence of risky behavior is indeed _____, but not to the extent that professionals would prefer.

26) Numerous _____ systems, especially those in urban locations, now make condoms available.

27) The fact remains, however, that for now _____ condoms represent one of the best protections against HIV transmission in sexual encounters.

28) A recommended guideline for having safer sex is to use a _____ _____ during oral contact with the vulva or anus.

ESSAY QUESTIONS
[Answers are provided at the end of the study guide.]

1) Describe demographic and cultural variables that affect rates of HIV transmission.

2) Briefly describe the stages of HIV infection/disease.

3) Describe the two tests commonly used for HIV antibody testing as well as the potential results of testing.

4) Describe social tension and ethical issues surrounding HIV/AIDS.

5) Describe six methods for reducing the risk of contracting HIV.

CHAPTER RESOURCE REFLECTIONS

The Global View

Reading about the teenagers in Cape Town evokes what emotions? What do you think about the power-based interplay between the adolescent boys and girls? Does it remind you of gender relations in the U.S.? What is your opinion about the statement, "what teenagers really need is to be terrified" to help prevent the spread of HIV? Realistically, what, if anything, can you do to address this problem?

Susan's story reminds us that anyone can be infected with HIV. Although we are constantly reminded of this fact, many of us don't take this message to heart. What keeps you from taking this message as seriously as you need to? If you believe you take the message seriously, when was the last time you had any element of risk in your sexual activities? What was the level of risk? What do you need to do to reduce and eliminate your risks?

Facing the Possibility of HIV

What do you think about Paula's reaction to the news of her current boyfriend's ex-girlfriend contracting HIV? What do you think about Paula's current boyfriend knowing his ex's status and continuing to have sex with Paula? Is this a realistic situation? What can you do to avoid the situation Paula is in?

HIV as My Reality

This is a particularly powerful piece that illustrates the isolation that HIV+ people can feel. What do you think about Jason's statement, "We feign monogamy while we slip away to parks, bookstores, campus library bathrooms, bathhouses…and engage in sexual liberation with a reckless abandon." Do these locations only serve to provide opportunities for gay men? What might your location list look like?

Case Study

After reading Brent's story, what do you believe he could have done differently to reduce his risk of infection? If you were Brent, how would you have reacted under these circumstances?

The Down Low

After reading the article, place yourself in the position of a "Down lower." How would you personally respond to the homophobia in the African-American community? Should "Down low" campaigns be developed for other clandestine homosexuals, bisexuals, and heterosexual men who have sex with men? Why or why not?

Self-Evaluation: Assessing Your Knowledge, Attitudes, and Circumstances Relating to HIV/AIDS; Considering Being Tested for AIDS

HIV and AIDS certainly have changed the face of sexual behaviors around the world, but what is most important is that this virus changes the face of your sexual behaviors. Take a few moments to assess your knowledge/attitudes about HIV/AIDS. What changes have you seen since 1992? Why do you believe the changes have occurred? The more challenging aspect of the self-evaluation may be assessing your getting tested for HIV antibodies. No matter if you have been tested repeated times, or never, assessing your thoughts, feelings, and emotions is important. Complete the assessment and reflect on your "readiness" to be tested.

Remember that this section of the study guide takes you beyond the text to explore other resources in the field of human sexuality. The experience attempts to expand upon at least one concept covered in the chapter.

Access the McGraw-Hill Web pages associated with sexuality at:
   http://www.mhhe.com/socscience/sex

Scroll down and "click" on the hyperlink for "Resource Room."

Scroll down and "click" on the hyperlink for "Web Resources."

Scroll down and "click" on the hyperlink for "The Body."

Scroll down and "click" on the hyperlink for "Access Your Risk for HIV and Other Sexually Transmitted Diseases."

Complete and submit the survey. What are your perceptions of the results? More importantly, as you completed your survey, what changes in your behavior do you need to consider in order to reduce your risk of infection? How can you minimize or eliminate your risks of infection? What behaviors keep you from eliminating your risks? Develop a plan or seek assistance with changing your behaviors to eliminate your risks.

CHAPTER 18
SEXUAL DYSFUNCTIONS AND THEIR TREATMENT

CHAPTER OUTLINE

Learning Objectives

UNDERSTANDING SEXUAL DYSFUNCTIONS

BEHAVIORAL APPROACHES TO SEX THERAPY

A CRITICAL LOOK AT SEX THERAPY

CHAPTER LEARNING OBJECTIVES

1. Describe the rates of and complexities in defining a sexual dysfunction.

2. Describe personal, professional, and cultural factors that influence perceptions concerning sexual dysfunction.

3. List and describe mythical performance standards for each gender and the consequences of such standards.

4. List and describe eight terms associated with labeling sexual dysfunctions.

5. List and describe the three-phase model of sexual response.

6. List rates of various sexual dysfunctions.

7. Briefly describe factors that may influence sexual desire.

8. List and describe three types of sexual desire disorders.

9. List and briefly describe two types of arousal disorders.

10. Describe the physiological process of penile erection and the methods to determine if a dysfunction is physical.

11. Briefly describe challenges faced by women concerning sexual arousal.

12. Define vaginismus and briefly describe relational consequences of this dysfunction.

13. Define dsypareunia and briefly describe potential causes of this sexual dysfunction.

14. Define anodyspareunia and briefly describe potential causes of this sexual dysfunction.

15. Describe the general rates and nature of orgasmic disorders.

16. Describe rates of and definitions used for premature ejaculation.

17. Describe perceived physiological and behavioral causes of premature ejaculation.

18. Briefly describe causes of and behavioral changes seen in males with dyspareunia.

19. Describe three generalizations regarding causes of sexual dysfunctions.

20. Briefly describe when a physical exam is suggested for sexual dysfunction.

21. Describe physical illnesses that can impact sexual functioning.

22. Describe how the use of alcohol, illegal drugs, and medications can impact sexual functioning.

23. Describe cultural and psychological factors that impact sexual performance.

24. Briefly describe relationship factors that can influence sexual functioning.

25. Describe some of the personal and professional challenges with treating sexual dysfunctions.

26. Describe five medicinal treatments for sexual dysfunctions.

27. Briefly describe two general types of biomedical devices used to treat sexual dysfunctions.

28. List and describe five types of psychotherapeutic treatments for sexual dysfunctions.

29. Describe reasons for a combination treatment approach for sexual dysfunctions.

30. Briefly describe the general backgrounds and therapeutic goals of sex therapists.

31. Describe challenges faced with finding a sex therapist.

32. Briefly describe therapeutic concerns when treating sexual dysfunctions.

33. List and describe five goals of behavioral sex therapy.

34. Describe two self-help techniques used in treating sexual dysfunctions.

35. List and describe five stages of partnership treatment for sexual dysfunctions.

36. Define sensate focus and describe the three phases associated with this technique.

37. Describe the rationale for the step approaches, culminating in sexual intercourse, for treating sexual dysfunctions.

38. Briefly describe behavioral approaches for treating vaginismus.

39. Briefly describe behavioral approaches for treating ejaculatory sexual dysfunctions.

40. List and briefly describe two categories used to validate sex therapy treatments.

41. Describe the general and research concerns regarding sexual dysfunction treatment effectiveness.

42. Briefly describe general ethical considerations faced by sex therapists.

43. Describe three main ethical issues for conducting sex therapy.

KEY WORDS

Acquired dysfunction: a difficulty with sexual functioning that develops after some period of normal sexual functioning.

Anodyspareunia: pain associated with anal intercourse.

Behavior therapy: therapy that uses techniques to change patterns of behavior; often employed in sex therapy.

Dyspareunia: recurrent or persistent genital pain related to sexual activity.

Female sexual arousal disorder: difficulty for a woman in achieving sexual arousal.

Hypoactive sexual desire disorder (HSDD): loss of interest and pleasure in what were formerly arousing sexual stimuli.

Impotence (IM-puh-tense): difficulty achieving or maintaining erection of the penis.

Lifelong dysfunction: a difficulty with sexual functioning that has always existed for a particular person.

Male erectile disorder (ED): difficulty achieving or maintaining penile erection (impotence).

Normal asexuality: an absence or low level of sexual desire, considered normal for a particular person.

Premature ejaculation: difficulty that some men experience in controlling the ejaculatory reflex, resulting in rapid ejaculation.

Preorgasmic: a term that has been applied to women who have not yet been able to reach orgasm during sexual response.

Sensate focus: early phase of sex therapy treatment, in which the partners pleasure each other without employing direct stimulation of sex organs.

Sex therapist: professional trained in the treatment of sexual dysfunctions.

Sexual aversion disorder: avoidance of or exaggerated fears toward forms of sexual expression.

Sexual surrogates: paid partners used during sex therapy with clients lacking their own partners; used only rarely today.

Spectatoring: term used by Masters and Johnson to describe self-consciousness and self-observation during sex.

Systematic desensitization: step-by-step approaches to unlearning tension-producing behaviors and developing new behavior patterns.

Vaginismus (vadg-ih-NISS-muss): involuntary contraction of the outer vaginal musculature when vaginal penetration is attempted.

SELF-TEST

When responding to the following multiple-choice questions, choose the "best" answer. The "best" answer is the one that corresponds to the information contained in your text.

1) Which book authored by Masters and Johnson assisted medical practitioners, psychologists, counselors and social workers clearly define guidelines for treating sexual concerns and complaints?
   a) *Human Sexual Concerns and Complaints*
   b) *Human Sexual Inadequacy*
   c) *Human Sexual Problems*
   d) none of the above

2) Approximately what percentage of women aged 18 – 24 have never had an orgasm?
   a) 8%
   b) 26%
   c) 33%
   d) 47%

3) Helping people with sexual dysfunction requires all but one of the following:
   a) creativity.
   b) a willingness to share your values.
   c) human sensitivity.
   d) well honed skills.

4) Which of the following is not one of the mythical standards of performance?
   a) There is a lack of male sexual pleasure without an erection.
   b) Women are expected to reach orgasm without difficulty.
   c) Men reach orgasm without difficulty
   d) Women are passive and nonsexual.

5) All of the following are labels for sexual dysfunctions *except*
   a) impotence.
   b) lifelong dysfunction.
   c) primary.
   d) tertiary.

6) This population has moved professionals to discuss whether sexual problems should be considered actual sexual dysfunctions.
   a) boys 11 – 17 years old
   b) girls 9 – 18 years old
   c) older age people
   d) housewives

7) The term used to describe low sexual desire is
   a) hyperactive sexual desire disorder.
   b) hypoactive sexual desire disorder.
   c) pseudohypoactive sexual desire disorder.
   d) pseudoypteractive sexual desire disorder.

8) The average age for men with hypoactive sexual desire disorder (HSDD) is _____, whereas the average age for women is _____.
   a) 45; 27
   b) 50; 40
   c) 55; 33
   d) 60; 38

9) Female sexual arousal disorder was previously referred to as
   a) sexual rigidity.
   b) female impotence.
   c) frigidity.
   d) nonorgasmia.

10) Male erectile disorder (ED) can affect men in any age bracket and can be caused by all but one of the following:
   a) depression
   b) excessive consumption of alcohol
   c) fatigue
   d) too many erections in a short period of time

11) The major cause of unconsummated marriages is
   a) vaginismus.
   b) impotence.
   c) erectile disorder.
   d) dyspareunia.

12) This term is used when women experience pain persistently during sexual intercourse:
   a) dyspareunia.
   b) vaginitis.
   c) vaginal pain disorder.
   d) disparaging pain disorder.

13) One explanation for male orgasmic disorders is
   a) the male's focus on his own sexual arousal.
   b) that the male may have a "numb" erection.
   c) that the male lacks psychological motivation.
   d) the male's partners are non-responsive to sexual behaviors.

14) The definition of premature ejaculation has included all of the following *except*
    a) ejaculation within one minute of intromission.
    b) ejaculation prior to achieving 8 to 15 pelvic thrusts.
    c) reaching orgasm prior to one's partner in 50 percent or more of one's coital experiences.
    d) ejaculation prior to one's personal expected length of sexual activity for personal. enjoyment

15) Premature ejaculation may be related to
    a) lack of voluntary control over the ejaculatory reflex.
    b) lack of involuntary control over the ejaculatory reflex.
    c) lack of control over frictional stimulation of penile glans.
    d) nonhabitual masturbation practices.

16) All of the following are considered factors that cause sexual dysfunctions *except*
    a) predisposing.
    b) maintaining.
    c) precipitating.
    d) postdisposing.

17) All of the following have been shown to impact sexual functioning *except*
    a) herbs.
    b) alcohol.
    c) hallucinogenic drugs.
    d) medications.

18) Another term for sexual "stage fright" is
    a) viewer's complex.
    b) spectator's complex.
    c) spectatoring.
    d) detached sexual performance.

19) Performance pressure is often rooted in an excessive need to
    a) be an outstanding lover.
    b) please a partner.
    c) fulfill traditional gender role expectations.
    d) feel powerful.

20) Effective treatment for sexual dysfunctions must be
    a) carried out in a step-by-step mechanical way.
    b) carried out as generalized treatment plans for all clients.
    c) designed and improvised for diagnostic groups.
    d) designed and improvised for particular clients.

21) Viagra was first approved for use in treating ED in
    a) 1994.
    b) 1996.
    c) 1998.
    d) 2000.

22) Which of the following is not a biomedical device used to treat sexual dysfunctions?
   a) semirigid rods
   b) inflatable tubular devices
   c) leather "cock" rings
   d) band placed at base of penis

23) Which of the following forms of psychotherapeutic treatments used systematic desensitization?
   a) behavior therapy
   b) group therapy
   c) hypnotherapy
   d) couples therapy

24) There is growing evidence that enhancing the ability for the female genitals to become engorged with blood is
   a) taking care of most women's complaints.
   b) leading to assured orgasm.
   c) the first step out of three in solving dysfunction.
   d) not going far enough in resolving most female arousal problems.

25) Sex therapists often have training in the following fields with the exception of
   a) psychology.
   b) religion.
   c) counseling.
   d) education.

26) One of the professional associations that an individual looking for a sex therapist can check with is
   a) AASECT.
   b) AASIECUS.
   c) the American College of Sexologists.
   d) the Better Business Bureau.

27) All of the following are goals of behavioral sex therapy *except*
   a) gaining a sense of permission to value one's sexuality.
   b) eliminating elements that are blocking full sexual response.
   c) reducing the amount of time to make sexual activity a priority, thereby reducing anxiety.
   d) reducing performance pressures.

28) Which of the following are two self-help techniques used to treat sexual dysfunctions?
   a) masturbation and therapy
   b) masturbation and body exploration
   c) body exploration and therapy
   d) masturbation and sexual surrogates

29) Various types of mutual body pleasuring exercises used by sex therapists are referred to as
   a) erotic focus.
   b) sensual focus.
   c) genital focus.
   d) sensate focus.

GUIDED REVIEW AND STUDY
[Answers are provided at the end of the study guide.]

1) Many of the newer medical treatments for sexual dysfunctions seem to be most effective when combined with some of the more traditional _____ techniques.
2) Treatment of sexual problems cannot be reduced to a series of _____ steps, although there are specific skills that may help a great deal.
3) One cannot attempt to change sexual functioning without being prepared also to examine sexual _____, _____ influences, the quality of _____ and other highly subjective life issues.
4) Sexual performance standards for men have been fairly _____, while those for women have been more _____ and mysterious.
5) Helen Singer-Kaplan identifies three phases of human sexual response: _____, _____, _____.
6) _____ phase is controlled by the autonomic nervous system.
7) Dysfunctions may be _____ when the problem occurs in all of an individual's sexual encounters, or _____, meaning that it happens only under specific conditions.
8) Sexual desire disorders seem to be more common in couples where there is less _____ with sexual behaviors and a low level of pleasure associated with such _____.
9) A nonpathological way of life, when choosing to be celibate or sexually inactive, is referred to as normal _____ and need not be considered a problem or dysfunction.
10) Sexual _____ disorder is characterized by fear or disgust about sex and avoidance of sexual activity.
11) What was once referred to as impotence in men is now termed _____.
12) One means of determining if male erectile disorder has a physical cause is to measure _____ penile tumescence.
13) Vaginismus is now considered to be one of the sexual _____ disorders.
14) It is not unusual for women who experience vaginismus to have had an unpleasant or _____ early sexual experience.
15) _____ orgasmic disorder is one in which an individual has never been able to achieve an orgasm.
16) The term associated with the male sexual disorder in which a male reaches orgasm too early is referred to as _____ ejaculation.
17) Male dyspareunia is apparently caused by involuntary contraction of the ejaculatory _____.
18) Men who experience postejaculatory pain often develop a pattern of general sexual _____.
19) Sexual dysfunctions are most often caused by _____ factors.
20) Complex circulatory and neurological mechanisms are involved in _____.
21) There is evidence that the _____ muscle, deep in the pelvis, must have good tone to permit a full orgasmic experience.
22) Men have invented their own techniques for delaying ejaculation, including _____ just prior to shared sex.
23) Masters and Johnson realized that they needed techniques to help patients _____ and _____ their behavior.
24) Although more research is needed, it does seem clear that the use of _____ can increase sexual desire in both men and women.
25) One of the most significant medical advances to treat sexual dysfunctions in recent years has been the popularly known drug _____.

26) Medical treatments for sexual dysfunctions have come increasingly effective, continued attention needs to be paid to _____ approaches.

27) Clients in behavioral therapy who need to practice therapeutic exercises, and who do not have partners, may use sexual _____.

28) Focusing solely on psychological or relational problems for sexual dysfunctions may ignore legitimate _____ conditions that are playing a primary role in these conditions.

29) A primary principle of sex therapy is lending a sense of _____ that it is all right to be sexual.

30) There is general agreement among sex professionals that _____ is an important aspect of good sexual adjustment.

31) An added positive outcome of sensate focus can be the reduction of the _____ imbalances in the sexual relationship.

32) The first phase of sensate focus activities involves _____ touching.

33) Men who need to delay their ejaculation may need to identify pelvic sensations so that they can prevent orgasm before they have passed the "point of _____ _____.

34) Couples who continue their _____ activities, such as sensate focus into the late stages of therapy, seem to have a better chance of positive outcomes.

35) Sex therapists should provide a foundation for change within the individual and the relationship so that a _____ can be prevented.

36) Work in sexology demands the highest standards of professionalism, _____, and informed consent.

ESSAY QUESTIONS
[Answers are provided at the end of the study guide.]

1) Describe personal, professional, and cultural factors that influence perceptions of sexual dysfunctions.

2) Describe both sexual desire and sexual arousal disorders.

3) Describe how physical illnesses as well as the use of alcohol, illegal drugs, and medications can impact sexual functioning.

4) Describe medicinal, biomedical, and psychotherapeutic treatments for sexual dysfunctions.

5) Briefly describe the ethical issues related to sex therapy.

CHAPTER RESOURCE REFLECTIONS

Viagra for Women

After reading about Viagra for women, are these researchers "trying too hard" to address an issue? Why or why not? Do you think drug companies should make more or less money available for researching chemical treatments for female sexual dysfunction? Why do you think Viagra has been available for so long, yet there is not an equal treatment available for women?

Case Study

After reading about Rudy's dilemma, what should he consider doing to address his concerns? Why are you making these particular recommendations? If you were Rudy, would you follow your own advice? Why or why not? If you were Rudy's partner, how would you deal with his concerns?

Case Study

After reading about Elizabeth's dilemma, what should she consider doing to address her concerns? Why are you making these particular recommendations? If you were Elizabeth, would you follow your own advice? Why or why not? If you were Elizabeth's partner, how would you deal with her concerns?

Cross-Cultural Perspectives

Although many of the traditions used to treat sexual dysfunctions in other cultures may seem "odd" to us, the reading indicated that in these cultures they are quite successful. Why do you believe they may be successful? If these methods were subject to rigorous scientific testing standards, what do you believe the results would be? If something is effective in a culture, must it be "proven" scientifically? Why or why not?

Curing a Dysfunctional Male Patient in the Mid-1700s'

If you were the patient being treated in this piece, how would you have reacted to the physicians' treatment? Is it really "mind over matter"?

MCGRAW-HILL RESOURCES
REFLECTING ON SEXUALTY

Remember that this section of the study guide takes you beyond the text to explore other resources in the field of human sexuality. The experience attempts to expand upon at least one concept covered in the chapter.

Access the McGraw-Hill Web pages associated with sexuality at:
       http://www.mhhe.com/socscience/sex

Scroll down and "click" on the hyperlink for "Resource Room."

Scroll down and "click" on the hyperlink for "Web Resources."
Scroll down and "click" on the hyperlink for "Go Ask Alice," or "www.goaskalice.colombia.edu."

Scroll down and "click" on a hyperlink for a topic under "About Sexual Difficulties."

Read the question and respond. If you were the individual who posed the question, do you believe the advice from Alice was beneficial? Why or why not? If Alice made a reference to other questions or resources, access one of those resources. What additional and beneficial information was obtained from that resource?

ANSWER KEY

Chapter 1 Multiple Choice
1) b
2) d
3) c
4) c
5) b
6) d
7) c
8) a
9) c
10) a
11) d
12) d
13) b
14) d
15) c
16) d
17) a
18) b
19) c
20) c
21) c
22) b
23) a
24) a
25) d
26) a
27) b
28) c
29) b

Chapter 1 Guided Review
1) ignorance
2) permissiveness, nonpermissiveness
3) competition, conquest
4) individual development
5) sex, love
6) provider, servant
7) Metrosexual
8) social constructionists
9) sex
10) many, drunk
11) biology, environment
12) contradictory
13) sin, ill
14) double standard
15) Heterosexual
16) 1970's
17) sexual rights
18) statistical analysis
19) Comprehensive
20) sexual
21) randomly
22) science, ideology, philosophy
23) assumptions
24) sexually
25) laboratory
26) variable
27) physical, psychological
28) Internet, sexuality
29) ethical dilemma

Chapter 2 Multiple Choice
1) c
2) d
3) a
4) b
5) c
6) a
7) c
8) c
9) d
10) d
11) a
12) d
13) b
14) b
15) a
16) a
17) a
18) c
19) d
20) b
21) c
22) a
23) c
24) c
25) b
26) c

27) a
28) d

29) b
30) c

Chapter 2 Guided Review

1) erogenous
2) clitoris, engorged
3) introitus
4) clitoris
5) smegma
6) Female genital cutting
7) sensitive
8) Vaginismus
9) cleansing mechanisms
10) imperforate
11) E. coli
12) atrophy
13) cervix, fundus
14) 21 or 3
15) speculum
16) spontaneous abortion
17) Oocytes
18) fimbriae

19) cervix
20) higher
21) Endometriosis
22) areola
23) visual, manual
24) Mammography
25) menarche, menopause
26) ovulation, menstruation
27) luteinizing
28) dysmenorrhea
29) menstruation, having sex during their period
30) dysphoric
31) Birth control pills
32) psychological
33) Prostaglandin
34) osteoporosis
35) hot flash
36) uterine, breast

Chapter 3 Multiple Choice

1) b
2) a
3) c
4) d
5) a
6) d
7) b
8) a
9) c
10) d
11) c
12) b
13) a

14) b
15) d
16) c
17) c
18) b
19) c
20) a
21) d
22) b
23) d
24) c
25) d
26) c

Chapter 3 Guided Review

1) bodies, issues
2) interstitial
3) inguinal
4) temperature
5) 25
6) Cryptorchidism
7) uncomfortable
8) frenulum, corona

9) spinal reflex, involuntary
10) bulbocavernosus, ischiocavernosus
11) Cyclic GMP
12) suction
13) 2.8, functional
14) smegma
15) hypospadias, epispadias
16) Anticircumcision

17) Peyronie's
18) bulbourethral glands
19) seminal
20) Prostatitis
21) hyperplasia

22) epididymis, ejaculatory duct
23) Orgasm, ejaculation
24) Testosterone replacement therapy (TRT)
25) reflexive
26) Biochemical

Chapter 4 Multiple Choice

1) c
2) b
3) a
4) d
5) b
6) b
7) c
8) d
9) a
10) b
11) c
12) c
13) a
14) b
15) d

16) b
17) c
18) c
19) c
20) b
21) d
22) a
23) c
24) a
25) d
26) c
27) b
28) a
29) d

Chapter 4 Guided Review

1) muscular, circulatory systems
2) excitement
3) psychological
4) plateau
5) subjective
6) biological
7) Evolutionary theorists
8) psychological
9) excitation, inhibition
10) controlled
11) learn
12) emotional processing
13) vasocongestion
14) sex flush
15) suspension
16) potential

17) pudendal, pelvic
18) Grafenberg
19) pubococcygeal (PC)
20) pregnant
21) Vasocongestion
22) penis
23) involuntary, involuntary
24) 50
25) gradually
26) hormones, activation
27) testosterone
28) Organizing
29) androgens
30) Attitudes
31) use, lose
32) failure

Chapter 5 Multiple Choice

1) b
2) d
3) c
4) c

5) a
6) a
7) b
8) d

9) c

10) b

11) c

12) d

13) b

14) d

15) a

16) c

17) d

18) b

19) c

20) a

21) d

22) b

23) c

24) a

25) d

26) b

27) c

28) a

29) a

30) b

31) d

32) d

33) c

34) a

35) c

36) c

37) b

38) a

39) d

40) c

41) d

Chapter 5 Guided Review

1) one-sexed

2) berdache

3) ambiguous

4) role

5) differentiation

6) active participants

7) self-fulfilling prophecies

8) Conception

9) default

10) masculinizing

11) hemisphere functioning

12) male

13) sexual

14) reproductive

15) DHT-deficiency syndrome

16) adrenarche, gonadarche

17) Testosterone

18) imagery, fantasy

19) oblique

20) Hyperfemininity

21) androgynous

22) Transgenderism

23) Germany, 1882

24) statistical

25) cerebral

26) orientation

27) acquires

28) aschematic

29) heredity, environment

30) hierarchies

31) stereotypes

32) repression

33) 30

34) doctoral degrees

35) slaves

36) invulnerability

Chapter 6 Multiple Choice

1) c

2) d

3) a

4) b

5) b

6) c

7) b

8) b

9) d

10) a

11) a

12) c

13) c

14) d

15) c

16) a

17) d

18) b

19) a
20) b
21) d
22) a
23) c
24) d
25) b
26) d
27) c
28) c
29) c
30) c
31) d
32) a
33) b

34) c
35) b
36) a
37) c
38) c
39) a
40) c
41) a
42) c
43) c
44) b
45) c
46) a
47) d

Chapter 6 Guided Review

1) critical
2) drive
3) sexual drive
4) polymorphously
5) latency period
6) Conditioning
7) psychosocial
8) validation
9) economics
10) erogenous
11) autoerotic, interaction with other people
12) multisexual
13) Exposure
14) attitudes, lifestyles
15) discomfort
16) Adolescence
17) masturbation
18) older
19) experimentation
20) oral sex

21) carry through the rest of a person's life
22) intimate
23) sex related, morality
24) males and females
25) sexual and reproductive activities, confidentiality
26) Intimacy
27) expansive
28) sexist
29) romantic, sexual
30) cohabitation
31) desire, satisfaction
32) intercourse
33) Polygamy, polyandry
34) starter
35) sexual
36) nonprocreative
37) medications
38) Ignorance
39) adjustment

Chapter 7 Multiple Choice

1) d
2) c
3) b
4) d
5) c
6) a
7) c
8) b

9) d
10) c
11) b
12) a
13) d
14) c
15) a
16) d

17) b
18) c
19) d
20) b
21) c
22) a
23) d
24) b
25) c
26) c
27) c
28) a
29) d

30) d
31) c
32) b
33) a
34) d
35) d
36) c
37) b
38) a
39) d
40) b
41) c
42) c

Chapter 7 Guided Review

1) normal, abnormal
2) sociocultural
3) values, mores
4) heterosexual
5) affectional
6) transvestite
7) natural
8) religious
9) libertarians
10) Nonreligious
11) heterosexism
12) Moral
13) pleasure
14) Augustine
15) 8, 10

16) consistency
17) abstinence
18) religious
19) may not be
20) cultural
21) sexuality
22) ten
23) anxious
24) impediments
25) Physical, mental
26) organs, function
27) spinal
28) heart attack , stroke
29) neuromuscular

Chapter 8 Multiple Choice

1) d
2) b
3) c
4) c
5) b
6) b
7) d
8) d
9) c
10) c
11) a
12) b
13) c
14) c
15) d
16) b

17) d
18) a
19) d
20) b
21) d
22) c
23) d
24) a
25) c
26) d
27) c
28) d
29) a
30) a
31) b
32) b

33) a
34) c

35) d

Chapter 8 Guided Review

1. problems, communication
2. imperfect, imprecise
3. taboo
4. scientific
5. vocabulary
6. stifle
7. strategy
8. unresolved, emotional
9. demonstrated, communicated
10. thinking ahead
11. self-talk
12. Introverted
13. Personality
14. express, needs
15. differential
16. personality, gender
17. constructive, destructive
18. mutuality
19. relational impasse
20. mutuality
21. mathematical
22. Damping
23. double standard
24. Passion, intimacy, commitment
25. imprinting
26. orgasm, prolactin
27. communication
28. romantic
29. heterosexual
30. superficial, destructive
31. Fearful
32. uncoupling
33. rebound

Chapter 9 Multiple Choice

1) c
2) a
3) b
4) a
5) d
6) c
7) b
8) c
9) d
10) d
11) b
12) c
13) a
14) c
15) b
16) d
17) d
18) b
19) d
20) a
21) b
22) c
23) c
24) d
25) c
26) b
27) a
28) b
29) c
30) d
31) a
32) c
33) c

Chapter 9 Guided Review

1) zygote
2) dizygotic, monozygotic
3) blastocyst
4) Ectopic pregnancies
5) fetus
6) Gene therapy
7) stem cells
8) eugenics
9) psychological
10) Cloning

11) embryo
12) reproductive
13) Amniocentesis
14) Ultrasound imaging
15) infertility
16) 40
17) commitment, intimacy
18) obstetrician-gynecologists
19) toxins, radiation
20) 35
21) 20
22) Fetal alcohol syndrome

23) sexually transmitted diseases
24) hormonal, psychological
25) oxytocin
26) afterbirth
27) Lamaze
28) midwives
29) bond
30) higher
31) premature birth
32) 8
33) RhoGAM
34) overweight

Chapter 10 Multiple Choice

1) c
2) a
3) b
4) d
5) d
6) b
7) c
8) c
9) a
10) d
11) b
12) b
13) c
14) b
15) d
16) a
17) c
18) d
19) b
20) a
21) c
22) d

23) c
24) b
25) c
26) d
27) c
28) d
29) b
30) c
31) d
32) b
33) c
34) c
35) d
36) b
37) d
38) c
39) a
40) c
41) d
42) b
43) c

Chapter 10 Guided Review

1) sex and fertility
2) Birth control
3) middle ages
4) Comstock Laws
5) zero growth
6) parenting
7) Americans
8) 5
9) gynecologist
10) biological, reproduction

11) medical
12) risks
13) effectiveness
14) well-educated
15) pregnancy prevention, disease prevention
16) abstinence
17) ovulation, implantation
18) overweight
19) patch
20) spermicides

21) instruction
22) diaphragm
23) 5 to 10
24) pelvic inflammatory disease
25) vasectomy
26) Essure transcervical sterilization procedure
27) 72 5

28) testosterone implants with progestin injections and levonrgestrel implants with testosterone injections or patches
29) *Roe vs. Wade*
30) fewer risks
31) beliefs, values

Chapter 11 Multiple Choice
1) d
2) b
3) c
4) a
5) b
6) a
7) c
8) b
9) d
10) b
11) a
12) c
13) b
14) c
15) a
16) a

17) d
18) c
19) a
20) d
21) b
22) d
23) b
24) c
25) b
26) a
27) c
28) d
29) d
30) a
31) c
32) b

Chapter 11 Guided Review
1) pleasure
2) negatively, man's
3) earlier, pleasure
4) clitoral Glans
5) autofellatio
6) loved partner
7) masturbation
8) Guilt
9) hooking up
10) erogenous zone
11) Cunnilingus
12) rubber dam

13) private, intimacy
14) White, better educated
15) fantasy
16) alcohol, marijuana
17) cantharides
18) negative
19) dildos, vaginal penetration
20) hymen
21) precoital
22) stand
23) marriage
24) sex

Chapter 12 Multiple Choice
1) a
2) d
3) c
4) b
5) c

6) a
7) b
8) c
9) c
10) c

11) d
12) c
13) b
14) a
15) c
16) d
17) b
18) c
19) a
20) d
21) d
22) d

23) c
24) a
25) b
26) d
27) c
28) a
29) d
30) c
31) d
32) c
33) a

Chapter 12 Guided Review

1) clusters
2) political
3) behavioral patterns, identities
4) stigma, discrimination
5) attraction, appeal
6) gender, position
7) educated, middle, high
8) berdache
9) homosexuality, psychiatric disorder
10) purity, fallen
11) medicalized, disease
12) psychodynamic, biological, socioenvironmental
13) biological, social influences
14) Evelyn Hooker
15) depression, anxiety

16) familial
17) males
18) suprachiasmatic
19) hormone
20) multifactorial
21) "repairative" therapy
22) indistinguishable
23) heterosexist, minority
24) significant others
25) heterosexual
26) sexual
27) bisexuals
28) Gaydar
29) guilt
30) Vermont

Chapter 13 Multiple Choice

1) c
2) c
3) a
4) d
5) b
6) c
7) d
8) a
9) c
10) d
11) d
12) c
13) b
14) a
15) c
16) d

17) d
18) b
19) c
20) d
21) a
22) a
23) c
24) b
25) c
26) c
27) d
28) a
29) b
30) c
31) c
32) d

33) c   35) d

34) c

Chapter 13 Guided Review

1) erotic
2) sensuality
3) negative
4) Promiscuity
5) anger, mistrust
6) double standard
7) heterosexual
8) Autogynephilic
9) hormonal, surgical
10) none, regret
11) appropriate
12) sex organs
13) neutral, positive
14) Vibrators
15) impersonal, romantic
16) Fetishism
17) paraphilia
18) extrarelational
19) sex workers
20) decriminalized, regulated
21) insecurity, inadequacy
22) confident, powerful
23) Toucherism
24) sexual
25) sadist, masochist
26) low self-esteem, sexist
27) Judeo-Christian-Muslim
28) pansexual

Chapter 14 Multiple Choice

1) b
2) c
3) d
4) a
5) c
6) c
7) b
8) a
9) d
10) c
11) b
12) d
13) c
14) d
15) b
16) c
17) b
18) c
19) b
20) d
21) b
22) c
23) b
24) d
25) c
26) b
27) c
28) d
29) b
30) d
31) c
32) b
33) b

Chapter 14 Guide Review

1) pornography
2) Artists
3) Surrealism
4) more explicit
5) Pietro Aretino
6) *Lady Chatterly's Lover*
7) music
8) *Playboy*
9) willing
10) 3 and 75
11) stereotyped
12) tolerant
13) *Boys Don't Cry*
14) romantic, sexual
15) Aggressive
16) pedophiles

17) legitimate, non-pornographic
18) sexual, sex
19) embedding
20) First Amendment
21) aroused, guilt
22) political
23) did not seem
24) physiological
25) egalitarian
26) nonaggressive
27) older

28) speech, press
29) solitary, intercourse
30) purient
31) demeaning, "consenting adults acting in private"
32) Colorado
33) HIV/AIDS
34) property
35) private
36) 1960s
37) confidentiality

Chapter 15 Multiple Choice
1) d
2) b
3) a
4) b
5) d
6) a
7) c
8) b
9) b
10) d
11) d
12) b
13) c
14) a
15) b
16) c
17) a

18) d
19) a
20) d
21) d
22) b
23) b
24) d
25) c
26) c
27) d
28) b
29) d
30) b
31) b
32) c
33) b
34) d

Chapter 15 Guided Review
1) feminine
2) stereotypes
3) lower self-esteem, sexually depressed
4) anger, rage
5) rationalization
6) psychological
7) alcohol
8) Sexual harassment
9) men
10) hostile environment
11) grievance
12) consensual, cohesiveness
13) policies, publicized
14) psychological
15) guilty

16) civil, criminal
17) masculine, machismo
18) to be abused again
19) rape
20) Statutory
21) communication
22) duty
23) Muslim
24) persuasion, intoxicated, love
25) Women
26) changed
27) posttraumatic
28) humiliation
29) secondary
30) family member, known

31) verbal
32) emotional distress, thinking clearly, concentrating
33) physical, sexual
34) Crisis
35) deter further abusiveness

36) incest taboo
37) emotional
38) overachievers
39) touching
40) Communication

Chapter 16 Multiple Choice
1) c
2) c
3) d
4) c
5) c
6) b
7) b
8) a
9) c
10) c
11) b
12) d
13) a
14) b
15) b
16) b

17) d
18) a
19) c
20) b
21) c
22) d
23) a
24) b
25) b
26) d
27) c
28) b
29) d
30) b
31) d
32) b

Chapter 16 Guided Review
1) retribution
2) moralistic
3) symptoms
4) less likely
5) Gonorrhea
6) sterility
7) Syphilis
8) Conjunctivitis
9) college campuses
10) lower, genital herpes
11) *Candida*
12) eyes

13) blisters
14) herpes
15) cancerous, precancerous
16) parasitic
17) lindane
18) Molluscum contagiosum
19) microbicides
20) penetration, bodily
21) condoms, vaginal pouch
22) spermicide
23) responsible
24) Diabetes

Chapter 17 Multiple Choice
1) c
2) b
3) c
4) a
5) d
6) b

7) b
8) a
9) c
10) d
11) b
12) c

13) b
14) a
15) c
16) c
17) d
18) b

19) c
20) b
21) a
22) d
23) b
24) c

Chapter 17 Guided Review

1) Medical
2) sexually active, pregnant
3) 4th
4) anal
5) heterosexual
6) blood, delivery process
7) Urban, poor
8) rural areas
9) Opportunistic infection
10) thrush
11) RNA, DNA
12) Antibiotics
13) late
14) ELISA

15) anonymity
16) notified, HIV+
17) anonymous
18) resistant, side, hide out
19) vaccination
20) Quarantines
21) judicial
22) governmental action
23) privacy
24) "cleansing", drugs
25) increase, declining
26) school
27) latex
28) rubber dam

Chapter 18 Multiple Choice

1) b
2) a
3) b
4) b
5) d
6) c
7) b
8) c
9) a
10) d
11) a
12) a
13) b
14) a
15) b

16) d
17) a
18) c
19) b
20) d
21) c
22) c
23) a
24) d
25) d
26) a
27) c
28) b
29) d

Chapter 18 Guided Review

1) psychotherapeutic
2) mechanical
3) values, religious, relationships
4) generalized, situational
5) desire, arousal, orgasm
6) Orgasm
7) rigid, vague
8) experimentation, experimentation

9) sexuality
10) aversion
11) erectile disorder
12) nocturnal
13) pain
14) forced
15) Lifelong
16) premature

17) musculature
18) avoidance
19) multiple
20) arousal
21) pubococcygeus
22) masturbating
23) relax, restructure
24) androgens
25) Viagra
26) psychotherapeutic

27) surrogates
28) medical
29) permission
30) self-awareness
31) power
32) nongenital
33) no return
34) homework
35) relapse
36) confidentiality

CHAPTER ESSAY POINTS

Chapter 1 Essay Points

1)

2)

- Eurocentric perspective, generally an either-or or black-white viewpoint
- Influence of Caucasian European ethnic groups
- Religious influence of Judeo-Christian perspectives
- Homogeneous cultures are generally smaller
- Homogeneous influence; people are supposed to be alike and maintain conformity
- Heterogeneous cultures are generally larger
- Heterogeneous cultures have a great deal of human diversity and less emphasis on conformity
- Heterogeneous cultures have little training in "appropriate" sexual conduct, conflicting messages about sex

3)

- New approaches to morality and personal autonomy – resistance of centralized, institutionalized authority; more social mobility with resultant independence
- Changing roles of women and men – roles are more individualized, more freedom to socially adopt different roles, women can initiate whereas men can express more emotional aspects of life
- Scientific research and technological development – increased scientific research,

research challenges myths, technological use of contraceptives, and safe abortion procedures
- Media and Internet attention to sexuality – change from the 1950s to a society in which, through the media one cannot escape sexuality, media may perpetuate myths, computers are making accessibility easier
- HIV and AIDS as agents of change – awareness of concern has increased, yet use
- of protective measures or changes in behavior are not reflective of this concern.

4)

- Krafft-Ebing viewed masturbation as a behavior that contaminated noble and ideal sentiments, leaves an animal desire for sexual satisfaction, declines attraction in opposite sex, and decreases sexual desire
- Others have blamed masturbation for causing homosexuality, insanity, sterility
- Prevailing professional opinions see masturbation as a normal part of human sexual expression, common in youngsters, and it can continue into later life
- Masturbation is healthy outlet for sexual tension and can teach about sexual responsiveness

5)

- Selecting population samples should be through a sampling process to allow for generalization of findings
- Sampling is best undertaken randomly and with a sufficient number of people, including demographic issues of diversity

- Volunteer bias when individuals volunteer for a study, indicates they are more sexually experienced, more interested in sexual variety, more interested in sex
- Response bias may result in underreporting or concealment of sexual behaviors or others may exaggerate or embellish the reported information

6)
- Informed consent involves giving research participants ; complete prior information about the purpose of the study, the manner of their participation, the lack of coercion and dishonestly in presenting information, protecting confidentiality, and being protected from physical and psychological harm.
- Ethical concern regarding inclusion of racial grouping when researching sexual behaviors. Difficulties concern sharing of the same heritage, same racial or ethical group, and determination of race.
- Ethical concern regarding the use of the Internet for subject recruitment, informed consent, and the protection of the data

Chapter 2 Essay Points
1)
- External sex organs: mons, labia majora, labia minora, clitoris, prepuce, Bartholin's gland, urinary meatus;
  Internal sex organs: ovary, fimbraie of fallopian tubes, fallopian tubes, uterus, and vagina
- Female genital mutilation, concerns regarding presence or absence of hymen

2)
- Acute urethral syndrome – frequent sexual intercourse - antibiotics
- Interstitial cystitis – chronic bladder condition - antibiotics
- Vaginal atrophy – lower estrogen levels – hormone replacement therapy
- Vericose veins of vulva – aching heavy sensation
- Vaginal atresia – non-closure of vagina – surgical reconstruction

- vaginal fistulae – abnormal openings connecting bladder, urethra, or rectum and vagina – surgical treatment

3)
- Recommendation of annual exam
- Detect cervical cancer, not other disorders or STDs
- Detect abnormal cellular changes – prior to cancer
- Check internal organs
- Test suspicious cells
- Uterine or cervical cancer
- Endometrial hyperplasia
- Endometrioses
- fibroid tumors

4)
- To detect abnormalities of the breast
- Increase survival rate if abnormality detected
- Monitor in event of "faulty" genes
- If high risk, early detection
- Visual examination - describe
- Examine around time of ovulation
- Manual examination – describe

5)
- Perimenopause – years surrounding menopause
- Gradual hormonal output
- Ovary insensitivity to stimulation
- Gradual cessation of menstruation
- Uterine and breast decrease in size
- Vaginal lining thins
- Color and textual changes
- Osteoporosis
- Hot flashes
- Risks – uterine and breast cancer, negation of estrogen benefits if used with progesterone
  Benefits – longer life, less heart disease,

Chapter 3 Essay Points
1)
- Testes – produce testosterone and produce sperm
- Scrotum – regulate temperature of testes

- Seminiferous tubules – where sperm cells formed
- Interstitial cells – produce testosterone
- Vasa efferentia – transportation of developing sperm
- Epididymis – where sperm mature
- Vasa deferens – transports sperm to seminal vesicle
- Seminal vesicle – stores sperm during sexual activity
- Penis – sexual intercourse – transportation of sperm/semen

2)
- Use adequate lighting
- Be alert for soreness
- Generally after hot shower – looser scrotum
- Roll each testicle between thumb and fingers
- Feel for small hard lumps
- Importance – especially for younger adult males
- Early detection of any potential problems
- Cancer and possible death
- If caught – merely removal of testis

3)
- General perception of males – not large enough
- Related to perceptual self worth
- Nonerect or flaccid measurements do not have great meaning
- There is equalizing effect
- Functionality is not related to size
- Use of suction devices – can cause injury
- Surgical techniques – risk of scarring

4)
- Prostatitis – antibiotics for acute conditions – difficulty in treating chronic conditions
- Benign prostatic hyperplasia – nonmalignant prostatic enlargement – use of medications
- If enlarged prostate – may surgically remove or may remove only parts of organ

5)
- Psychological and social changes – related to family and work
- Possible midlife crisis – andropause

- Gradual decline in testosterone – significance debated
- Less testosterone – may increase depression
- Testosterone replacement therapy
- Need for supportive help – counseling
- Use of medications

- stroke, and broken bones

Chapter 4 Essay Points
1)
- Masters and Johnson – physiologically based, researched in laboratory, details as to physiological responses for each phase, difficulty in clear separation of stages of excitement, plateau, orgasm, and resolution phases,
- Kaplan's model – introduction of a desire phase that is more psychological in focus and not seen in the Masters and Johnson model, responds to neurophysiological mechanisms of body, vasocongestion phase and orgasmic release, model is used in treating sexual dysfunctions

2)
- Males reach orgasm more rapidly during intercourse
- Orgasms very similar in both sexes
- Pelvic vasocongestion and muscular tension experienced for both sexes
- Women more orgasmic from masturbation
- Subjective differences in orgasmic perception
- Women capable of "faking" an orgasm
- Women tend to "romanticize" sexual desire
- Men "sexualize" sexual desire
- Men, sex is a goal, women focus on arousal
- Women focus on partner, men focus on physical or sexual attractiveness

3)
- Females can be multiorgasmic, men have a clear phase on non-restimulation
- Women can have sequential orgasm
- For women the type of sexual stimulation can be important

- Orgasm is not sole sexual satisfaction for women
- Types/controversies or orgasms: uterine, vaginal, and blended orgasms
- Issue of G spot and the relationship to orgasms and sexual pleasuring

4)
- Direct correlation between hormones and sexual behavior is not entirely accurate
- Female hormones related to menstrual cycle may impact them sexually
- Hormonal concentration is not apparently a factor
- Testosterone has more direct physiological impact on males
- Some males with low testosterone can have erectile difficulties
- Testosterone levels in both males and females increase after sexual activity

5)
- Gradual decrease in sexual desire and frequency of sexual activity
- Thinning of vaginal lining, reduce vaginal lubrication, increase in uterine cramping with orgasm, increased amount of time for sexual arousal and vaginal lubrication, increased time to reach orgasm and fewer muscular contractions, no change in resolution period for women and if multiorgasmic – generally remain so
- atrophy of testicular tissue, less preejaculatory fluid and semen, testes don't elevate as much, increased time to full penile erection, increased time and stimulation to orgasm, and strength of muscular contractions in orgasm is less, resolution quicker, and refractory period elongated

Chapter 5 Essay Points
1)
- Intersexuality accepted as a "third sex"
- American Plains Indians – social status of berdache – men who did not have skill or interest for masculine/aggressive pursuits – considered to have special powers and possibly a shaman

- In India the third sex called hijra and included both male and female roles and considered sacred
- Sambia tribe of Papua, New Guinea, generally hermaphrodites, and not expected to take either male or female roles in society, are allowed to be shamans or spirit doctors
- Western cultures – have a two-sex model – and children with ambiguous genitals are subjected to hormonal and surgical treatments – others are pressing for more understanding regarding intersexuality

2)
- Egg contains only X chromosome, sperm can be either X or Y chromosome, and at conception "sex" is determined. Some research indicates that on Y chromosome an area labeled SRY helps to determine sex, but new research of X chromosome and region called DAX-1 may play a role in sex determination
- Up to 8th week of fetal development can not determine sex of human embryo – the Müllerian ducts represent potential female reproductive organs, while Wolffian ducts represent potential male reproductive structures, and presence of SRY or DAX-1 can influence development of these structures
- Hormonally, if chromosomes programmed to produce female, this will occur – but if chromosomes programmed to produce male then a more complex process. H-Y antigen chemical agent that helps transformation of testes and produces testosterone promotes development of Wolffian ducts, and SRY gene activates anti-Müllerian hormone, which suppresses development of female organs

3)
- Physiological effects include: developing body cells of genetic males unable to response to testosterone – result, develop normal-appearing female genitals while internal structures are not fully developed female organs. Breasts develop at puberty

and short vaginal canal, no uterus so no menstruation.

- Some genetic males with AIS and raised as females tend to exhibit traditional feminine traits and desired roles. They report desiring male sexual partners and dream of raising a family.
- AIS girls have difficulty adjusting to their infertility, and feelings of inferiority may result from surgery to increase vaginal size

4)

- The continuum of transgenderism includes: transvestites, transsexuals, and transgenderists
- Transvestites – engage in cross-dressing, varying degrees and for various periods and times of life
- Transsexuals – have the mind and personality of the opposite sex and may be either low-intensity or high-intensity. High-intensity are likely to desire a change in their sex while low intensity do not have a high enough level of motivation to undergo sex reassignment
- Some transgenderists assume the "other" gender social presentation on a permanent basis, essentially living their lives as the "other" sex
- Socially and professionally these individuals may meet with harsh treatment and prejudice and generally experience a lack of understanding – may be professional resistance to allow some individuals to undertake reassignment surgery

5)

- Feminism: Women are oppressed and are considered as secondary in status as compared to men: therefore, we must reject prejudices that imply inferiority of either gender; work together to achieve equality and balance with regard to rights and opportunities; and women should be considered equal participants in sexual activity.
- Asserting masculinity: Men are trapped by certain roles of injustice and discrimination: therefore, we must encourage men to confront and share feelings more openly'

celebrate masfculinity in non-traditional ways" and new roles to adopt such as metrosexuality and retrosexuality.

Chapter 6 Essay Points

1)

- focuses on the working dynamics of the mind
- relies on concept of instincts
- concept of unconscious mind – controls much of human development and behavior
- infants are born with store of sexual energy – libido
- libidinal energy first undifferentiated and indiscriminate
- infants polymorphously perverse
- libidinal energy centers in body parts at various developmental periods
- latency period – sexual energies lie dormant

2)

- John Gagnon and William Simon, sociologists, developed theory
- Sexual behavior socially constructed
- Sexual conduct derived from social and cultural contexts
- Scripts acquired via lifelong acculturation to suit own needs
- Scripts have cultural scenarios
- Interpersonal scripts
- Intrapsychic scripts

3)

- UCLA study: 77 percent of parents – children had engaged in sex play prior to age 6 including masturbation. Nearly 47 percent interactive sex play by same age. Age 2 or 3 exploring playmates' bodies ranging from embraces to stroking, kissing, and touching genitals. Playing doctor or nurse. Ages 3 to 5, more gender awareness seen in social markers of clothing.
- Mayo Clinic study: children observed ages 2 to 12. Behaviors seen: self-exploration, exposing body to others, rubbing against another person. More intrusive behaviors: oral-genital contact, limited insertion of objects into vagina or rectum. Sexual behaviors decline as years increase.

4)
- narrowing in the differences of teen sexual behavior patterns
- across socioeconomic, racial, and ethnic groups
- sexual intercourse is a transition to adulthood
- fears of pregnancy, disease, or parental disapproval cited for not engaging in premarital sexual intercourse
- society expects heterosexual behavior
- less attention to same-gender orientations
- discourages positive gay role models
- conflict with school environments
- developing intimate emotional attachments when many social prohibitions

5)
- Sociobiological assumptions: human beings use sexual strategies in mate selection – related to evolution, which contributes to survival of species. Mate selection differs for short-term and long-term couplings, and sexes differ on mating objectives.
- Emotional systems include: craving for sexual gratification, attraction focusing, and mate attachment.
- Evolutionary theory: short-term partners more important to men and men identify with sexually accessible women. In short-term partner, men minimize commitment. Men want to find mates who will likely bear children, and women want male partners who can provide adequate resources.

Chapter 7 Essay Points

1)
- To be normal is to be attracted sexually to members of the opposite sex
- Normal is to desire penis-in-vagina intercourse – is ultimate expression of sex
- All else is considered, to some degree, abnormal
- Yet, historically humans have been very diverse and variable
- Literature and art are influences portray sexual activities

- Religion generally influences codes of sexual conduct
- Cultures express acceptance by awareness – example of more known about prostitution than same-gender behavior
- Cultural values and mores also influence society and individuals

2)
- Deviation first used by psychologists, and seen as straying from normal pathway – also is seen as being more emotionally charged
- More recent label – variation or variance – still implies somehow different – generally negative connotation
- Within last decade use of paraphilia, meaning a "love beside" – a sexual attachment or dependency on some unusual or unacceptable stimuli
- Statistical normalcy based on population characteristics – use of sex surveys
- Normalcy by expert opinion – educational and professional credentials – example psychiatrists or psychologists – use of DSM-IV
- Moral normalcy – uses religious traditions – generally dominant one in society
- Continuum of normalcy – situational morality – sex seen in relative terms – is behavior healthy, safe, and non-exploitative

3)
- Although "phobia" is used, a true fear is not usually involved
- For homosexuals their life is considered, by about 50% of people surveyed, to be morally wrong and more than half say sexual orientation is chosen
- Certain occupations evoke more negative attitudes, such as teaching and the perceived role modeling for students
- Misperceptions of sexual abuse committed by homosexuals
- For gay students, more harassment, misunderstanding, and discrimination including more physical violence
- Biphobia results in prejudice and discrimination – and may be more prevalent on college campuses than homophobia – in part because of perceived responsibility for

spread of HIV to heterosexual population – also a denial of the existence of this human sexual orientation

- When externalized can see name calling, prejudice, and discrimination – may be the result of questioning one's own sexuality
- When internalized can be seen in high-risk behaviors, depression, and other personal problems

4)

- Effect parent-teenager communication is a major barrier
- Parents' lack of comfort with subject
- Teens' uneasiness with subject
- Parents unprepared
- Comprehensive sexuality education – see teens as likely to be sexually active, need to see people being prepared – is more sex positive. A concern from opponents is that permissiveness should be combated. Proponents counter, comprehensive sexuality education is in only reaches 5% of youngsters. Also cite lower rates of pregnancy.
- Abstinence programs – value chastity. Abstinence is until marriage and as a result solves social problems associated with teen sexual behaviors. Opponents maintain this is not realistic, and even if chastity is taught there have been and will be sexual problems. Others are concerned about the reliance of scare tactics and fear that are part of these programs, and that many are religious is their philosophy.

5)

- In an estimated 25-50 percent of SCI patients there are reported sensations in genital area
- Capable of having sexual intercourse by the third year in most patients
- Erection of penis and lubrication of vagina is partially controlled by localized spinal reflex
- Through direct stimulation – may achieve orgasm and/or ejaculation
- Face challenge of learning new forms of sexual expression

- Need to learn new positions and techniques to minimize effects of catheters
- May use electrodes to potentially increase blood flow to penis
- Need to resolve emotional issues, including emotional and sexual issues in relationship
- May need to seek counseling but many do not

Chapter 8 Essay Points

1)

- Operating by "The Rules" – playing hard to get (generally women) – some say they work – others see as less than honest
- The Power Games – sex used to express struggles – can exert direct power or passive power resistance - use of "right" time
- The Relationship Games – bringing unresolved conflicts and emotional problems into new relationships – if trust lacking then barriers generally stay
- The Communication Games – common one, push for resolution – may involve avoidance of confrontation
- Ground Rules:
- Degree of commitment of relationship – helps to focus level and type of communication
- Know your values – where do you stand
- Keep yourselves on equal ground – equality not "one-up or one-down" position
- Build trust for one another – issue surrounds trust
- Pick the right location and time for talking – need to be relaxed and comfortable

2)

- Boys more hierarchical – groups have leader – elaborate rules filter through group – struggles for status – vie for attention – use of threats to get way
- Girls smaller groups or pairs – intimacy and community are focuses – allow all to have a turn – generally no winners or losers – harmony and compromise
- Women – more agreeable and congenial
- Men – more personal reaction to verbal rejection – resist doing what told – don't like being dominated

- Talking over problems –men less likely to communicate feelings – men more forceful and loud – women not being told feelings feels like rejection – softer and more emotional
- Asking for directions – men resist – women welcome chance
- Expressing needs – women may express needs indirectly and focus on intimacy – men may respond directly and feel pressured
- Talking and listening – men talk more than women in public situations – more questioned focuses – more lengthy and more interruptions – while at home, roles reversed – women talk more but about feelings and problems

3)

- Intimacy – emotional component – involves closeness, support, and sharing. Increases gradually and steadily at first. In well-established relationship, may not be readily seen, but in crisis is becomes evident
- Passion – motivational component of love. Manifested desire to be united, leading to sexual arousal. Likened to addictive substance and if withdrawn quickly then other person may experience depression, emotional pain.
- Commitment is the cognitive side of love. It grows over time and then levels off, and if relationship fails, or begins to, it will decline as well.

4)
- In women attraction may be between one exclusively same-gender person and a more bisexual person, in women.
- Males potentially drawn into romantic attachments out of their being different and self completion
- Historically there were romantic, but potentially non-sexual, relationships "Boston Marriages"
- Heterosexual model for dating and marriage is one pattern for same-gender relationships
- Marked model is another pattern – older paired with a younger person
- Friendship model is the third pattern – emphasis on sharing and equality

5)
- Impact: Internet dating is feared as enemies to human intimacy.
- Implications: Internet dating, somestudiews are indicating, often lead to very positive interpersonal relationships.

Chapter 9 Essay Points
1)
- Identical or monozygotic twins formed by single ovum and sperm and fraternal or dizygotic twins formed by two zygotes
- Other mothers prone to having multiples
- Other cause is the use of fertility drugs, especially in infertile couples
- Risk of premature births and birth defects
- Risk of death of fetus
- Selective reduction is a risk reduction technique. Involves aborting one or more of the fetuses.

2)
- Two-step process: secure the viable sperm and ova, then bring both together to maximize conception
- Process occurs in a laboratory and sometimes referred to as "test-tube" babies
- Ovum are harvested from ovaries via surgical procedure
- Sperm are collected via masturbation
- If fertilization occurs, then egg is implanted in uterus
- One variation is zygote intrafallopian transfer
- Controversy of using preimplantation genetic diagnosis – to detect defects and destroy embryo
- Controversy regarding claims made by clinics regarding success rates

3)
- General concern of the reliability of the technology to assure outcome
- Social and psychological factors can potentially determine sex – the "returning soldier effect" – as well as age of father (older) and mother (younger) – male child

- Can use sperm sorting when combined with artificial insemination
- Prevalent medical view – patients should have choice
- Ethical issue that surrounds termination of pregnancy if child not of desire sex
- Social policy, such as China, may promote the termination practice
- Ethical concerns regarding use of costly medical resources and procedures

4)
- Environmental pollutants may be increase infertility
- In women histories of pelvic inflammatory disease, endometriosis, diabetes and hypertension increase chances
- Men generally a result of low sperm count or sluggish sperm
- Infections of testes can cause infertility
- Some drugs, alcohol, and tobacco can potentially cause infertility
- Psychological impact of disappointment and deprivation
- Limited success of treatments as to disappointment and frustration
- Can create relational stress and anxiety, but more in women
- Feelings of inadequacy

5)
- Pregnancy-induced hypertension – formerly called toxemia. Rise in blood pressure, swelling in ankles, and protein in urine. Could progress, if not treated, to blindness, convulsions, and coma.
- Premature birth – a birth prior to the 37th week. Involves more male fetuses. More premature the greater chance of death. Have respiratory can cranial abnormalities.
- Rh Incompatibility – a blood factor – if baby and mother different – mother produces antibodies that destroy red blood cells in the fetus
- Breastfeeding is one adjustment but may be restricted by work decisions – while benefits of this practice have been documented
- Relational adjustments – as baby needs care – loss of sleep – and so individuals are tired and irritable

- Post partum depression – low-energy levels, feeling overwhelmed

Chapter 10 Essay Points

1)
- Americans more skeptical about effectiveness of birth control, and blame unwanted pregnancies on societal problems
- Ethical concerns rooted in "purpose" of sex – biological reproduction versus prevent unintended pregnancies – also recreational view of sex
- Roman Catholic and Muslim religions oppose use of birth control and abortion
- Politically – various country factors – Japanese sexual morals prevented approval of contraceptives – United States, which party has power at a particular time – can be legislative restrictions

2)
- Theoretical rate or the "perfect"/"lowest observed" – percentage of failures when used exactly and without error or technical failures
- Typical use failure rate – takes into account human error and carelessness and technical failure rates
- Contraceptive failure rates are measurable – while actual rates of effectiveness are elusive – no study can ascertain pregnancy if they had not used method – so really an expression of how "likely" they are to fail
- Although concerns – rates in text are based on the best designed and statistically valid studies

3)
- Combined oral contraceptives – contain both estrogen and progestin and "inert" ingredients – taken for 21 days
- Progestin-only pills – or minipills – contain only low does of progestin
- Oral contraceptives – changes in menstrual cycle that interrupt ovulation or implantation
- Combined pills – high estrogen – inhibiting release of FSH and LH –

- Progestin – change in cervical mucus – sperm cannot pass easily, and uterine lining less receptive to implantation
- Progestin-only works same way and may prevent ovulation

4)
- Male condoms – controversies over type to use – latex best – skin are porous and not acceptable for HIV prevention – store in cool place and do not use "oil" based lubricants as they weaken latex - Polyurethane – individuals with latex reaction
- Male condoms – can fail from breakage or slippage – estimate under 7 percent – polyurethane condoms higher rates of both
- Best way to prevent STDs, but not used with consistency
- Controversies with distribution in schools and in clinics
- Female condoms – lubricated polyurethane – contains rings and one is placed by cervix and one ring placed around labia
- Female condoms – preferred by women over male condoms – need to use extra lubricant – advantage woman can take responsibility for protection and not relying on male partners
- Failure rates are moderately high at slightly more than 20%
- Use problems – with edges can enter vagina – permitting spillage of semen

5)
- Legal medical abortions – fewer risks than giving birth
- Estimate 1 in 100,000 if performed by week 12 – rates increase with length of pregnancy – rate is 20 to 100,000 in continued pregnancies and births
- First-trimester – safest abortions and few complications – yet possible infections if all fetal tissue not removed
- Later abortions – higher risks of bleeding and infection – fatal complications minimal
- Multiple abortions – may lead to ectopic pregnancy

- Psychological effects – related to beliefs and values of female – and degree of care of decision
- Serious emotional complications following abortion is rare
- May experience depression, grieving, regret and sense of loss – and more likely reactions in second- and third trimester abortions

Chapter 11 Essay Points
1)
- Not always a guilt-free practice – guilt reported in about half of both genders – yet does not affect male rates of masturbation – affects rates for women – if guilty than less positive physical and psychological reactions
- Moral implication – Judeo-Christian-Muslin once predominantly antimasturbation – but now a moderated position based on medicine and psychology – may relate to scriptures – in Judeo/Christianity with Onan and Onanism

2)
- Fellatio – kissing, licking, sucking on the penis – or mouth stimulation of penis – stimulation of frenulum on underside of penis
- Cunnilingus – kissing, licking, sucking of clitoris – labia – vaginal opening – inserting tongue into vagina
- If performed on each other – slang term "sixty-nine"
- Risks of transmitting sexually transmitted diseases – including HIV – concerns if prostate infected
- Reduce risk with use of latex barrier protection – rubber dams over vulva – condoms over penis

3)
- Vibrators- Aids to sexual stimulation and can be shared
- Electric – used in masturbation – can provide intense sexual pleasure
- Can view pornographic materials together – others enjoy reading books with explicit language

- Men achieve sexual arousal using vibrator and erotic videos
- Fantasy can be integral to sexual experience – some couples act out fantasies
- Aphrodisiacs – food and chemicals purported to act as sexual stimulants – some of concern – cantharides – southern European beetle – causes inflammation of urinary tract – considered dangerous
- Some see alcohol and marijuana as an aphrodisiac – but if used in large quantities – they may inhibit sexual desire and arousal

4)
- Intercourse – surrounded with moral and social values
- Most society – some limitations on heterosexual coital behavior – goal preventing enjoying bodily behaviors
- Vaginal sex is most common sexual activity
- Sexual intercourse – prefunctory/hurried or lengthy and sensual
- Personal needs and characteristics determine depth and degree of pleasure
- Factual knowledge – and attitudes are also factors
- Vaginal intercourse – a route of HIV transmission – via semen or vaginal secretions
- Risk is your partner has had other partners –
- Safest if male uses condoms – with spermicide nonoxynon-9

5)
- Reclining face-to-face – most common used – good facial contact – reclining positions preferred
- Man on top – woman supine – most common in European and American societies - some see as only "normal" way to have intercourse
- Other variations on face-to-face – including both partners seated – woman on edge of bed or chair – both partners standing
- Both partners standing – most difficult to manage and sustain – need to maintain balance and stability – not a popular position – deep penetration is difficult
- Real Vaginal Entry – position used by most mammals – if employed seen as comfortable and exciting – employed in many world cultures – intimacy may be lost
- Both partners kneeling, rear entry – woman holds upper part of body up with arms – man kneels behind –

Chapter 12 Essay Points
1)
- Kinsey seven-point scale heterosexual to homosexual rating
- 0 – exclusively heterosexual
- 1 – predominantly heterosexual – only incidental homosexual
- 2 – predominantly heterosexual – more than incidental homosexuality
- 3 – equal heterosexual / homosexual
- 4 – predominantly homosexual – more than incidental heterosexual
- 5 – predominantly homosexual – incidentally heterosexual
- 6 – exclusively homosexual
- Benefits – "stroke of political genius" seemed to resolve issues and a new way of understanding
- Demonstrated that same gender behavior more common in U.S. population – so comforting for homosexual individual and supporters
- Removed the either/or perception of sexual behavior – orientation
- One problem – the continuum that maintains in some fashion – a modified either/or model
- Issue remains more complex – within dimensions of sexuality

2)
- Same-gender orientation much higher in cities and suburban and rural locations
- More pronounced in gay men than lesbians
- In 12 largest cities in U.S. – more than 9 percent of men – 3 percent of women – same gender identified –
- So cities – and sexual cultures and communities are a factor
- Also – people raised in cities are more likely to be gay than people raised in suburbs or rural areas

- European studies – lower rates of same gender orientation than NHSLS
- In France – higher in Paris than in rural areas
- British study – male same-gender activity – about 6 percent had some self-defined homosexual experience
- Younger men more likely to report homosexual activity
- High percentage in the London area
- American Plains Indians – the berdache tradition
- Brazil – gay subculture in masculine society – some levels of violence and murder against gays – Mexico – also a machismo culture –
- Russia – imposed strong sanctions against same gender behaviors

3)

- Hormones – could play a role in animal behaviors – endocrinologists speculated hormone levels may play role in same gender orientation
- Findings – prenatal hormonal factors – might influence later gender identity
- Certain brain structures – masculinized and defeminized by male hormones produced in fetal testes – lead to predispositions after birth
- No clear relationship demonstrated in humans regarding sexual orientation
- Yet, females with CAH – more masculinizing hormonal influences on CNS
- Random physical and developmental characteristics
- Genetic factors – genes exert influences over human behavior – pinning down exact influence a challenge
- Gay males – higher likelihood of a male gay relative – similar for lesbians
- Twin studies – also provide some support for genetic connection
- "Hand characteristics" of fingerprints or handedness

4)
- Cass Model of Sexual Identity Formation

- Stage 1 – Identity Confusion – same-gender orientation realization may apply to them – cannot be ignored
- Stage 2 – Identity Comparison – examine broader implications of being gay – begin to feel different – may devalue heterosexuality – or may "pass"
- Stage 3 – Identity Tolerance – accept same gender orientation – recognize sexual, social, emotional needs – increased involvement in homosexual community – if negative experiences – may not move beyond – if positive – develop commitment
- Stage 4 – Identity Acceptance – when accept self-image as homosexual – increased connection with subculture – positive identification –
- Stage 5 – Not using heterosexuality as a standard – pride in accomplishments of community – may become politically active – can involve anger -
- Stage 6 – Identity Synthesis – realization world not divided – not all heterosexuals viewed negatively – nor same-gender viewed all positively –

5)

- Military – previously asked about sexual orientation – now a "don't ask, don't tell" policy –
- In military only sexual behavior between married individuals acceptable
- If openly declare homosexuality – can be discharged – as "incompatible with military service"
- New training programs to prevent harassment
- In other countries – allow homosexuals to serve
- Governmental positions – legalized partnerships receiving attention – but not sanctioned –
- Some state positions – New York – long term gay relationships constitute family
- Some cities – register domestic partners – including same gender orientated individuals
- Congress passed – Defense of Marriage Act – to not recognize same sex marriages

- Vermont – homosexuals should enjoy benefits as heterosexually married couples – Supreme Court of State

Chapter 13 Essay Points

1)
- Ertophilia – consistently responding positively to sexual cues –
- Erotophobia – responding negatively to sexual cues
- Degree of either – includes learning in childhood and adolescence
- Erotophobia – little interest in sexual activities – less likely to use contraceptives – experience more guilt
- Hypersexuality – very high level of sexual desire
- Hyposexuality – abnormally low level of sexual interest
- Can be fundamental asexual - while most fall between this bipolar positions
- Erotomania – more compulsive form of hypersexuality – referred to as nymphomania in females and satyriasis in males – females more negative viewed
- As a clinical condition – erotomania is a rare disorder

2)
- Transgender behaviors are a range of expressions of identity - recall information from gender identity chapter – gender identity a continuum of social and personal identity
- Cross-dressing – transvestite – clothes of opposite sex – sometimes for sexual arousal - found most in heterosexual people
- Some transvestites – practice is a fetish
- Transgenderism – cross-dressed roles for an extended period of time – more sustainable identity
- Transsexuals – both high and low intensity - high intensity – discomfort and disgust with their bodies – desire sex change operations
- Sexual orientation – independent of transsexual identity – may be a male to female transsexual and lesbian

3)

- General considerations – sensory input, emotions, and thoughts – processed in brain and impact arousal
- Sexually explicit media – magazine, videos – associated with sexual arousal
- Habituation – at least in males regarding use of pornographic materials
- Used by between 23 percent of males and 11 percent of females
- Vibrators – most common for of sexual aid used – provide intense vibration to genitals – sometimes recommended for individuals who have orgasmic difficulties
- Dildos are historical – can be used in masturbation – and inserted both vaginally and anally
- Men may use "cock rings" made of leather, rubber or metal – some use to help maintain an erection – but no research to support this contention

4)
- Western cultures – concerned about sex with more than one person at a time
- In other cultures – part of rites or religious ceremonies
- In our society – more of an experiment
- Threesomes – troilism or ménage à trois
- Or large groups – orgy – more an occasional episode
- May involve elements of exhibitionism, voyeurism, same-gender sexual interaction
- May create relational discord – possessiveness and jealousy

5)
- Sadomasochism probably least understood
- Sadism and masochism opposite sides of coin and individuals may enjoy either
- Is a matter of degree – from tight gripping to cutting
- Variants of stimuli – for arousal and gratification
- Submissive person may yield more power in encounter
- Acting out of fantasy may be related to activity
- Bestiality or zoophilia – some animals may make sexual advances

- More rurally based –
- Seen as experimental – not necessarily seen as serious psychological disturbance

Chapter 14 Essay Points

1)
- Prehistoric representations – related to fertility symbols
- Sex organs – objects of worship
- Religious portrayals – sex as important
- Culturally – seen in all – artists test limits – and are very sexually explicit
- Some erotic art – educational functions – "bride scrolls"
- 16th century – engraving – woodcutting – expanding availability of erotic art
- Puritan attitudes – began repression
- In early decades of 20th century – Surrealism – sexual fantasy – now more realistic in photography, video, and films
- Brooklyn Museum – Mayor of New York – wanted to censor "Sensational" – and works have been censored in Paris

2)
- System has changed over years – no longer use rating of "X" – replaced with NC-17 – no children under 17 allowed
- Other ratings – PG – general audiences – PG-13 - and R
- Rating system was an outgrowth of the Legion of Decency – started by the Roman Catholic Church in 1934
- Levels of self censorship by film industry to avoid the NC-17 rating or previously the X rating
- Censorship of women in films – of same-gender relationships – throughout history – with a movement to change and openness of portrayals
- Pornographic films not part of mainstream industry – evolved independent of those structures
- Before 1925 made with 35mm cameras
- Then 16mm and 8mm equipment – and now video equipment – made both professionally and personally

- Now pornographic films are available at over 25,000 stores in the U.S.

3)
- Presidential Commission – recommended repeal of legislation prohibiting sale, exhibition or distribution to consenting adults
- Found no evidence – materials pay a significant role in delinquent or criminal behavior
- No cause of social or individual harm
- Report rejected by President Nixon
- Minority questioned – lack of use of imitation studies and actual youth reports
- Attorney General's Commission – charged with making recommendations regarding how "spread of pornography can be contained"
- Premise was – pornography as serious national problem
- Members chosen – for antipornography positions
- Used witness testimony – no new research
- Concluded – violent pornography caused sexually aggressive behavior

4)
- For success pornography must produce arousal – these are motivators
- Most people have pleasurable responses to such materials
- Men – respond to more sexually explicit material – women to emotionally charged material
- If behavior is self perceived as bizarre – then generally negative response
- Attitudinal effects – believed to be in arousal – as peripheral processing and not more permanent – as not central processing
- Men – more exposure – not more negative attitudes toward women – more gender egalitarian
- Attitudes unaffected – even when stimuli are more aggressive while egalitarian
- Behaviorally – some increase in sexual behavior after exposure
- Behaviors would normally be participated in

- Institutionalized individuals – less exposure to such materials – responses that involved more emotional guilt – adult responses more typical of adolescents – especially if behavior led to masturbation

5)
- To regulate access to sexually explicit materials – governmental bodies use the legal definition of obscenity – and courts have moved to a community based standard
- Court standard – work as a hole must lack serious literary, artistic, political or scientific merit
- States also see use of law to enforce social morals – vs. some who say law should protect not prohibit
- Various laws to regulate aspects of sexual behavior – nature of sexual act – where the act takes place – criteria of consent
- Use of sodomy laws – deviate sexual intercourse – can include mouth genital contact/ mouth anal contact/ manual genital contact – depends on state
- Constitutional principles – "independent rights" restrictions on state laws - "right of privacy" – regarding private acts – "equal protection" clause of Fourteenth Amendment – laws cannot be discriminatory – "void of vagueness" in that laws must be explicit, to a certain degree, so individuals can know what constitutes a violation of law

Chapter 15 Essay Points
1)
- There are generally elements of mutual seduction in most shared sexual experiences
- Consent is an issue – and knowledge related to this process
- Persuading may involve coercion – some people use emotional blackmail
- Generally imbalance – such as age, status, or power to take advantage of
- Rationalization to justify behaviors
- Prejudice – can affect those who are openly different – especially when not based on fact as prejudice generally is
- Results in stress – may result in lack of self-respect/self-esteem

2)
- Sexual harassment can be subtle forms of coercion and exploitation
- Both women and men can be harassed
- Perceptions are a factor – most men perceive woman's behavior as sexy not harassing
- Courts – can be same sex/gender sexual harassment
- Bases of harassment - Coercion and bribery or quid pro quo harassment – Hostile environment – work/school uncomfortable sexual innuendoes, uninvited advances – Aggressive acts – unwanted embraces, kissing, fondling – Third-party effects – student getting better grade because of sexual relationship with professor – impacts other students

3)
- Twenty to 33 percent of female college students have been victims
- Use of alcohol and drugs – by both individuals – very common
- Athletes and fraternity members associated with this behavior
- Use of "date rape drugs" – Rohypnol – to spike drinks – result is unconscious woman
- Need to be aware of relationships with coercion
- Issue is difficult as the perpetrator is normally a befriended individual
- Some consent to satisfy needs of partner
- Misunderstandings and lack of communication can be keys – mixed signals
- Some women don't mean "no" when said – so confusing messages

4)
- Acute or disruptive phase – related to posttraumatic stress disorder – involves stress, anxiety, depression, lowered self esteem
- Victim may deny and put out of mind – yet agitated, hyperalert
- Recovery phase – may last months – long-term reorganization – relationships disturbed – victims are angry
- First treatment phase – early crisis intervention – goal see self as survivor not

victim - accept consequences while reestablishing personal competence/control
- Long-term focus – sexual and relational problems – and reactions to depression and physical symptoms
- Also need to deal with loss of interest and sexual dysfunctions

5)
- Adult sexual abusers – may be rooted in own treatment as child – possible past sexual abuse - lacked confidants as children – sex as an escape from emotional pain – see sexual meanings in behaviors of children
- Adult male abusers – rejecting and controlling families – disturbed relationships with fathers – some prior trauma – fantasize about children
- Little known about adult female abusers – marginal intelligence – history of sexual and physical abuse – dissatisfaction with sex lives – may act out anger
- Child abusers – generally abused themselves – tend to respond to counseling
- Adolescent abusers – abuse younger children and adolescents – usually males – come from dysfunctional families – have serious developmental and psychological difficulties

Chapter 16 Essay Points

1)
- Throughout history – STDs have represented scourges on society – such as syphilis – seen as retribution of gods
- Societies have blamed each other for the diseases (French/Italians/Turks)
- Were a problem during WWII with U.S. troops
- In 1940s with penicillin and antibiotics – looked like VD (old name) was "cured"
- Possible mixed feelings on part of health policymakers – about curing STDs as related to illicit sexual behavior
- Moralistic stance may have prevented eradication
- Many STDs lack clear symptoms – also issue of the stigma associated with them

- Avoidance of public discussion and potentially health care provider education
- Older individuals may not take threat seriously
- CDC considers many STDs reportable – may private physicians do not comply
- Public clinics – report more identifiable – yet others may not have technology or money to diagnosis
- Reporting problem with "cases" vs. patients

2)
- An infection of vulval region and vagina
- A common type of STD
- Any imbalance of pH in vagina may make vagina more vulnerable to infection
- Symptoms – discharge – the color, thickness and odor varies with type of infection
- Types of: Bacterial vaginosis – caused by Gardnerella vaginalis – men can carry without symptoms – treated with antibiotics – sexual partners usually treated as well – Yeast infection – monilial vaginits – growth of fungus *Candida albicans* – treated with fungicides – *Trichomoniasis* – caused by *Trichomonas* – residence in vulva and vagina or male urethra – a common vaginal infection – frequently no noticeable symptoms – Atrophic vaginitis – low estrogen levels – most likely after menopause – not sexually transmitted

3)
- [Only one example provided]
- Gonorrhea – the "clap" – caused by bacterium Neisseria gonorrhoeae - transmitted exclusively by sexual contact
- More riskier for women than men with 50% chance of infection in woman with one exposure
- Can infect – cervix, urethra, rectum, or throat
- Symptoms – often mild or absent – discharge from penis – vagina – rectum – can burn during urination – generally appears within two weeks – in women discharge may be green or yellow
- Treatment – with antibiotics – but penicillin-resistant cases developing

- Diagnosis – smear of discharge – looking for bacteria – culture may also be made – used more with women

4)
- Viral STDs no cure – so need to use effective prevention measures
- Role of abstinence from sex is a rational choice
- Sexual sharing does not need to include internal penetration
- Avoid multiple partners – especially those not well known to you
- Take responsibility for own protection
- Use condoms, vaginal pouches, spermicides
- Get medical screenings – seek prompt medical attention
- Inform sexual partners – urge them to seek treatment when necessary

5)
- Concerns about being sued if you transmit a STD
- Need to be responsible – as that is what law requires
- Need to protect others from harm
- Some states have passed laws against transmission or potential transmission of STD – HIV legislation was some of the first passed in this area

Chapter 17 Essay Points
1)
- AIDS is now fourth largest cause of human death
- More blacks become majority with fewer deaths with deaths at 50% and infections at 60%
- Initially gay men and intravenous drug users
- Hemophiliacs via blood products
- Male transmission to females more than reverse
- Most global infections via heterosexual conduct
- Southern and Southeast Asia and sub-Saharan African countries hardest hit
- Not rampant on college campuses – about 1 to 3 percent

- Urban areas more concentrated with HIV infection – in poorer areas and areas with use of intravenous drugs – so others may deny risks
- Cultural need for a sustained "bridge" to heterosexual community – a condition not currently met
- Economic challenges if not perceive as a social disease – that is not part of privileged class

2)
- Predictable stages of undermining of immune system
- Primary HIV disease – soon after contracting HIV – some develop fever, swollen glands, fatigue, rash – and symptoms disappear
- Chronic Asymptomatic Disease – gradual decline in immune system – no particular disease symptoms – may experience chronically swollen lymph nodes
- Chronic Symptomatic Disease – increasing vulnerability to opportunistic infections – one common one is thrush –infections of skin – inner membranes of body –
- AIDS diagnosis after 1 or more of 26 diseases have been manifested in HIV-infected individual

3)
- ELISA is most common test – inexpensive – completed within 5 hours – not technically difficult to interpret – can give high rate of false positives – test for presence of antibodies
- Western blot – immunoblot test – more accurate that ELISA – more expensive and lengthy –
- Tests can be undertaken via blood or now swabs from mouth or in urine
- New tests extremely sensitive – can distinguish different strains of HIV
- Possible results: Clear confirmation of the presence of HIV antibodies - Clear confirmation that the antibodies are absent – An uncertain result that leaves patients unsure

4)

- Social concerns with how to treat infected – should they be quarantined like for other diseases
- Yet, society has precedents of individual freedom, privacy, confidentiality
- Socially a stigma remains – and certain rights have been denied – yet covered under the Americans with Disabilities Act
- Some states require premarital HIV testing – but may drive some people underground
- Ethical issues of: Confidentiality – within health care has been a long standing practice in medicine – yet in counseling may violate if a third party is facing some danger – any actions have possible legal implications – Cost of caring for HIV-infected patients and supporting research - other diseases are not getting as much funding even though they impact more individuals – Legal ramifications of HIV/AIDS- judicial system being called upon to resolve issues

5)
- Know your sexual partners and sexual histories
- If new partner – and no absolute guarantee that HIV not present – not to have sex outside that partnership – agree to testing – wait to have sex –
- Use latex or polyurethane condoms throughout sexual encounter
- During vaginal intercourse – use spermicidal foam containing nonoxynol-9
- Avoid direct contact with any bodily fluids or excretions
- Use rubber dam during oral contact with vulva or anus

Chapter 18 Essay Points
1)
- If a person is satisfied and can not perform to social or professional "standards" – then should it be considered a dysfunction
- Need to allow for individual differences
- Some estimated 20 to 33 percent of women do not see a lack of orgasm as a problem
- Treatments based on assumptions and values of both patient and therapist

- Need human sensitivity and well-honed skills
- Limited by statistical and clinical evidence that is limited
- Need to consider person's own history and feelings
- Some professionals if couple or individual identifies a concern than a dysfunction
- Culturally there are "mythical performance standards" such as: for men – need erect penis for successful sex – need to postpone ejaculation – men reach orgasm without difficulty   ---for women – perceived as more passive – new standards of pressure for intense arousal –

2)
- Desire disorders:
- Low levels might be related to lack of activity in brain centers that control sex drive
- Above may affect levels of hormones
- Sexual boredom a possible factor
- In couples may be less experimentation and low level of pleasure
- Some may have low desire levels even in sex saturated society
- As a disorder – hypoactive sexual desire disorder – loss of attraction to formerly exciting stimuli
- Arousal disorders:
- Male erectile disorder – penis fails to become erect
- Female sexual arousal disorder – lack of vaginal lubrication
- Could have orgasm without arousal – as control mechanisms separate
- Brain input important for male penile erection – although spinal reflexes are involved

3)
- Physical exam needed to determine medical causes
- If ejaculatory control abrupt – could be neurological or urological - same for vaginismus
- Vaginismus may be related to past stimuli

- Illnesses of general malaise, fever, exhaustion can cause desire disorders
- Any medical condition that interferes in circulatory and neurological mechanisms can cause disorders
- Pain can interfere – heart, back, cysts
- Specific illness that can impact – Multiple sclerosis, brain disorders, lung/kidney disease
- Depressant drugs, barbiturates, narcotics, alcohol – with built up concentrations – inhibited responses
- Hallucinogenic drugs – unpredictable effects – some may, depending on circumstances, can stimulate response – while other times – magnify preexisting disorders –
- Anabolic steroids associated with erectile disorders

- Ethically therapists must have adequate training
- Strict standards of confidentiality – no disclosure without individual's written consent
- Welfare of patients must be protected

4)
- Medical treatments – medications – hormone injections – muscle relaxants – antidepressant drugs – antianxiety drugs – injections/suppositories directly into penis – use of Viagra
- Biomedical Engineering Devices – vacuum devices – 90% effective- low drop-out rate - if organic- prosthetic devices: semirigid rods, inflatable tubular devices
- Psychotherapeutic treatments – Couples Therapy – as sex dysfunction a shared problem – Hypnotherapy – relaxation and suggestions and mental imagery – Group Therapy – provides support and information – Behavior Therapy – systematic desensitization - Surrogates – practice therapeutic exercises with nonpartnered persons

5)
- High standards of professionalism
- Confidentiality
- Informed Consent
- Ethical dilemmas – in couple therapy – one person admits contracting an STD extramaritally - although confidentiality is involved – risk of exposure to other partner
- Who decides what is and when a problem exists